Mr. R. Hawkins
46 Birch Grove
Dunfermline
Fife
KY11 5BE
TR14/AH6

D0246754

RAILWAY LIVERIES

SOUTHERN RAILWAY

Brian Haresnape

LONDON

IAN ALLAN LTD

Acknowledgements

H. C. Casserley

T. J. Edgington

M. L. Harris

A. A. Harrison

C. J. Leigh

S. W. Stevens-Stratten

R. White

P. Winding

Front cover — coats of arms
Top left: Southern Railway
Bottom left: Great Western Railway
Top right: London & North Eastern Railway
Bottom right: London, Midland & Scottish Railway.
Crown copyright, National Railway Museum, York

Rear cover
Top: Great Western Railway 'Castle' class 4-6-0 No 5028 *Llantilio Castle* serves to demonstrate the Collett express passenger livery in all its glory; pictured here at Swindon in 1934 when the engine had just been constructed.
British Rail

Bottom: London Midland & Scottish Railway 'Coronation' class 4-6-2 No 6229 *Duchess of Hamilton* serves to demonstrate the 'photographic grey' livery in which many locomotives were recorded for offical purposes.
Real Photos

First published 1989

ISBN 0 7110 1829 4

Published by Ian Allan Ltd, Shepperton, Surrey; and printed by Ian Allan Printing Ltd at their works at Coombelands in Runnymede, England

Contents

Preface

In choosing to initiate a book on the subject of British railway liveries, past and present, the Author is deeply aware of the dangerous arena he is entering! Probably no other aspect of railway history and folklore is so ridden with speculation, debate, contradiction and simple lack of reliable evidence or contemporary records. Nevertheless, it is an aspect which deserves to be considered in its own right and one which holds a great deal of interest for many people, and by presenting these books to the reader it is hoped that a clearer and more concise record will eventually be achieved, covering the whole span from the pre-Grouping era to the present day.

Colour is both an emotive subject and an abstract quality. To write about colour is rather like trying to describe in words the flavour of a cheese, a glass of beer, or a good wine. To describe a colour can be as misleading as trying to put a word to a particular sound, or a smell. *Exactly* what, for example, is meant by apple green? A quick glance in the nearest greengrocer's window reveals a wide variety of apples, and shades of green to go with them. Yet apple green is acknowledged to be the LNER locomotive green in railway folklore. The fruit garden, the vegetable garden and the herb garden are well represented in colour descriptions — sage green, olive green, holly green, pea green, etc — but what purports to be a particular colour quite often does not match its natural namesake. Beware then, the easy trap of naming colours! In this series I will use names only where they have already been applied in contemporary sources; I will not add to the confusion. As even a single colour can vary considerably in shade, or tone (by the addition of white, or perhaps black) it is simply not enough to describe it with one overall name. For example, olive green can range from a pale yellowish shade to a dark bluish shade, and still one can find olives on a French market stall to match.

Each individual sees colour uniquely. No two people possess exactly the same colour perception and in many cases a definite colour deficiency exists in one eye, or both. Diminished eyesight comes with increasing age and so too does diminished colour memory. The amount of contentious debate likely to arise if two or more people are asked to remember a certain colour — malachite green for example — and then afterwards to select it from a colour chart has to be seen to be believed! Some people are actually born colour-blind or partially so, without even knowing it until many years later they take a test; perhaps whilst learning to drive a car. One curious feature is that each eye, even in a person who can perceive the entire spectrum of colours, ie the colours of the rainbow — red, orange, yellow, green, blue and violet, can vary these by seeing them either 'cold' or 'hot'. [Cold colours are those tending towards a blue tint. Hot, or 'warm' colours tend towards a yellow tint.]

Another important factor in colour perception is the effect of the play of light upon a colour. Daylight varies according to both the season of the year and the time of day. Photographs taken on a hot summer day often have deep blues in the shadows (hence those curious blue smokeboxes so often gracing a highly-polished preserved steam locomotive for example), whereas on a dullish day the same colours will appear soft, or muted, in intensity and tone. An interesting and readily observable example of the effects of light upon a railway livery is the present day BR blue. This looks well in sunlight, when it seems to possess a certain depth and richness, but grey winter days rob it of this quality completely. The yellow front ends, however, can tolerate a much greater range of lighting and still remain effective. It was, of course, for exactly this reason that the yellow (of the shade used) was chosen by BR for the end of locomotives and multiple-units, in order to give maximum visual warning of their approach at speed. For generations beforehand a red bufferbeam had been used (originating from the earliest days of steam when a man preceded the train, carrying a red flag), until scientific study in the early 1960s revealed that yellow was actually a more efficient warning colour.

Most people have at some time or another encountered another difficulty relating to colour; namely that a small patch of colour chosen from a colour chart or sample, can look completely different when applied in quantity to a large surface area. How many housewives one wonders have been disappointed by the finished result of a decorative scheme for a room which looked fine on the colour chart but which turned out to be quite different once completed? This is a problem of tonality. Generally speaking a small area of colour appears darker in tone than a large area of the same. To produce an exact match some modification may therefore be required. The expert colour matchers employed by industrial paint manufacturers have constantly to allow for this factor when producing a shade to a given specification. Today it is possible to produce exact colour matches by scientific analysis and quantity control of the pigments used; but the tonality problem remains. To give an example of what I mean, let's take a popular railway colour like the crimson lake of the Midland Railway. If a batch of paint was produced by present day methods matching exactly the shade used on the preserved Compound, No 1000, it would nonetheless be hopelessly dark in tone if applied to a scale model of the same locomotive. The final judgement as to shade and colour must always rest with the individual and the particular application involved

If I paint (no apologies for the pun) a complex picture about the problems of colour matching, then I do so in order to emphasise, as I have just said, to the reader that a good deal of personal judgement must be applied; according to the particular job in hand. Even the texture of the surface upon which the colour is to be applied can change the final effect. A coat of varnish can bring to life a colour which has dulled because it is on a rough surface or absorbent one. The same coat of varnish, on paint on a smooth and reflective surface can considerably heighten the colour effect. If for example many prewar LNER or GWR locomotives appeared to have colours of greater intensity and hue than their postwar nationalised counterparts, then this was largely due to the basic fact that they carried more coats of paint and varnish. The actual *colour* of the pigment in the paint, could well have been identical. Postwar economies prevented the same elaborate painting procedures from being applied, and as a result the finish quickly lost its true colour and either faded or darkened.

Today various methods exist whereby colours are standardised and classified by numbers. There is, for example the BSS (British Standard Specification) range, and the well known Munsell method. Within these ranges many of the colours used for railway liveries can be accurately matched. but I have chosen not to refer the reader to these directly. Instead, each book in the series will have a colour sample range, matched by the printer as accurately as possible (allowing for the difference in luminosity and depth between printing inks and paint) and these will be numbered, with a prefix denoting the railway concerned, and all references in the text will refer the reader to the colour chart which appears in Ernest F. Carter's book *Britain's Railway Liveries*, published by Harold Starke Ltd. This chart contains no less than 50 colours all pertaining to railway liveries, and it is quite unsurpassed as a reference work. The text of the book, alas, is not so comprehensive and does not clearly define many of the variations as it consists of a collection of references concerned with liveries culled from contemporary magazines and other sources. This limits its value, because many of the contradictory statements reprinted therein are not resolved, but rather left to the reader. The range of colours produced by Mr Carter's own research work are, however, quite superb. These are referred to in this series by the prefix C followed by the number on the colour chart; eg C39.

Having forewarned the reader of some of the problems related to colour matching in general, it is as well to take a look at some of the more specific problems related to railway liveries. Various

3
Comparison with the next picture speaks for itself! Here is Class I3 4-4-2T No 2091, posed outside Brighton shed in prewar days, displaying to perfection the Maunsell green livery and the skills of the paintshop. Such a lovely finish deserved the high standard of cleanliness seen here. *Ian Allan Library*

3

researchers (including members of the Historical Model Railway Society) have discovered that actual paint samples taken from surviving relics of rolling stock or structures show surprising variations in shade. Quite simply this is because each batch of paint ordered could vary slightly (perhaps emanating from different manufacturers) and the constituents of the paint could also vary. For example some pigments produced from chemical or vegetable dyes can fade quickly if exposed to sunlight. Others perhaps with oxide as a constituent can darken. A classic example is the first shade of SR green used by Maunsell for passenger rolling stock and (from about 1926) locomotives (SR1/C21), sometimes referred to as 'Parson's Green'*. This had a definite tendency to go blue, of a Prussian shade, when exposed to sea air or general weathering, because Prussian blue was the dominant pigment in its composition.

It should also be remembered that each workshop had its own stock of paint. Ashford, we are told, tended to paint with a darker shade of green than Eastleigh, for instance, and many small details of lining and lettering varied slightly. This is not surprising, but it can give the researcher plenty of headaches when trying to establish a standard for any period!

To establish colour standards for railway liveries it is best to visualise the colour in its pristine state, just applied by the paintshop and given the final coats of varnish. One day, the engine is put to trials or traffic, and from that moment on the paintwork is subjected to weathering and discolouration by dirt. Even cleaning the paintwork, perhaps with oily rags, can alter the colour by giving a patina of a yellowish hue, whilst the effects upon paint subjected to heat — boilers, fireboxes, smokeboxes etc — is generally to darken the paint, sometimes almost to black (if not black already, of course) and in extreme cases to peel the paint off completely. Carriages cleaned by hand display a finish totally different to those cleaned by mechanical means, and generally speaking hand-cleaning of locomotives and carriages retains the paint finish in better condition. Freight stock once painted, is rarely if ever, cleaned, and gradually darkens down, or fades.

Beware another trap! This is the practice, still commonplace today, of 'patch-painting'. Workshops do not necessarily completely repaint a locomotive or carriage every time it passes through for repair or overhaul. If the paintwork is generally sound, only damaged areas are repainted, and the ensemble cleaned and perhaps re-varnished. This often shows the newly applied patches as darker and richer than the rest, which is of course no longer the original shade, due to weathering and fading (even if only slight). The SR established a comprehensive re-varnishing programme at its Selhurst depot for suburban electric stock, and it was quite surprising to see how the new varnish could revive the paint, although the *original* shade could not be recovered by this practice.

**Throughout this book I shall use the description 'Maunsell Green' rather than 'Parson's Green', in order to reduce confusion.*

4
Another of the Brighton line's Class I3 4-4-2Ts, No 2090 provides the contrast and is seen in the plain black livery of World War 2; evidently not cleaned for some time. Bulleid's lettering is on the side tanks. The small yellow triangle on the bufferbeam, above the number, denotes it conforms to the composite SR loading gauge (allowing it to work on other sections). Photographed passing Hurst Green junction on a Victoria-Tunbridge Wells train. The leading set, No 473, of five coaches, had recently been outshopped in malachite green livery; c1947.
C. R. L. Coles

4

5

Much railway rolling stock remains in everyday service for up to 10 years before *complete* repainting — a practice of today, and one which was commonplace in previous decades. This means that subsequent livery variations can take 10 years to apply to all stock, and examples of the out-dated colour, or livery scheme, continue to run alongside the new. When this out-dated scheme receives the 'patch-painting' process, it prolongs its life, although usually beginning to look rather shabby by comparison with the new colours. (Numerous BR Class 47 diesel-electrics for instance, were 'patch-painted' to retain their original two-tone green livery for some time after BR had adopted blue as their new standard colour.)

A final word of warning on the subject of colour research is offered to the reader, regarding the study of old monochrome photographs. These can be very misleading about colours (despite being sepia, or black and white), because if they were taken prior to the invention of the panchromatic emulsion, they do not portray the correct colour *tones*, in relation to one another. Red lining-out or buffer beams, and the background to nameplates appear as dark areas on these old negatives and prints, and in some instances the reds are completely invisible if upon a very dark colour. Blues of the lighter shades are bleached-out to become almost white, or grey. With modern black and white panchromatic film, these colours have their correct tone values.

And so to the theme of this new series; Liveries. In its original sense the word dates back to medieval days and beyond, to the colours of select bands of men worn, often together with heraldry, to identify themselves; perhaps for commerce, or perhaps for more involved religious, political or even sinister reasons. In nature, the plumage of some birds — striking and distinctive for sexual attraction or as a warning, or camouflage — is known as their livery. In modern terms, a livery is a uniform treatment of colours and style for a group, be it people or their possessions and present day jargon talks of 'corporate identities'; 'company images'; 'house styles', etc. Put simply, a livery is a visual identity, using colours and symbols.

The most important reason for painting the locomotives, rolling stock and other structures of a railway system, is however for *protection*, not identity. Both steelwork and woodwork suffer from exposure to the elements, and consequent deterioration. Regular repainting is one of the best methods of preservation, and it also maintains an attraction to the eye. Thus from the very beginning of railways, colours had to be chosen which whilst offering protection, also looked 'well' on their subjects. No-one would, for example, seriously entertain pale pink or mauve for the bold masculine forms of a steam locomotive!

5
When a locomotive, or carriage, has just been outshopped, and carries a gleaming varnished livery, it most accurately displays the correct colours as envisaged by the engineers, or designers. New North British Loco Co-built 'King Arthur' class 4-6-0 No E769 *Sir Balan* is seen in positively pristine condition, undergoing inspection at Gorgie junction, en route from the makers to the SR, hauled dead in a goods train and minus motion. *P. Ransome-Wallis*

6
From mid-Victorian times it was the custom of locomotive and rolling stock manufacturers to photograph their new products, for record and publicity purposes, using a special matt 'photographic grey' paint finish. This avoided reflections and loss of detail due to shine, or glare, upon the paintwork but, although giving truly excellent mechanical detail, it gave a very erroneous idea of the livery. The grey areas are too light to represent the tone of the Maunsell green in this picture, whilst those below the running plate (except wheels and cylinders, and footsteps) would in reality be black. The locomotive is Class N 2-6-0 No 1410, built at Ashford Works in 1933. *Ian Allan Library*

6

The use of identifiable liveries for each railway company became important when the boom in Victorian railway building was bringing rival companies to the same town or county, and it became necessary for commercial reasons to make the public — their customers — aware of the existence of each company plying for their trade. From this time, the use of heraldry (some of distinction, and some distinctly dubious), became a striking feature on railway trains, together with bold lettering denoting the name or initials of the company. Individual locomotives were identified by a name, a number or both, and rolling-stock carried numbers.

To begin with it was not unusual for the basic colour of the locomotives of several companies to be the same; perhaps a deep green, commonly called 'engine green'. This was because the locomotive *builder* had his own colour and used it for all construction, as it had proven to be a good colour in terms of wear and durability. By mid-Victorian times this practice was giving way to individual colour schemes chosen by the Board of Directors or the locomotive engineers of the railway companies. These colours often became identified with these autocrats, giving rise to such descriptions as 'Stroudley's Improved Engine Green', 'Marsh's Umber', etc. The wide variety of the pre-Grouping liveries made the railway scene a colourful one; in particular at busy junctions where several railways met.

The 1923 Grouping, with which I have chosen to commence this series, brought the 'Big Four' railways into existence reducing the variety of liveries considerably. However, quite quickly each of the four established its own livery and identity and not until 1948 when they were nationalised did the overall 'British Railways' image begin to emerge, gradually leading-up to today's blanket of 'corporate identity' blue and grey. It is certainly a pertinent moment in time in which to record this aspect of railway history.

In this series of books, the emphasis is understandably upon the liveries of the locomotives and rolling-stock — the figureheads of the railways. But a railway livery applies to a wider spectrum and I have decided to include architecture (mainly stations), road vehicles, publicity and some other elements to a degree at least offering a general idea of what occurred at any given period. The specialist in search of deeper knowledge of these associated elements is referred to the excellent work being done by the members of many societies at the present time. In particular I would mention the Historical Model Railway Society and the Railway Correspondence & Travel Society, both of whom publish very detailed information upon railways, their stock and their liveries, from time to time.

With so many preserved railways in existence today, and with an array of operational rolling-stock restored to what purports to be its original livery, or style, a strong temptation existed to take a camera and record these in colour for use throughout the series. For two basic reasons I have decided not to do this. One is that wherever contemporary evidence of a livery exists, I prefer to use it, as it is of course completely authentic even allowing for the known vagaries of film emulsions and suchlike. The other reason is that, sad to say in a fair number of cases, what is otherwise truly excellent restoration work is spoiled by inaccurate livery details — perhaps due to lack of professional painters, or lack of proper lining-out and final varnishing. In the worst instances some of these preserved items are in the wrong colour, or shade, for the period which identifies the mechanical condition of the locomotive or carriage concerned. There is no point in perpetuating errors or omissions of this kind. Happily there are a good many really authentic museum-restored pre-Grouping locomotives and rolling stock in existence, and for this period, prior to the availability of colour film, I will be making some use of them. For the Grouping (certainly from mid-1930 onwards) a considerable amount of original colour material has been unearthed in recent years, in particular by the diligent efforts of Ron White of 'Colour-Rail', and by the now defunct 'Steam & Sail', and wherever possible I will use this rare and interesting collection. Some of these early colour photographs have faded, some have the blues and magentas too evident, but even allowing for this they bear the stamp of authenticity and carry with them a fine air of nostalgia.

My own interest in liveries extends to a professional level and I have been concerned as a consultant in recent years with the new freight rolling stock liveries of BR in particular, during which I learned a great deal about the problems of the railway operators, the engineers and the marketing and advertising departments in trying to

7

8

achieve a brighter appearance for trains which ran 24 hours a day, all the year round, year in and year out, in all weathers! (It makes the Sunday morning car-cleaning ritual look like a child's game by comparison.) Early on in my freelance career I was involved in the selection of liveries for the 'Western' class diesel-hydraulics then under construction at Swindon. The amount of loyal resistance to *any* change from GWR green was admirable, but quite out-of-context because this excellent colour — marvellous to behold on a polished 'King' or 'Castle' — simply looked drab on the shapely box-on-wheels then being built. Alas, the Stroudley LBSCR golden ochre colour looked no better (my contribution) but the maroon scheme sat quite well upon them. How many times in the past 150 years had such aesthetic arguments taken place on this emotive subject, one wondered? Perhaps Henry Ford had it right when he declared that they could paint his Model 'T' Fords any colour they liked — provided it was *black*!

Finally my thanks to Ian Allan, to whose personal inspiration this new series of books owes its existence, and to A. B. MacLeod of the Ian Allan Library and Ron White of Colour-Rail, for attentive and helpful assistance throughout.

Brian Haresnape FRSA NDD
RAMATUELLE
FRANCE
December 1981

7
Photographs in general, and of railway subjects in particular, if taken prior to the invention of the panchromatic emulsion, gave false readings of the tone values of some colours. The red bufferbeam of this Adams 4-4-2T No E0125 was in reality a light vermilion, but the film has rendered it as a dark area. This was a particular problem with red lining-out on engines, which tended to disappear completely! This was, of course, one reason for the use of 'photographic grey' for official photographs (in which case the red lining would be painted on in white), which could show up the colour breaks clearly in a monochrome photograph.
Ian Allan Library

8
Painting and lining a steam locomotive is a lengthy job and sometimes it took place during repair or overhaul, if time was pressing. Otherwise it was the practice to send the locomotive to the paintshop after all other work was completed. This SR Urie/Maunsell Class H15 mixed-traffic 4-6-0 is seen at Eastleigh in the late 1930s, having its valves set. Painting is incomplete (note grey undercoat in readiness for black edging to the lining-out on the running plate, and on cylinder covers. The green and black areas are varnished on the wheels, but the green is matt on the engine, and the chalk marks of the lining-out (to guide the painter) can be seen at the leading end, and on the cylinder. *Ian Allan Library*

A note on locomotive numbering

In the pictures that follow it will assist the reader to understand the livery changes which relate to the renumbering of locomotives, to have the following general guide:

After the Grouping, former LSWR engines had 'E' for Eastleigh added to their numbers. Former LBSCR engines had a 'B' for Brighton and former SECR engines an 'A' for Ashford. These former railway systems became the Western, Central and Eastern Sections of the SR respectively, and engines built by the SR were allocated to the sections from which the designs originated. This of course did not prevent them from being used on the other sections.

In 1931 the system of section letters was altered and Eastern Section engines had 1000 added to their numbers, Central Section engines, 2000, and Western Section engines retained their numbers. The E, B and A prefixes were deleted. (An exception were the Class Z 0-8-0Ts, originally Nos A950-957 which were re-allocated to Eastleigh and kept their numbers; minus the 'A'.)

Also in 1931 Brighton Works was closed, and engine repair work shared between Ashford and Eastleigh. A small plate with either an 'A' or an 'E' was fixed to the cab side, by the driver's lookout, on Brighton engines to show at which works they were repaired.

Bulleid introduced his own scheme for numbering his new locomotives, with the class number and the wheel arrangement shown. Thus in 21C1, the 2 signifies the number of axles in front of the coupled wheels; the 1 gives the number of axles behind the coupled wheels the letter C, the number of coupled wheel axles (A1, B2, C3, etc); and the last figure is the engines number, so that No 21C1 means 4-6-2 No 1.

Some locomotives, on the Western Section only, carried a 'haulage classification' mark, consisting of a single letter painted on the side of the footplate framing near the front bufferbeam. The letters indicate the powers of haulage, A being the most powerful and the other classifications graded down to K, the lowest.

1: The Maunsell Years, 1923-1937

The Board of Directors of the newly formed Southern Railway soon set about establishing a company livery and namestyle. Rather than use the initials SR, they chose to place the word 'Southern' upon locomotives and 'Southern Railway' upon carriages; reserving the initials for use only on goods stock. The CME, R. E. L. Maunsell, came from the South Eastern & Chatham Railway, but the battleship grey livery he had used for that company's locomotives was not favoured by the Board, and the only Ashford features in the new locomotive livery were the large numerals and (except for Eastleigh painting) the bufferbeam numerals . The other two main pre-Grouping constituents of the SR were the London, Brighton & South Coast, which painted its locomotives and coaches in umber brown, and the London & South Western Railway which used green; one shade for locomotives and another (recently adopted), for coaches.

The SR Board evidently favoured the green (for a while rumour had it they would choose the umber, and blue was evidently considered, because a coach appeared in blue on the Eastern Section in 1923), but the exact green shade was, it seems, determined by existing paint stocks. Eastleigh was painting locomotives in the sage green (SR1/C21) adopted by Urie during World War 1, and coaches in the darker 'Parsons green' (first applied to the new electric stock in 1915). These *two* colours were used up by Maunsell until 1925/6, when he adopted the darker coach colour for locomotives as well. This we will now refer to as 'Maunsell green' (SR2/C20*) and it remained standard for the SR until the final months of Maunsell's regime at Waterloo.

**For some reason Carter does not specify No 20 on his colour chart, for the SR. But it certainly matches the available contemporary evidence.*

Various contemporary sources refer to the green becoming darker, or bluer, in the early 1930s. This was almost certainly due to the paint manufacturer modifying the specification (perhaps at Maunsell's request) in efforts to prevent it from fading to blue/green, which was a known weakness of the colour. Better quality pigments would have resulted in a richer effect, and then varnishing would emphasise this. No *official* record of the deliberate change of the shade of green in the period 1925-1935 has come to the Author's attention. Further to confuse the issue, it should be noted that from time to time Eastleigh used-up all its old stocks of transfers (also those from Ashford and Brighton) for bufferbeam numerals and tender or bunker end numerals; also applying some ex-LBSCR gilt numerals to the sides of some tanks and smaller tenders.

Maunsell nevertheless achieved a very high standardisation of livery during his term of office, and it was not until 1935 that a shareholder voiced an opinion at the Annual General Meeting of the company, that something should be done to brighten-up the appearance of the trains. Presumably the taste of the mid-1930s was reacting against the trends of the 1920s; the normal trend in taste, which later of course reverts back with a sense of nostalgia! Evidently the directors considered a change a good idea too, and in 1936 the first sign that a change in colour was being considered was the appearance in traffic of an electric train in a 'brighter shade'; *not* identified specifically as malachite. Maunsell then painted quite a number of locomotives in a mid, or light, olive green (SR3/C12) a paler version of the Urie sage green (SR1/C21.) It was however discovered after a few months of trials to turn khaki in colour and to flake badly.

The origin of this trial with mid olive green is described by C. F. Klapper in his book *Sir Herbert Walker's Southern Railway* (Ian Allan Ltd), but unfortunately Mr Klapper assumes, incorrectly, that it was the malachite green that resulted. This colour came later, when the olive shade was observed not to be coming up to specification. Mr Klapper records, on pages 261/2, the events which took place on a train journey to Portsmouth with Sir Herbert Walker, Maunsell and other SR personages present. The year, it is important to stress, was *1936*. I quote:

'All the way down to Portsmouth and across on the paddle steamer *Duchess of Norfolk*, and then on the train to Sandown, a triangular conversation went on while three of the four eminent men in the compartment argued about the effects of rolling stock colour on passenger bookings. Cox wanted a lovely green with golden lining; Bushrod thought green all over could be attractive; Maunsell plunked for dark unlined grey, with large white numerals on the tenders of engines — just the finish he had produced for his first 2-6-0 under the stress of war in 1917. Sir Herbert took no part, but evidently thought a lot about colour schemes. After the gloomy news from the hotel industry was confirmed by actual observation and Sir Herbert had insisted on paying for the lunches of the two aides, who had not the opportunity of Lucullian lunches in the ordinary way, Sir Herbert went across to an optician's shop, where reels of spectacle cord were displayed in the window. He dashed in, emerged quickly with a length of green cord, produced nail scissors, and cut off a piece for each of the officers. He still had an abundant part of the reel, "Now, argument shall cease; that will be the colour Southern engines and coaches shall be painted in future. This reel shall remain in my office safe as the standard to which reference shall be made." When Oliver Bulleid became responsible for the painting of Southern locomotives and coaches the choice of malachite green was thus made inevitable by a general manager who had retired a fortnight before Bulleid's appointment began.'

The assumption made in the last sentence is not borne-out by the facts, which are that during late 1937/8 locomotives and stock were tried out in the mid-olive, which I suggest is the colour Sir Herbert Walker chose. Maunsell retired in October 1937; Bulleid had been appointed the previous May and for the month of September the two men were both at Waterloo, when no doubt the subject of the experimental livery was discussed.

I now quote from page 93 of *Bulleid of the Southern*, by his son H. A. V. Bulleid (Ian Allan Ltd) who states:

'Then there was the interesting matter of the colour. All the railways had adopted their distinctive colours at the Grouping, and they were generally well liked. In particular the Southern had adopted green and used it everywhere and Bulleid agreed it was an excellent choice, specially for trains without engines. The only thing was, *he didn't like the olive green chosen* [Author's italic]. Rather typically, he unearthed a technical disadvantage in the paint used in that its yellow pigment was less stable than the blue. Hence the colour gradually became more bluish, which had the twin disadvantages of looking sombre and accentuating rust staining. The brighter, bluer, and less conservative malachite green favoured by Bulleid avoided these disadvantages, had a more modern look and would make his new designs that bit more distinctive; but how to sell the idea? Offering a choice of colours always causes dissension because each alternative gathers a few adherents so that the majority will not favour the ultimate choice. So he offered only one choice — malachite green — on a beautifully painted carriage brought to Waterloo for Board inspection. There was much discussion and many opinions were freely aired and debated. Bulleid always preached and practiced debate-without-vulgarity, and when he overheard one of the anti-malachites remark with emotion that "it ought to be spelled with an 's' instead of a 'c' " he wittily dismissed this as "rather a gutteral remark". When, some years later, I asked my father exactly how the colour was decided he wrote that "The Chairman and several directors liked the malachite but some of the older directors thought it was too light. Finally, to get a decision, I suggested we made it just a tone darker, and they all agreed. I have never known just what a 'tone' would be like." So he used the original malachite.'

With that, I let the matter rest regarding the *final* livery of the Maunsell years. the broad specifications throughout were as follows:

Locomotives

Passenger livery

ex-LSWR Urie sage green (SR1/C21); from 1923 until 1925/26.

Maunsell green (SR2/C20) from 1926 onwards.

White lining, black edging, green wheels, black tyres and centres, mid chrome yellow lettering and numerals. Red bufferbeams; no lining.

Goods livery

Black; dark green lining; later emerald green (only on some types of locomotive).

Mid chrome yellow lettering and numerals. Red bufferbeams; no lining.

(Plain black livery for all classes after 1935/36.)

Passenger Stock

Maunsell green (SR2/C20) sides.

Chrome orange lining; black edging.

Black ends, underframes and bogies.

Gold block lettering and numerals; shaded black

White, or mid grey, roof.

(Driving ends on electric stock, etc, were finished in green.)

Other Stock

General utility vans/Livestock vans

Maunsell green (SR2/C20) sides. No lining out.

Black ends, underframes and wheels.

mid chrome yellow block lettering, shaded black

White, or mid grey, roof.

Goods wagons

Dark brown bodywork, sides and ends.*

**The dark brown often extended over the solebars and headstocks as well, with black patches painted on to carry white-painted inscriptions, or chalked dates.*

Black underframes, wheels, etc.
White lettering.
Vermilion red ends on brakevans; including headstocks.

Insulated and ventilated vans
Light stone; sides, end and headstocks.
Dark brown; solebars.
Black buffers, wheels, undergear etc.
Red lettering and company initials.

Refrigerator vans
Light stone; (as above) for ex-LSWR stock.
White; for SR-built stock.
Black underframes, etc.
Black lettering.

Containers
A variety of colours were used, to denote the purpose of the container; ranging from the standard brown, to unpainted aluminium (mid-1930s onwards). Colours listed by Historical Model Railway Society in their livery register No 3* are as follows: Stone; Venetian Red (vermilion); standard brown; sea green; red oxide; yellow; standard green; orange; Portland stone. Furniture containers carried advertisement-style liveries.

**The reader in search of the most detailed list of container types and liveries is recommended to this publication.*

9

LOCOMOTIVES

9
Urie Class H15 4-6-0 No 473, ordered before the Grouping as one of a batch of 10 locomotives Nos 473-478, 521-524 and delivered to the SR in 1924 by Eastleigh; without change to their design. Maunsell finished these in the existing shade of sage green used by Urie, with white lining and black edging. The new style of lettering in expanded Egyptian serif forms was applied to the tender sides, with large SECR-style condensed sans-serif numerals below. The prefix E — for Eastleigh — appeared in a small bold serif letterform above the number. Letters and numbers were in medium chrome yellow to simulate gilt. No cabside numberplates fitted and the only identification of the engine itself was the hand-written number on the bufferbeam (which was in block yellow, black shaded LSWR-style sans-serif).
Ian Allan Library

10
From the commencement of the SR's livery scheme, the goods locomotives were painted black with fine dark green lining, and with lettering and numerals to the same style as that adopted for passenger engines. The green lining was too subtle, and apt to disappear after some months in service, and (to judge from photographs) it was later made thicker and lighter (an emerald shade, according to A. B. MacLeod) in an effort to make it more effective. Class G16 4-8-0T No E492 is illustrated; the lining-out is barely visible on the original photograph!
Ian Allan Library

11
Standard letterforms and numerals for locomotives, introduced by R. E. L. Maunsell. The colour of these varied in everyday observations (no doubt according to age since application) from Primrose yellow to Strong orange — but the true shade was medium chrome yellow to imitate the appearance of gilt. They were hand-painted.

12
Application of the new livery scheme to locomotives of all the pre-Grouping constituents seems to have proceeded apace, and after an initial period during which Eastleigh's stock of Urie's LSWR sage green was used-up, Maunsell changed the shade to match that he used on the carriages in June 1925. This was darker and had been known in LSWR days as 'Parson's green', (having been introduced on the electric suburban stock). Hereafter it is referred to as Maunsell green. It had more of a bluish shade than the Urie colour, which tended towards yellow. Ex-LBSCR 'Baltic' tank No B333 *Remembrance* is seen in its first SR repaint, still carrying the name in LSBCR style letterforms, but hand-painted *without* shading, on the tanksides. (Brass war memorial plaque below.) The legend 'Southern' appears in special small-sized letters on the bunker. *Ian Allan Library*

10

11

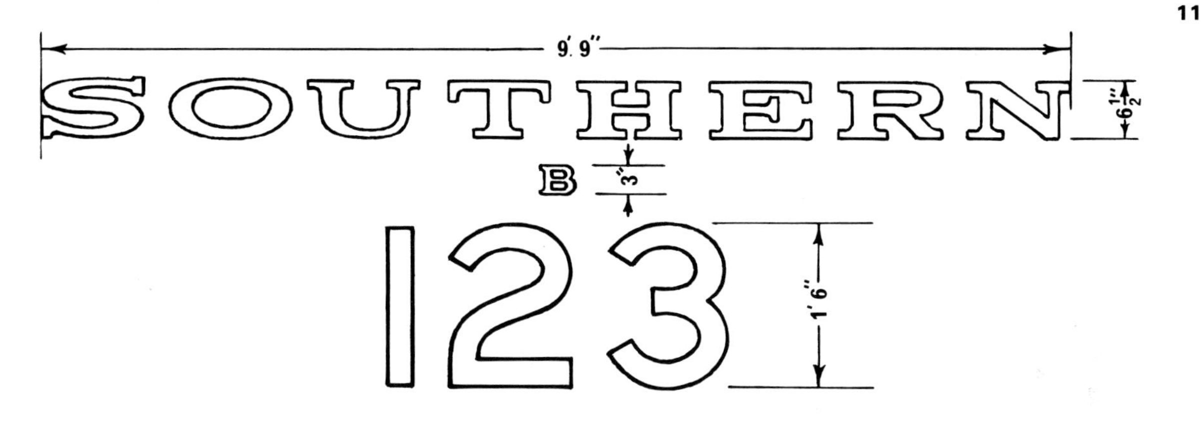

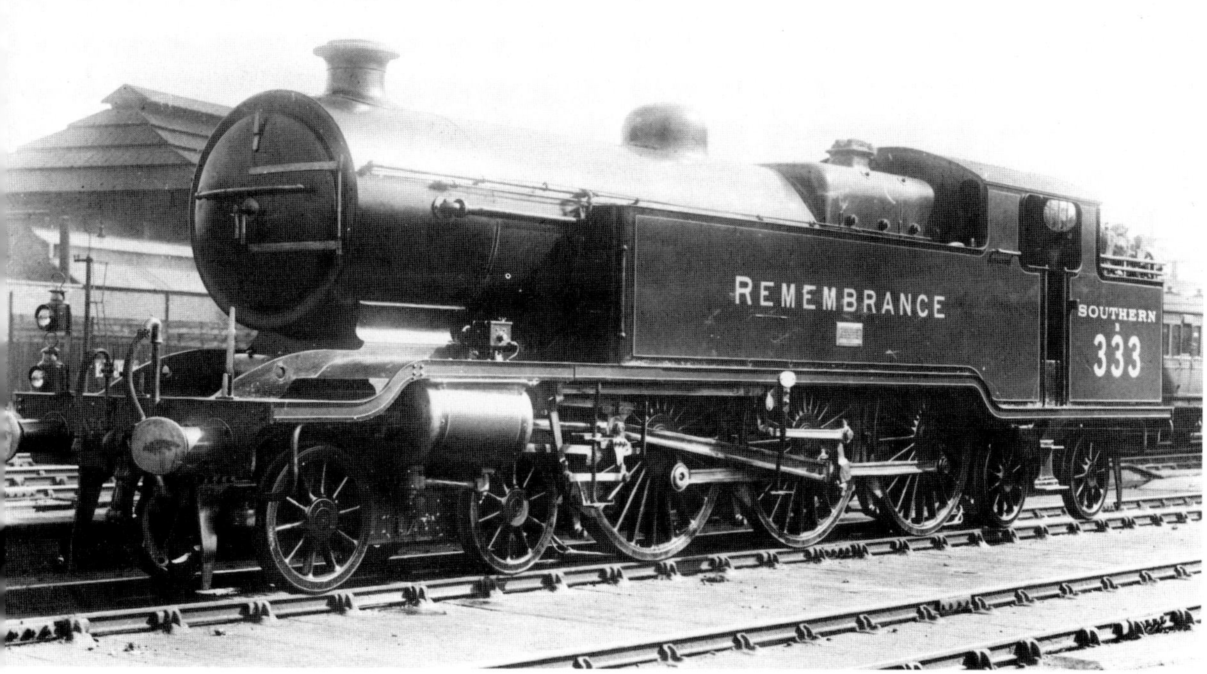

12

13

14

15

13
By mid-1924 the future SR locomotive livery scheme had been decided upon and apart from the change in shade mentioned already, to Maunsell green, only one other subsequent change was made, this was to place the engine number on the cabsides of tender engines, on an oval brass plate. This carried the words Southern Railway, the number and the prefix A, B or E (see text for details). From the same time, tank engines carried one plate on the rear of the bunker, and tenders also carried a plate, on the rear. Maunsell 'King Arthur' class 4-6-0 No E795 *Sir Dinadan* demonstrates the standard passenger livery, as outshopped by Eastleigh in 1926. The one item which was still a variant of Eastleigh at that time was the use of LSWR-style sans-serif numerals on the bufferbeam. At this time the South Eastern and the Brighton engines were carrying serifed yellow and black transfers on the bufferbeams; believed to have come from Inchicore. The background to the numberplates and nameplates was red. *Ian Allan Library*

14
Throughout Maunsell's régime the design of nameplates remained basically the same, except that some were horizontal and some were curved to match the splashers of the locomotive's driving wheel. Illustrated is the nameplate for 'King Arthur' class No E770.

15
Nameplate of 'King Arthur' class 4-6-0 No E770 *Sir Prianius*; for comparison with drawing. Finish was polished brass, with red background. *J. Scrace*

16
The Maunsell livery seemed to suit every type of locomotive and its only problem was a tendency to lose its true shade and become bluer. One of the ill-fated 'River' tanks, No A790 *River Avon* is seen here on the turntable at Victoria. The tank engine in the righthand background is still in the LBSCR umber brown livery. *LPC*

17
It has often been suggested that the choice of the expanded Egyptian lettering, and the use of the single word 'Southern' was influenced by contemporary North American practice for liveries. It certainly had much the same style. Hence it sits quite prettily upon the typical American features of the Lynton & Barnstaple's Baldwin 2-4-2T No E762 *Lyn*; photographed in 1934, at Pilton. The handpainted numerals are slightly bolder and smaller than normal. *A. B. MacLeod*

16

17

18

19

20

18
Rebuilt from a 'River' class 2-6-4T, at Eastleigh in 1928, Class U 2-6-0 No A793 (formerly *River Ouse*), was photographed at London Bridge. Full Maunsell green livery, but only single lining-out on cylinders (compare with Photo 13) and *black* background to cabside numberplate. Rounded-serif shaded numerals on bufferbeam; badly spaced between the 7 and the 9. It was this style of transfer numerals which are believed to have been purchased secondhand from Inchicore Works, Dublin, by Maunsell, perhaps in his SECR days. Note the set number 465 painted in chrome yellow upon the black end of the leading carriage, which is finished in the same shade of green as the locomotive. *LPC*

19
For his fine new 'Lord Nelson' class 4-6-0s Maunsell applied his standard green finish, but he used large LSWR-*style* numerals in yellow, shaded black, on the red engine bufferbeam, on some of the class, when new. No E855 *Robert Blake* (note that the E prefix only appeared on the tendersides and numberplates, not the bufferbeam), is seen heading the up 'Golden Arrow' soon after entry into service, c1928/9. *F. R. Hebron*

20
Close-up, in photographic grey finish, of bufferbeam numerals on 'Lord Nelson' class 4-6-0 No E850 *Lord Nelson*, as first delivered. When new, No 850 had chrome yellow lining-out; later changed to white.
Ian Allan Library

21
Detail of the rear of tender of No E850, in photographic grey finish, showing the standard cast brass numberplate. Final painting reversed the tonality, with the red background to the plate appearing *lighter* than the dark green livery colour. *Ian Allan Library*

22
Dimensions and style of standard numberplates as first applied, with A, B or E prefix. Originally to be painted black, or green, but soon changed to red.
A. B. MacLeod collection

21

22

23

24

23
For a period engines began to appear with the works initial, or prefix, painted upon the bufferbeam instead of the abbreviation: No. In large shaded serif style, No E859 *Lord Hood* displays this feature. The engine is in modified condition, with smoke deflectors (black) added and attached to a Urie 8-wheeled tender; also, as an experiment, it had smaller 6ft 3in diameter driving wheels when photographed working a boat train near Dover. *M. W. Earley*

24
In 1931 the SR locomotive stock was renumbered (see text) and the works initial, or prefix, was abolished. Existing cast brass numberplates had the initial ground or chiselled-off. Two sizes of serifed bufferbeam numerals were then used. The larger size was for the three-figure Western Section based engines, as seen here on 'King Arthur' class 4-6-0s Nos 751 *Etarre* and 777 *Sir Lamiel*; photographed awaiting departure from Waterloo about 1934. No 751 is on the 4.50pm Portsmouth express and No 777 on the 5.0pm West of England express.
G. J. Jefferson

25

25
Rebuilt from the LBSCR 'Baltic' tank design (see photo 12) in 1934-36, the Maunsell 'N15X' class 4-6-0s carried the standard livery; being notable for the number of lined-out boiler bands, and only single lining on cylinders. No 2333 *Remembrance* shows the new curved nameplate and the original memorial plaque resited upon the centre splasher. Urie bogie tender, with lining-out to flared upper portion, (later replaced by plain black.) New-style cast brass numberplate on cabside, without works prefix, and with number in centre (see picture 28). Matt finish to black smokebox, chimney and smoke deflectors; lining-out to locomotive wheels.
Ian Allan Library

26
The smaller size of shaded serif numerals, needed for the four-figure numbers (after the 1931 changes), are seen here in this bufferbeam detail shot of ex-LBSCR Atlantic, SR Class H1 No 2039 *Hartland Point* (formerly *La France*), photographed hauling the 'Sunny South Express' in 1938. The yellow triangle above the abbreviation 'No.' indicates that the locomotive had been converted to the composite SR loading gauge. *O. J. Morris*

26

27

The Maunsell green passenger locomotive livery in all its finery, upon 'Schools' class 4-4-0 No 919 *Harrow*, built at Eastleigh in 1933. Features to note are the polished brass surround to the cab side window, double lining-out of the cylinders, lined green finish to the small splasher over the inner wheel of the leading bogie, and plain green finish (with black centres and tyres) to the locomotive wheels. The small letter A painted above the leading footstep, behind the buffer, denoted the 'haulage classification' (see text) and was carried on some types of locomotive on the Western Section only.
Ian Allan Library

27

28

Revised style of cabside numberplate, without prefix letter. Brass with red edges and background.
A. B. MacLeod collection

29
During the Maunsell period of the mid-1930s and following the renumbering of 1931, a move away from brass plates in favour of lettering was commenced, for the rear of tenders and the bunkers of tank engines. For four-figure numbers the same style as used upon the bufferbeam was generally favoured, as seen here upon ex-LBSCR Class D1 0-4-2T No 2215, c1940 hauling a freight train from the War Office depot through Grove Street, Deptford, past a Commer van. For locomotives with only three-figure numbers, the opportunity was taken to use up old stock of ex-LSWR and LBSCR shaded sans-serif numerals, at this time; the majority however carried a larger version of the shaded serif.
Ian Allan Library

30
For goods locomotives, the green lining was finally abandoned in 1935-36 and the livery became plain black, with yellow numerals and lettering and red bufferbeams. Mainly done for economy it was quite effective, if kept clean. 'W' class 2-6-4T No 1919 displays the scheme. *Ian Allan Library*

29

30

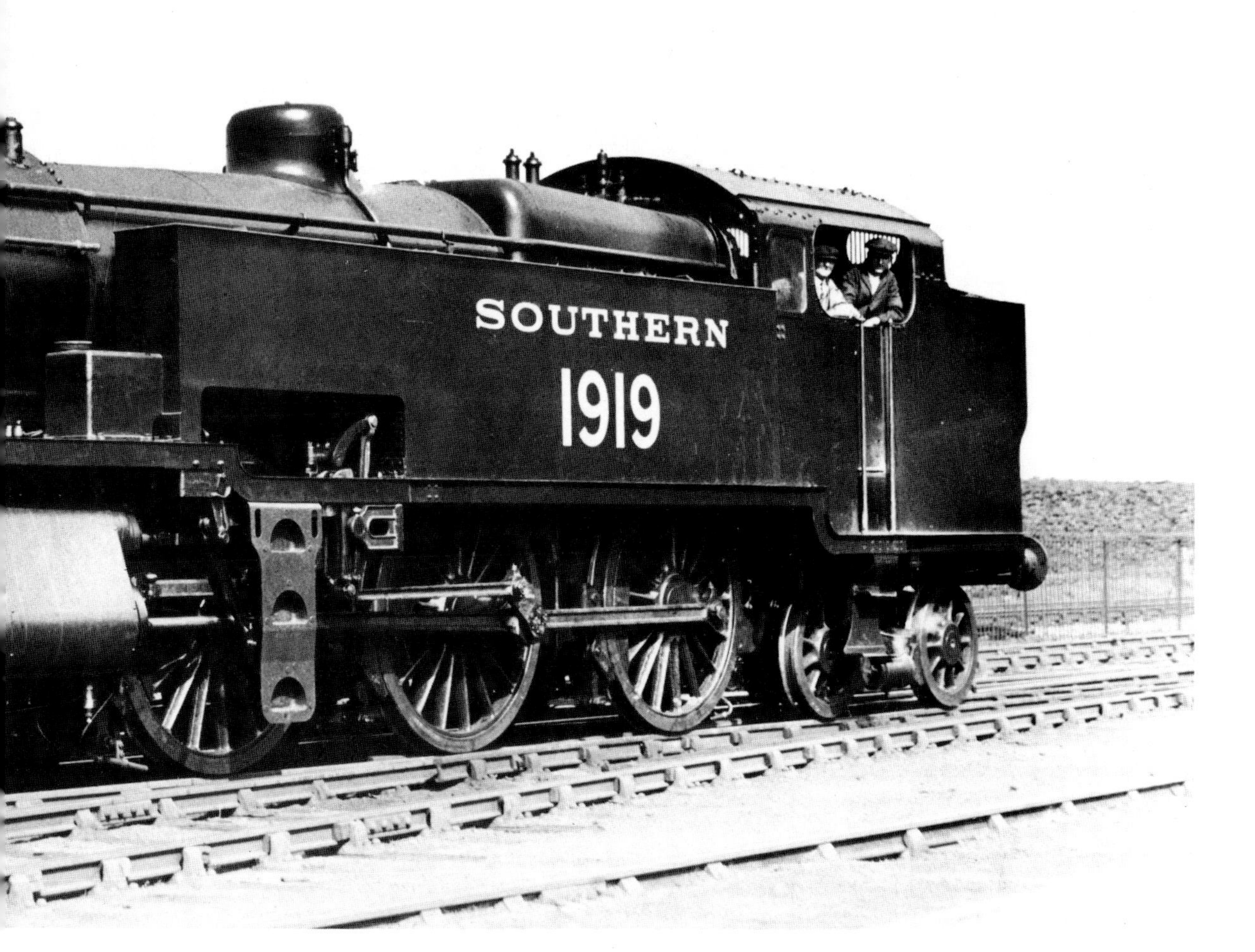

31

32

33

31
The word 'Southern' in the full sized lettering is more closely spaced than normal, and this and the large numerals completely fill the tank side on this 'P' class ex-SECR 0-6-0T ex-works at Ashford in black unlined livery. *H. C. Casserley*

32
By way of contrast to the preceding picture, the handpainted 'Southern' on ex-LBSCR 'Terrier' 0-6-0T No 2636 (formerly *Fenchurch*), is spaced normally, but the smaller numerals are old LBSCR gilt transfers, which a number of older-type locomotives carried in the period 1936/7; presumably to use up old stock. Captioned by the photographer 'A Couple of Terriers', this charming picture of the loco in black livery was taken at Newhaven Harbour (on the West quay) about 1937. The extremely light permanent way was laid on the harbour wall.
C. C. B. Herbert

33
Full passenger green livery (including lining-out on the wheels) applied to the Isle of Wight ex-LBSCR 0-6-0T No 1 *Medina*, with standard size lettering but smaller numeral on bunker side. Note the lining around the nameplate. *O. J. Morris*

34
Large numerals in ex-LBSCR gilt and black shaded transfers, applied to the rear of the flat-sided bogie tender of 'Lord Nelson' class 4-6-0 No 860 *Lord Hawke*; showing also black edging and lining-out standard for the rear panel of tenders on locomotives finished in Maunsell green livery. Brass numberplate on cabside also edged in black and finished with a single white line surround.
A. B. MacLeod

34

PASSENGER STOCK

35
The livery adopted by Maunsell for passenger rolling stock was a direct follow-on from the LSWR scheme known as 'Parson's green' or sage green, and which had first appeared on the London area electric stock of 1915. In the final years of the LSWR, about 1921, the Company had decided to apply this colour to all their coaching stock instead of the famous Salmon pink and brown scheme, but this policy had not got far before the Grouping. The lining was chrome orange, with black edging, and the coach ends, underframes and bogies were black. In the initial SR scheme the roof was white (soon turning cream or dirty grey) and the company name and numerals, also subsidiary lettering and numerals 'Guard', 'First', 'Third' etc, were in gilt or gold leaf, transfers shaded black. Where possible the legend 'Southern Railway' was carried above the windows in the most centrally sited cant rail panels, with the numerals in the same height panels at the extreme end of the carriage sides. With deep-windowed stock, such as seen here, the 'Southern Railway' had to be placed *below* the windows, at waist level. Illustrated, in 'photographic grey' livery is a side-corridor third class main line carriage, c1929. Note, no lining out or panelling below waist level. *Ian Allan Library*

36
The panelling above waist level was elaborately picked-out in orange and black on wooden-bodied stock, and an imitation of this was carried by steel-bodied stock, until 1930 when a more simplified style began to appear on the latter. This wooden-bodied Lynton & Barnstaple narrow gauge Brake Composite (1st Saloon, 3rd compartment and luggage/guard compartment) No 6991 was photographed at Pilton, freshly painted, in 1934/5. White roof, and red (smoking) and green (no-smoking) roundel transfers on outside of windows. *A. B. MacLeod*

35

36

37

2' $3\frac{1}{4}$" — 12" Min — 1' $9\frac{5}{8}$"

SOUTHERN RAILWAY

$3\frac{5}{16}$" — $\frac{7}{16}$"

1234

$\frac{7}{16}$" — 3" — 1' $2\frac{3}{4}$"

37
Standard lettering and numerals for SR coaching stock adopted in 1923, with gold leaf or gilt finish and black shading. Used throughout the Maunsell régime.

38
A simplified form of lining out, still retaining some illusion of panelling, was applied to the flush steel sides of the Brighton main line electric multiple-units, when first delivered. The standard Maunsell green (by this time generally stated to be somewhat darker and richer than had been the case in the 1920s) was carried around the driving ends, without lining. The lining was confined to the waist and window areas, with numbers and letters above. On motor-coaches, such as seen here, and Pantry Cars, the class was denoted by figures, whereas electric trailer cars and steam stock retained the full legends First and Third. Illustrated is a third class electric motor coach, No 11053, built by the Metropolitan-Cammell Carriage & Wagon Co in 1935. Window frames in the droplights was varnished teak; roof was lead white, underframes, bufferbeams, buffers and bogies black. *Ian Allan Library*

38

39

39
Perhaps it was simply economy, or perhaps commonsense, or perhaps a mixture of both, that resulted in the final version of the Maunsell carriage livery; produced just prior to his retirement. For modern flush-panelled stock, such as the new Portsmouth line electrics, all allusion to fake panelling was dispensed with and two parallel lines of chrome orange and black ran along the bodysides at waist level; as seen here on the side of a new electric kitchen car for the Waterloo-Portsmouth electrification; photographed in June 1937. Where a break in the lines occurred, such as a doorway, the two parallel lines were turned to meet each other vertically, with a radius to the corners.
Ian Allan Library

OTHER STOCK

40
The basic livery for SR goods rolling stock after the Grouping was dark brown, based upon the LSWR scheme, but evidence suggests that existing stocks of brown carriage paint from the LBSCR and possibly elsewhere were also used up. (The LBSCR carriage paint was a more rich reddish brown; the LSWR shade was more like bitter chocolate.) The block sans-serif lettering was white, unshaded. Illustrated is an ex-LBSCR 10ton cattle wagon. Note the details painted upon the end, rather than the side. The ends of goods brake vans (not illustrated) were painted vermilion red. *Ian Allan Library*

41
Standard unshaded sans-serif block lettering used by the SR for goods rolling stock and similar applications; such as containers. Colour was white,except when used on stone-coloured (insulated and ventilated) vans, when it was red, or on the refrigerated vans (which were white) in which case the lettering was black.

40

41

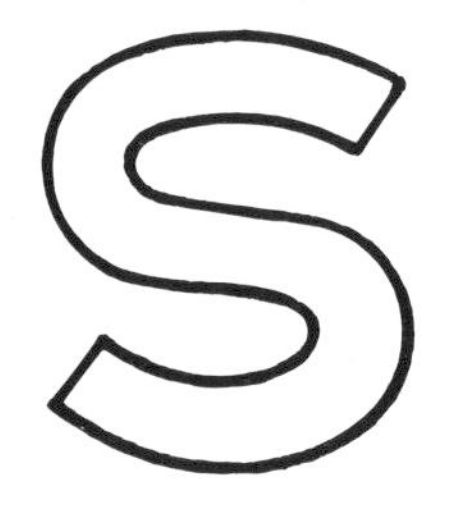

42

43

42
Standard chocolate brown livery, with white inscriptions on 12ton open wagon No 7606, photographed in September 1930. The brown extended over the solebars, in many cases even covering the axleboxes and undergear; otherwise these areas were black.
Ian Allan Library

43
Looking extremely smart are these two goods vehicles on the narrow gauge Lynton & Barnstaple line; photographed at Lynton in 1935. Nearest the camera is bogie covered goods wagon No 47045, in chocolate brown livery; beyond is a truly diminutive 4ton open wagon, No 28305, also in the standard brown.
A. B. MacLeod

44
Many departmental vehicles, such as breakdown and tool vans, were painted plain grey with white lettering. This scheme was also applied to the SR weed-killing train of the early 1930s; composed of converted ex-LSWR locomotive tenders. Seen here is No 573S; close-coupled footplate end to another one; forming a twin. Livery of plain grey included the ends, buffer beams and buffer stocks, and underframes. *Ian Allan Library*

44

45

45
More colourful than the goods stock were the general utility vans, which could often be found attached to passenger trains. These were finished in the standard Maunsell green, devoid of lining but with mid chrome yellow sans-serif with lettering and numerals, to match the gilt on the carriages. Roof when newly painted was white; body ends and underframes etc, were glossy black. Illustrated is No 2051, built in March 1928; with wheel rims painted white for photographic purposes. The four oblong panels on waist level, for chalked inscriptions, were painted matt grey. *Ian Allan Library*

46
Containers were finished in a variety of colour schemes, according to their purpose (see text). This small Type C $2\frac{1}{2}$ton open was built by the Birmingham Railway Carriage & Wagon Co and painted in the goods wagon brown livery, with white lettering. Note the full stops for S.R. — not standard practice. *Ian Allan Library*

46

2: The Bulleid Years, 1937-1947

We have already seen that Bulleid arrived at Waterloo in the midst of a period of change for rolling stock liveries, and we have his son's account of his reactions to the new olive green then being tried. Bulleid soon entered the debate, and added two important contributions. One was the change in style of the lettering for the word 'Southern', to a gilt or mid chrome yellow sanserif style with no shading and with a body colour (green or black) line within it, this appeared to 'line-up' visually with the numerals in black shaded san serif style on the cabside of tender engines. The brass numberplates on cabsides were then dispensed with. The second major contribution Bulleid made, after only a few months in office, was the trial in service of malachite green (SR4/C14) on both locomotives and carriages.

Events then overtook Bulleid's efforts to obtain a new brighter standard livery for the SR. As 1939 saw the nation drawn steadily closer to and into war, the workshops evidently commenced using-up all their existing stocks of paint, no doubt due to shortages. For a period, into 1940 the original Maunsell, the light olive and the malachite shades were all in use, some with lining-out and some without. The new style lettering and numerals were to be seen on all three colours, and on some black engines.

By 1941 it was apparent that shortage of paint would force the SR to paint all but its top rank express passenger engines in black. For the remaining green engines a revised livery, using less malachite, was proposed. For the 1,803 steam locomotives to be painted black, a revised style of lettering was then introduced, at the suggestion of A. B. MacLeod, then Assistant Stores Superintendent at Waterloo. This became known as the 'Sunshine' lettering because it used golden yellow instead of gilt for the transfers (making an estimated saving of some £2,049 a year in the process) and with green shading 'shot' with the yellow, to give a little touch of colour to the black engines. The malachite green (officially known as the new 'No 3 green' incidentally) for the express passenger types had black shaded gilt transfers designed for them, at the same time, in the new 'Sunshine' alphabet.

All attempts to paint even the express passenger locomotives in malachite green were abandoned the following year, and black was the official standard livery until the end of the war; although of course many engines survived this grim period still in prewar colours (including some in the pre-1938 Maunsell green with large numerals!). Characteristically, Bulleid used this wartime interruption to normal painting procedures to establish his ideas for a standard postwar livery.

When the SR began to repaint locomotives and rolling stock green in mid-1945, the standard shade was malachite throughout. By 1947 when nationalisation put an end to the individual company liveries, the SR was well on the way to achieving a bright and efficient modern image, using the new green and the 'Sunshine' lettering. (It was to take BR nearly 10 years to achieve anything remotely similar!) With the nationalisation, Bulleid remained in office for some time, but once Eastleigh, Brighton and Ashford had used up their stocks of malachite green, the new motley array of BR colours took their place.

The broad specification of the postwar Bulleid livery was as follows:

Locomotives

Passenger livery

New green No 3; malachite (SR4/C14).
Golden yellow lining; black edging. Green wheels (some classes), black tyres. Gilt transfer lettering, shaded black and 'shot' with golden yellow, gilt numbers, shaded black and 'shot' with yellow. Red bufferbeams; no lining.

Shortages of paint restricted the number of secondary passenger engines to receive green livery, but the ultimate intention was for them all to carry it.

Goods livery

Black; no lining-out.
Golden yellow lettering, shaded green and 'shot' with golden yellow. Red bufferbeams; no lining. (Basically the wartime livery, perpetuated.)

Passenger Stock

New green No 3; malachite (SR4/C14) no lining out. Black ends, underframes, bogies, etc. Golden yellow and black lettering and numerals. Mid grey roof.

Other Stock

Basically as in prewar days, except that malachite replaced the Maunsell green for general utility vans, post office carriages, livestock vans, etc; without lining. The vast majority of goods wagons remained in the patch-painted appearance adopted during the war years for economy purposes, with only the left hand lower corner properly painted, to carry the number and associated details.

LOCOMOTIVES

47
Just before Bulleid's arrival, the SR's General Manager had decided to brighten up the appearance of the trains so an experimental phase began for liveries. Bulleid added to this the new form of lettering for use on locomotives and carriages. The letters were actually adapted from a style of typeface which the SR's publicity department had been using for advertising and other printed matter for some years past (see picture 93). The block letters were in gold leaf, or gilt, unshaded, but with a body colour line *inside* it. The numerals, however, did not have the line. Bulleid changed the colour of the lining-out on some Maunsell green engines to yellow, in order to match this new lettering, when applied.
A. B. MacLeod collection

48
The new style sans-serif shaded numerals for use with the revised lettering, on green locomotives. Note that in this monochrome photograph the shading of the letters appear *lighter* than the background. This is incorrect; the shading was black and the background green.
A. B. MacLeod collection

47

48

49
Although many locomotives continued to be painted (or patch-painted) in Maunsell's green (some however had white lining, and some yellow) during the period late 1936-1939 Bulleid tried out one or two alternative greens, and varied the lining, in his search for a satisfactory new 'image' for the SR stock. One version on the 'Lord Nelson' class was a mid olive green (SR3/C12) with yellow lining and Maunsell green edging. Cylinder covers plain black, but entire area of smoke deflector green with yellow and black edging. Another version featured malachite green with dark green and yellow lining, but with plain black smoke deflectors and cylinders, as seen here on No 863 *Lord Rodney*; stove pipe style multiple-jet exhaust. *British Rail*

49

50

50
Malachite green was the shade favoured by Bulleid, and by mid-1938 he was sufficiently convinced to have the entire 'Bournemouth Limited' train repainted, including six of the 'Schools' class 4-4-0s rostered to haul it. No 927 *Clifton*, with white lining-out and black edging to the malachite, black smoke deflectors, and with extra large san-serif bufferbeam numerals, is seen at Waterloo on 21 July 1938. Class M7 0-4-4T No 40 is seen alongside. The coaches, with set 232 leading, were in unlined malachite. A colour plate of this scene, taken by the same photographer appeared in the *Railway Magazine* for December 1938. Unfortunately this colour plate tends to make the malachite look too yellow in shade; it was colder in reality. *O. J. Morris*

51
The new style gilt lettering and numerals gradually began to appear on iesser types of locomotive, immediately prior to World War 2. The Guildford Shed pilot, 0-4-0ST No 3458 *Ironside* displays them, on black livery. Some wit has placed a price label on the rear of the cab for 1s, 6d! *S. C. Townroe*

51

52

53

52
By 1939 Bulleid had refined the malachite green livery to achieve what would have become standard but for the outbreak of the war. This view of 'Lord Nelson' class 4-6-0 No 857 *Lord Howe* (with experimental round-top combustion chamber boiler and Bulleid-Lemaitre multiple-jet blastpipe fitted), shows the settled version, with green on the smoke deflectors and wheels, lined yellow and edged black, but plain black cylinders. Yellow lining and black edging on engine and tender but gilt lettering and numerals. Red background to nameplate and black-shaded gilt numerals (of same style as cabside) on the red bufferbeam. Photographed at Herne Bay in November 1939. Note the unusual elbowed smoke-deflectors then carried by this engine.
P. Ransome-Wallis.

53
Bulleid's first new locomotive design for the SR was an eye-opener in many respects; not least its outward appearance. No 21C1 *Channel Packet* was completed at Eastleigh in February 1941, and despite the severe economies of wartime, it was given a full passenger livery. The malachite green (for the entire sides of engine and tender, and rear of tender) was however of a matt finish. The three horizontal lines were in golden yellow. The nameplate was in polished brass with red background. but the new style numberplates on the front and cabsides and the ownership plates on the smokebox door and tender sides were in polished gunmetal, with red background. The front end was black with a red bufferbeam and the wheels were green, unlined, with black edging and centres. The roof above the guttering was finished in matt black. *Author's Collection*

54
Front end detail of No 21C1 *Channel Packet*, as built. The numberplate measured 30$^{13}/_{16}$in by 12$^{7}/_{16}$in overall and had numerals 9in high; the letter C was however 10in high. *Ian Allan Library*

55
The nameplates on No 21C1 set a completely new style for the SR and carried a coloured enamel plaque in the centre, depicting the House flag of the shipping service, or company, that the locomotive was named after. That on No 21C1 *Channel Packet* showed the SR House Flag, as carried by its cross-Channel steamers (see picture 92). Photographed 8 March 1941. *Ian Allan Library*

56
By 1941, with all the material shortages and the general pressures of wartime making themselves felt, the policy of painting locomotives green was in question. An attempt was made to keep the most important classes green — the 'Nelsons' 'Schools' and 'King Arthurs' whilst all others became plain black — following a period when the workshops used up the remaining stock of Maunsell green on lesser types of locomotive (often without lining and sometimes with Bullied lettering). This picture of 'Schools' class 4-4-0 No 938 *St Olave's* was taken at Eastleigh to show a revised style of painting with the malachite green restricted to the sides of the engine (including smoke deflectors) and the tender and with black (lined yellow) for the edging. The cylinders, entire cab front, and rear of the tender were black. No number on rear of tender, and cabside window removed and replaced by sheet metal (painted green) as an air raid precaution. 'Southern' in gilt on tender sides.
British Rail SR

56

57
The prototype Bulleid/Raworth Co-Co mixed traffic electric locomotive was completed in 1941 and turned-out for trials in a matt grey finish with white lining. No sign of ownership was carried, and the numerals CC1 only appeared on the red bufferbeams in white at each end. It is almost certain that this was the 'photographic grey' and that, but for the wartime conditions, the engines would have been finished in the same malachite and yellow scheme as used on the 'Merchant Navy' Pacifics. Photographed near Merstham on 5 December 1941. *British Rail SR*

58
In August 1941 it was decided that out of the total stock of 1,803 steam locomotives, only 127 main line locomotives would retain the malachite green (see picture 56) and the remaining 1,676 would be painted black. To retain some of the well-known SR green on the black engines a revised style of golden yellow lettering (old gold shade) was introduced, shaded in green and 'shot' with golden yellow. This was to become known as the Southern 'sunshine' lettering. The same style of lettering and numerals was adopted for the remaining green engines, but using gold leaf or gilt instead of the more economical yellow and with black shading 'shot' with golden yellow. (It is extremely doubtful if many, if any, green engines carried these gilt transfers until postwar days.) The new style for the black engines is illustrated. *A. B. MacLeod collection*

59
New style of old gold (golden yellow) numerals, with green shading, 'shot' with golden yellow, for black engines; introduced 1941. Numerals were 9in high to match the lettering. *A. B. MacLeod collection*

60
New style of Gilt numerals for use on the remaining malachite green engines (Class LN, V, and N15,) with black shading and 'shot' with golden yellow highlights 9in high. *A. B. MacLeod collection*

61
Bufferbeam numerals for black engines, in golden yellow (old gold) with black shading and golden yellow highlight on red. Those for the green locomotives were identical in style, 6in high, but finished in gilt.
A. B. MacLeod collection

62
Specimen 9in letter and numeral for black engines from the SR 'Sunshine' alphabet introduced in 1941, and specimen 6in figure from bufferbeam. *Ian Allan Library*

57

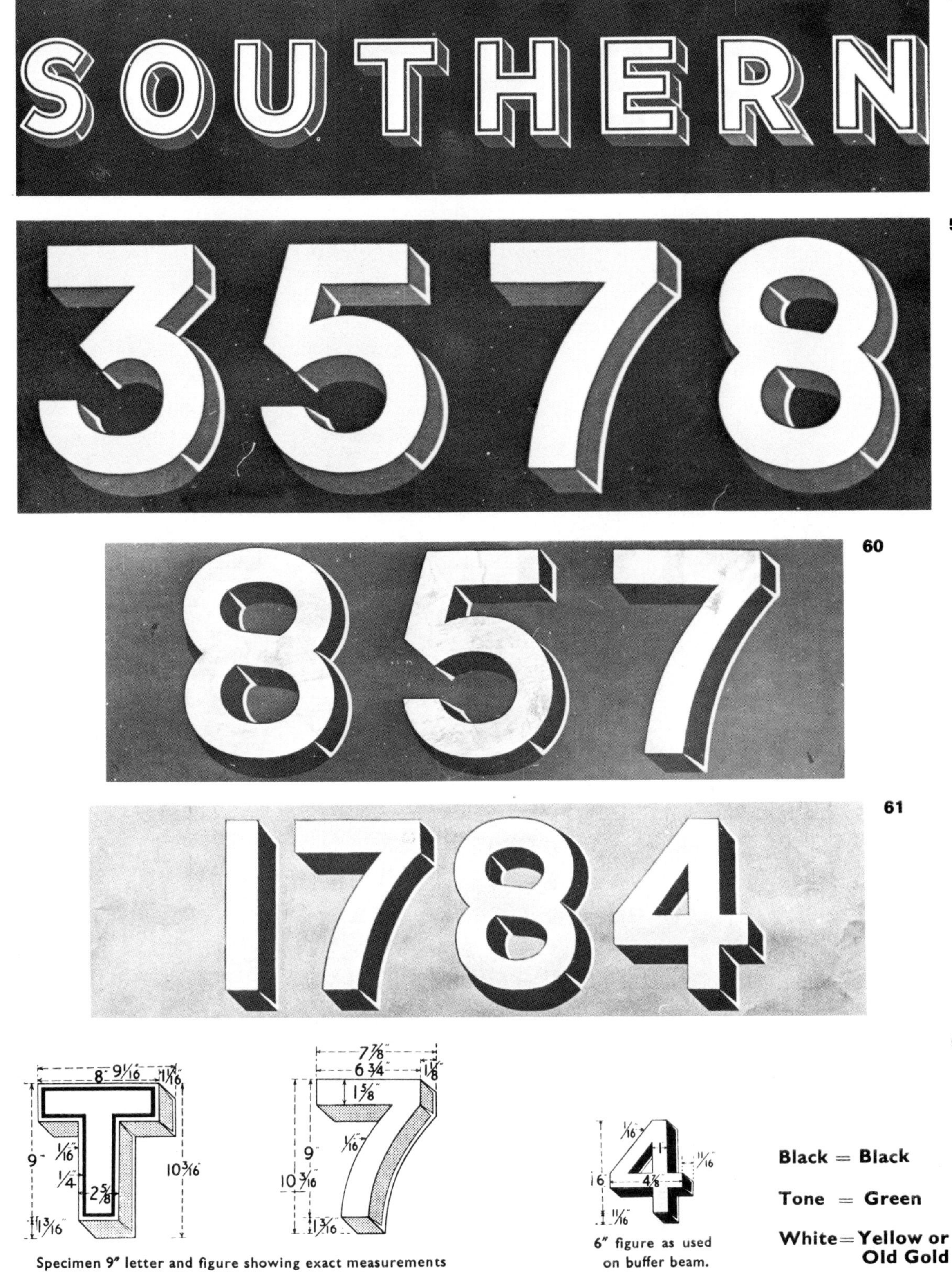

Specimen 9" letter and figure showing exact measurements

6" figure as used on buffer beam.

63
Scarcely had the SR produced its revised scheme for locomotive liveries when shortage of the green paint forced them to abandon all efforts to keep the 127 express passenger engines (or slightly more, if one includes the 'Merchant Navy' engines then completed) in green. Black, without lining became the order of the day, and the only green was in the shading of the 'sunshine' lettering and numerals. New 'Merchant Navy' Pacific No 21C8 *Orient Line* is seen here in new condition at Eastleigh in October 1942, finished in black overall except for the background to the nameplate, and ownership plate on the smokebox, and the bufferbeams, which were red. The smokebox ownership plate was changed to the complete roundel shown here after complaints from enginemen that the original 'inverted horseshoe' (see photo 54) was unlucky! The added lower portion carried the inscription 'Eastleigh 1942'. Incidentally, Bulleid himself ordered this photograph to be withdrawn from circulation when his attention was drawn to the fact that the front footsteps had been bent by accident! *A. B. MacLeod collection*

64
Overall wartime black, with green shaded 'sunshine' lettering and numerals and red-backed nameplate, on 'Schools' class 4-4-0 No 930 *Radley*; photographed at Eastleigh on 27 April 1943. *Ian Allan Library*

63

64

65

65
Despite a chronic shortage of cleaners and shed and footplate staff generally, the SR maintained a reasonable standard of cleanliness with the black engines, and the colourful lettering must have helped to keep up morale in these drab days. The Isle of Wight Class 02 0-4-4T No 33 *Bembridge* displays the cleaner's efforts, at Newport, date unknown, but possibly the immediate postwar period. *Mr Wickens*

66
The SR was commendably quick off the mark in restoring the use of malachite green for its more important locomotives, immediately after the war ended. Seen here is 'Merchant Navy' Pacific No 21C1 *Channel Packet* (somewhat modified at the front end compared to pictures 53/54), beautifully repainted at Eastleigh in April 1946 in readiness for working the restored Pullman car 'Golden Arrow' train. Livery was now *glossy* malachite, and the positioning of the horizontal yellow bands had been altered to make them more evenly spaced. Smokebox door plate changed to a complete roundel, and numberplate repositioned immediately above bufferbeam (compare with picture 54). *Ian Allan Library*

66

67

67
For his lightweight Pacifics, of both the 'West Country' and 'Battle of Britain' classes, Bulleid was able to standardise the livery from the outset, using malachite green and yellow but with the lower portion of the side sheeting on both engine and tender painted glossy black, Gilt version of 'sunshine' lettering and numerals, with black shading for *sides* but golden yellow version with green shading for the front numerals, painted upon black. Wheels were usually black, but some locomotives received green wheels, either for special occasions when new or during repaint. No 21C154 *Lord Beaverbrook* is seen here, making a splendid picture for the photographer. *E. R. Wethersett*

68
Both the versions of the lightweight Pacifics featured distinctive nameplate designs, complete with enamelled colour plaques. The 'West Country' class version is seen here on the second of the class to be built. No 21C102 *Salisbury*; photographed in malachite green on 4 July 1945. *Ian Allan Library*

68

69

The two Bulleid/Raworth Co-Co electrics, Nos CC1 and CC2 received malachite green livery in the postwar period, with two horizontal yellow bands down the bodyside at cantrail and baseline levels, and with large gilt, black shaded and yellow highlighted lettering 'Southern'. The numbers appeared only on each end, on the bufferbeam in large characters yellow shaded black, upon red. *British Rail SR*

70

Although postwar paint shortages meant that some locomotives had perforce to be returned to traffic in black, the SR made every effort to put the express passenger locomotives into malachite green, as they passed through the workshops. 'King Arthur' class 4-6-0 No 790 *Sir Villiars* is seen in a new coat of paint, passing Millbrook, Southampton in January 1947, en route to Waterloo. Note that the malachite green was carried up to the top of the tender side and that the lettering was placed in line with the numerals on the cabside. Dirty coal is obviously creating exhaust dispersal problems in this instance! *Frank F. Moss*

69

70

71

71
The standard postwar malachite livery graced some of the more elderly passenger locomotives with a charm almost like the livery they had carried in pre-Grouping days. Class H2 'Atlantic' No 2421 *South Foreland* carries the colours proudly in this view outside Newhaven shed, taken on 4 September 1947, after the locomotive had worked the down boat train from Victoria.
C. C. B. Herbert

72
Particularly pleasing was the return of the malachite green to grace the Isle of Wight passenger tanks, which were kept beautifully clean. Illustrated is No 18 *Ningwood*; photographed in April 1948. *D. Trevor Rowe*

72

73
For locomotives of lesser types, such as this delightful little Class C14 0-4-0T, which retained the black livery in postwar days, the 'sunshine' lettering gave a pleasing touch of colour. Photographed at Eastleigh on 26 July 1947. *J. H. Aston*

74
Although the 1948 nationalisation brought an abrupt halt to Bulleid's malachite liverv scheme for the SR, the colour lasted upon both rolling stock and locomotives for several years afterwards. (The malachite was however chosen as a standard colour for BR multiple-unit electric trains. Still sporting the full Bulleid postwar colour scheme in April 1951, is this Class L 4-4-0 No 1778, seen at Tonbridge with the through express from Birkenhead to Margate. Note that the cabside numerals had to be lowered to clear the beading of the splashers.
Rev. A. W. C. Mace

PASSENGER STOCK

75
One of the first demonstrations of Bulleid's originality in design matters was the revised interior of the Buffet cars for the Bognor Regis electrification in 1938. The exterior of these cars he had painted in unlined malachite green (the rest of the train was in Maunsell green) and this brochure produced by the SR shows that he intended to place the SR coat of arms on at least one. No photographic evidence of this has come to the Author's attention (evidence would be welcomed) and so far as is known only two cars carried coats of arms, and these were of the County of Sussex. Readers are invited to add any further details they may have on the subject. Note that this coat of arms is completely different from that reproduced in picture 2; which was apparently, produced to replace it. *A. B. MacLeod collection*

76
Unlined malachite green livery, with gilt numerals, shaded black and new style lettering for 'Southern' in gilt without shading, at waist level. Numbers instead of words for class. A 1932 Maunsell composite carriage, specially refurbished in 1938 for use on the 'Bournemouth Limited'. (See also picture 50.) *British Rail SR*

77
New rolling stock for the Waterloo & City underground line; introduced in 1940. Malachite green bodysides with aluminium/silver finish for the front ends, roof and sliding doors. New style lettering in gilt for 'Southern', and gilt numerals, shaded black, above end windows of each carriage. No 56 leading. *British Rail SR*

78
One of Bulleid's major contributions to the SR was the introduction of all-steel suburban electric carriages. The first of these appeared in 1941, 4SUB set No 4101, and this was painted in unlined malachite green; setting a trend that was to last for the rest of the SR's existence. Seen here is a later 4SUB unit, introduced in 1946. No 4111 has the 'sunshine' lettering in golden yellow shaded black and 'shot' with golden yellow on the ends and centre of the sides. Plain malachite green, mid grey roof, black underframes and bogies, and buffers and bufferbeam. Carriage numbers at extreme ends of carriages at what would normally be cantrail level. (The gutter was exceptionally high.) *British Rail SR*

75

THE NEW BUFFET CARS
FOR THE ELECTRIC TRAINS BETWEEN
LONDON AND BOGNOR REGIS
ELECTRIC TRAINS ARE ALSO NOW IN SERVICE
BETWEEN LONDON & LITTLEHAMPTON
AND WEST WORTHING & HAVANT

SOUTHERN ELECTRIC

76

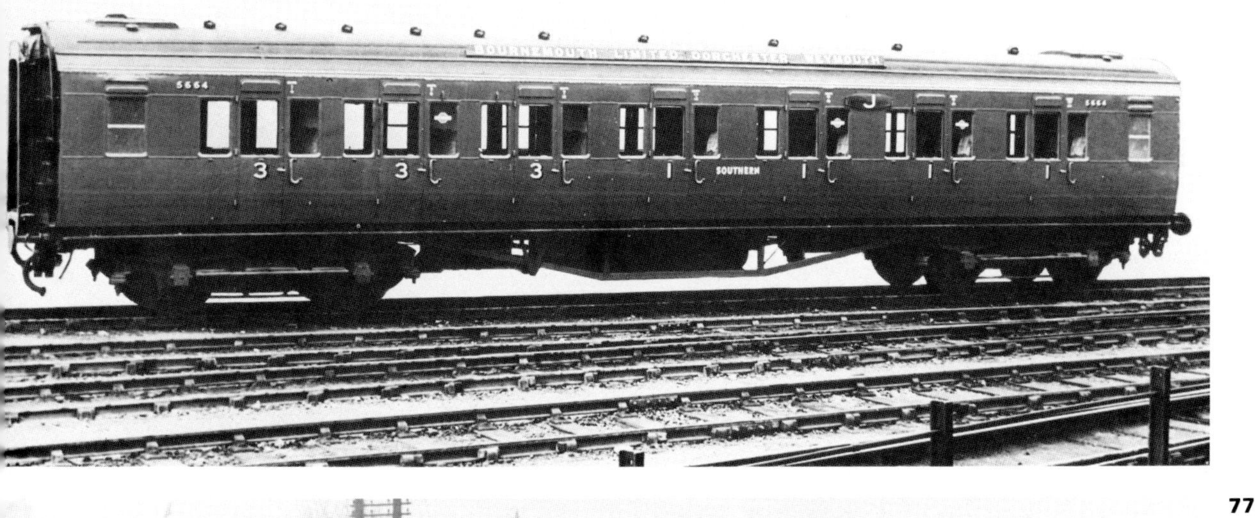
BOURNEMOUTH LIMITED DORCHESTER WEYMOUTH
SOUTHERN

77

SOUTHERN

78

SOUTHERN
4111
10962

79
Bulleid postwar main line loco-hauled corridor set No 290, with two restaurant cars. Plain malachite green, grey roofs, black underframes and bogies. (Some coaches had green ends; some black.) Set number 290 painted in golden yellow, unshaded. 'Sunshine' lettering in yellow and black on bodysides. *Ian Allan Library*

79

80

OTHER STOCK

80
Just prior to Bulleid's arrival at Waterloo the decision was taken to stop using the large white letters SR on the sides of goods stock, and to place it on each side in small letters, together with the number and other details, at one end in the bottom left hand corner. Bulleid did not alter this. Pictured here is a detail from a chocolate brown liveried SAW (shock abosrbing wagon) built in 1940. Three vertical white lines were painted on the sides to denote these special wagons. *Ian Allan Library*

3: Stations

The Southern had a very standardised livery scheme for its passenger stations, throughout its existence. The rather cold combination of green and cream or stone colour was perhaps a little depressing because of its monotony, but it proved to be very practicable and instantly recognisable. As with the rolling stock livery, the darker green tended to fade to blue with exposure and weathering, but it was otherwise a very robust colour scheme.

The broad specification for stations was as follows:

Light stone: For roof and valance interiors, interior walls, upper parts of buildings (under awnings) wooden gates and fences.
Dark stone: For valance exteriors, wooden walls, lavatory entrance screens, signalbox wooden planking and balustrades, wooden hut exteriors, close boarded fences (where not creosoted) and some gates.
White: For window sashes, flag poles, level crossing gates, wicket gates, railings at bridge approaches and (as distemper) for interior ceilings.
Mid chrome green: For drain pipes, valance mouldings, awning columns, railings, handrails, window frames, internal walls (up to 4ft from the floor), doors and frames, most metal fittings, lamp posts, etc. Also grounded carriage bodies (within station limits) signal/telephone boxes, etc.
Dark green: 4in border to poster boards.
Light green: Roofing steelwork (under awnings, etc) and ornamental brackets.
Deep green: Internal walls; upper parts.
Red: Fire buckets and cupboards, hose carts; level-crossing gate 'targets'.
Grey: Exposed point levers, gutter interiors, poster board centres, grounded bodies (outside station limits), water tanks, ladders, water columns, signalbox walkways.
Black: Metalwork on level crossing gates.
Signs: Green and white for the majority. Red and white for warning signs.

NB Some of the above shades were modified in later years but the overall appearance remained much the same.

81
The new Hastings station, officially opened on 6 July 1931, and showing the bold style of san-serif lettering then favoured for signs. The main lettering 'Southern Railway' is in relief letters in green with a white edging, fixed to the stone. All the subsidiary lettering is in white upon green enamel. Note the use of the initials SR. On the poster boards the larger ones carry the full railway title, the smaller ones only the word 'Southern'.
Ian Allan Libary

81

82

83

82
Typical green enamel nameboard, with bold san-serif lettering white (based upon Gill sans bold, but with modified characters). Concrete support and fence panels; a characteristic of many SR stations. *J. G. Glover*

83
Making an interesting comparison with Hastings (picture 81) is the facade of Southampton Central station photographed on 17 June 1939. Of 'Art deco' or 'cinema' styling, it had a white finish to the concrete exterior, and metal window frames painted green. The relief lettering for 'Southern Railway' is in green, and the style of the characters is much closer to Gill Sans than previously. *Ian Allan Library*

84
The late 1930s witnessed a creative approach to station architecture on the SR. No doubt influenced by the excellent work of Frank Pick for the London Transport system, the Southern's architects produced some stylish new stations for the electrification to Chessington, (intended to reach Leatherhead, but curtailed by the war). With a neat brickwork finish. Chessington North photographed in May 1939, had the company title in relief lettering of white with a green centre, flanked by two white flagpoles. The station name is in white on green glass; illuminated from behind at night. The lettering above the poster hoardings is in the sans-serif style with inner line, used for publicity purposes, and applied to rolling stock in the period 1938-1941 (see picture 47), from which the famous 'sunshine' alphabet was developed. *Ian Allan Library*

85
Many stations served by electric trains, and some road signs directing people to them, had the words 'Southern Electric' in white upon green enamel, with a white 'lightning' flash across the two words; linking them together in the middle. This example is seen over the corner of Eastbourne station (and survived there into the 1960s!), with the clocktower above. *British Rail SR*

86
'Southern Electric' logotype, with 'lightning' flash.

84
85
SOUTHERN
RAILWAY
CHESSINGTON NORTH STATION
SOUTHERN RAILWAY
EAST
SOUTHERN ELECTRIC
Information
KEEP LEFT

86

SOUTHERN ELECTRIC

87

87
The SR achieved a considerable uniformity of style in their station signposting; using white lettering upon green enamel. The letterforms were very legible, even when viewed from a passing train. Pictured here is a typical platform sign, with concrete support, at Swanage, still in situ in 1969. *John H. Bird*

88
This 1947 view of Woking station platforms shows all the standard forms of station name signs. Extreme left is a concrete support (similar to picture 87) on the platforms and on the concrete lamp post there is the standard SR roundel in green and white (closely related to the famous LT roundel in style). On the ends of the roof canopies large green and white enamal signs boldly display the name; the canopies were painted stone colour, with the inner steelwork supporting it painted light yellow green and the columns strong yellowish green. *British Rail, SR*

88

4: Miscellany

A few associated elements in the overall livery of the SR are shown, in order to give added detail. However, the reader in search of 'in-depth' descriptions for which space does not exist in this series, must search through contemporary publications where quite often a description of a new road vehicle, for example, will have some limited livery detail included. For the printed publicity of the prewar and postwar periods, a useful source can be found in the specialist journals of the day produced for the commercial art world. Much information on uniforms can be gleaned from the study of people in the backgrounds to photographs taken at stations, despite the fact that these nearly always concentrate upon the locomotive and train as their subject.

ROAD VEHICLES, ETC

89
This smart Horse box dates from June 1930, and is finished in Maunsell green, with gold leaf or gilt lettering shaded in black. The wheel centres were in Chinese red, also the rear fuel tanks; front mudguards and trim over rear wheels in glossy black; also the headlamps. White roof on cab and body. *Ian Allan Library*

89

90

91

90
This photograph is of particular interest because of the lettering on the nearest vehicle, the trailer, which has the inner line painted upon the words 'Southern Railway' and is *shaded*. Taken in April 1931, this is the earliest example of the alphabet adopted by the SR for publicity in the 1930s (and later as 'sunshine' for the trains), that has come to the Author's notice. The lorry and trailer are in the Maunsell green with gilt lettering, and dark red wheels. The containers are 'insulated' and were intended for fast road transport of meat from Southampton Docks to the principal towns in Hants, Sussex, Dorset and Wilts. (Publicity slogan was 'From Ship to Shop;) In view of this the inscription on the extreme left hand end of the trailer side valance — speed 12mph — makes amusing reading! The containers were stone coloured with black lettering. *Ian Allan Library*

91
The publicity lettering in white with an inner green line, upon a green body, became standard for SR road vehicles during the 1930s, and continued in use until nationalisation. The shade of green was distinctly lighter in postwar days and some vehicles were in a colour very similar to the malachite used on carriages in the final years; others were in a darker apple green similar to that used for buildings and name signs. This Thorneycroft vehicle was photographed new in September 1940.
Ian Allan Library

92

The standard livery for ships of the SR fleet, throughout the company's existence was a black hull, with white upper parts and a buff colour for the funnels, topped with black. The house flag is reproduced on the nameplate of Pacific No 21C1 *Channel Packet* (See picture 55.) Illustrated here is the turbine steamship *Dinard*, built in 1924 for the Southampton-St Malo night service and converted in 1947 to become a car-ferry for the Dover-Boulogne route. *Skyfotos Ltd*

93

Vandalism evidently reared its ugly head during the war! This March 1944 poster is of some social interest, but is reproduced here mainly to show a typical example of the use of the 'publicity' lettering for the words 'Southern Railway' *Ian Allan Library*

94

Typical of latterday steam locomotive enginemen in Britain, and on the SR throughout its existence, were the blue 'jean' type jacket and trousers, and the oilskin top to the cloth cap with stiffened peak. The footplate of a steam locomotive was no place for a glamorous uniform! Making a striking contast to the Mayor of Southampton in his civic regalia, the driver of the first postwar 'Bournemouth Belle' is greeted upon arrival, on 7 October 1946. Useful details of the 'sunshine' lettering on the Bulleid Pacific tender in the background. *Frank F. Moss*

93

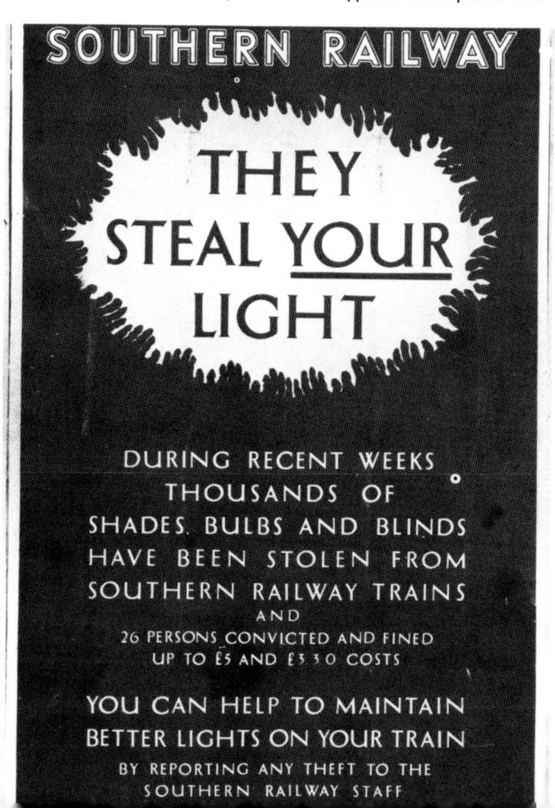
SOUTHERN RAILWAY
THEY
STEAL YOUR
LIGHT
DURING RECENT WEEKS
THOUSANDS OF
SHADES, BULBS AND BLINDS
HAVE BEEN STOLEN FROM
SOUTHERN RAILWAY TRAINS
AND
26 PERSONS CONVICTED AND FINED
UP TO £5 AND £3 3 0 COSTS
YOU CAN HELP TO MAINTAIN
BETTER LIGHTS ON YOUR TRAIN
BY REPORTING ANY THEFT TO THE
SOUTHERN RAILWAY STAFF

94

95

95

Passenger train guard's uniform of the early wartime period. Black with polished metal buttons and yellow trim and details upon the hat. The electric motorcoach alongside is in Maunsell's final green livery with lining out only at waist level; No 11195. *British Rail SR*

GWR
GREAT
WESTERN
RAILWAY
1923-1947

Previous page (inset)
GWR monogram, introduced 1934.

1 Below:
With a particularly brilliant shine to the copper chimney cap, 'King' class 4-6-0 No 6022 *King Edward III* is evidently being worked hard as it passes Tigley signalbox on the ascent of Rattery bank, heading the 3.30pm Paddington-Truro express one day in June 1939. *H. K. Harman*

The Grouping Years

Alone of the four major railway companies created by the 1923 railway amalgamation, known as the Grouping, the Great Western Railway (GWR) started life with an existing title and a very popular visual identity. This was due to the fact that in the main the geographical boundaries of the GWR were the same as those possessed by the pre-Grouping company of the same name, with the addition of a number of smaller Welsh companies and one or two minor outposts; notably in north-west England. Whereas the new LNER, LMSR and SR were all faced with the problem of creating a completely new public image, or corporate identity (in modern parlance), to replace the very varied images of their constituent companies — a huge task, which involved the repainting of all the locomotives, rolling stock and structures — the GWR simply extended its existing identity to encompass the absorbed companies and lines. Not a major problem!

Just prior to the Grouping the GWR had appointed C. B. Collett as Chief Mechanical Engineer, to succeed the famous G. J. Churchward; on 1 January 1922 to be precise. This change of Chief coincided with the start of a policy of improvement for locomotive and rolling-stock liveries, following the austere finishes used in World War 1 days and for the immediate postwar years; referred to below.

The pre-Grouping GWR liveries are not covered in this book, but a brief mention of these earlier liveries is necessary here in order to create an accurate picture of what C. B. Collett inherited when he took office. From the earliest days (1840), the GWR, under Brunel's guidance, had established a livery, and although variants occurred under successive CMEs, it was to last in basic form for the entire 112 year span of pre-Grouping and Grouping existence, and (partially) into BR days until the demise of steam. The choice of a dark green for locomotives probably came from the contemporary practices of the pioneer locomotive builders, who had apparently favoured this colour for its stable and lasting qualities. It was often referred to as 'Engine Green' by these builders. By the 1850s, the GWR was embellishing its new locomotives with polished brass details (eg *Lord of the Isles*, 1851) and by 1855 the famous copper-capped chimney had appeared. (Perhaps a more accurate description is copper-*topped*?)

Styles of lining-out, and the shade of green that Swindon used varied slightly from decade to decade, whilst the locomotives painted by Wolverhampton Works had for many years a very different shade of green to those painted at Swindon, but somehow a fairly cohesive GWR style was created, to some extent by means of the polished metal adornments and the characteristic lettering and numerals of the number plates and nameplates.

The year 1906 saw a middle chrome green shade (ref C19/GW1; see later), settled-upon, with black and orange-chrome lining. Basically this shade was retained for the rest of the GWR's days (except for a period during World War 1), but many people have observed that individual batches of paint from different suppliers did have variations; some being more inclined to blue, some to yellow. No doubt this was the case, and another contributory factor could have been the varnishing. I have already described these factors and others in the Preface to this book, to which readers are referred.

Until the outbreak of World War 1, the GWR retained a very consistent and high standard of painting and cleanliness for its locomotives, but as early as 1908/9 the carriage stock had suffered the indignity of being repainted in an all-over chocolate brown, losing the characteristic upper cream panels. In 1912 the brown was changed to crimson lake, and Churchward evidently gave some thought to painting the locomotives in the same colour.* These changes were undoubtedly made to overcome the expense of applying the two-colours and avoiding the problems of keeping the upper panels in a clean and presentable condition. Ever-increasing labour costs must have been a contributory factor. Whether or not Churchward would have gone ahead and applied crimson lake to locomotives generally remains a matter of speculation, because World War 1 enforced severe restrictions on both paint supplies and labour availability. As a result, by 1915 a khaki-green

'2221' class 'County Tank' No 2225 ran for some time in experimental crimson lake livery, from July 1909, and some auto-train locomotives were painted brown, later crimson lake, to match their trailers. The steam railcars were treated similarly to the coaches.

2
In the khaki green livery of World War 1, devoid of all lining-out, and with the brass and copper finishes either removed or else painted over (except the name and numberplates), 'Saint' class 4-6-0 No 2920 *Saint David* typifies the plain appearance of the GWR locomotive fleet at the time of the Grouping. *LPC*

2

shade was being applied to locomotives (oddly with an orange bufferbeam) and all lining-out was dispensed with. Perhaps the orange was used because a supply existed which had been ordered originally for lining-out purposes; the khaki-green sounds as though it came from War Department sources. At the same time the polished metal finishes were painted over, in either the green or black. By 1917 the supply of middle chrome green had been resumed, but still without any lining and this plain finish was still being applied when C. B. Collett took office.

Thus the typical main line GWR train of early 1922 consisted of a locomotive painted in the plain standard green (or perhaps still in khaki), devoid of all lining, with black frames, smokebox, wheels, etc and with the brass and copper finishes most probably painted over except for name and numberplates, although these were sometimes painted yellow. The coaches would be a mixture of all-over brown or crimson lake (perhaps even the occasional shabby pre-1908/9 chocolate and cream survivor). It was certainly not the classic GWR image so beloved by today's enthusiasts!

In the final year of its pre-Grouping existence and with Collett newly installed, the GWR decided to revert to chocolate and cream livery for coaching stock. Yet to come was any improvement in the austere locomotive livery.

However, before going-on to our story, which of course commences with the 1923 Grouping, I would like to re-emphasise one or two basic points about the subject of liveries, in particular with the GWR in mind.

First of all there is the confusion so often created by 'official' or 'works' photographs depicting the locomotive in a matt grey livery, but apparently fully lined and lettered. This practice was widespread, and Swindon was no exception. The idea was a sound one, in that the matt grey finish cleverly avoided problems of colour rendering with the quality of film available to the camera (black and white — or monochrome — of course) and the matt finish prevented unwanted highlights and deep shadows, or reflected shadows; particularly on sunlit days. On the credit side these photographs give excellent mechanical detail, and on the debit side they give false tonality to the livery scheme. They are however useful for details of lining-out, because this feature was painted in contrasting black and white and was therefore more photogenic. Even the polished brass details, such as name and numberplates which of course normally have a shine effect, were painted in black and white for these photographs.

From time to time locomotives have been released to traffic whilst still carrying a workshop grey livery. This was either due to an urgent need for all available motive power at a peak traffic period, or because the locomotive concerned was the subject of some trials under CME surveillance prior to final acceptance into stock. It would be a mistake to assume that these grey locomotives constituted a livery experiment!

Normally, when a locomotive entered traffic after receiving its livery scheme and final varnishing, a steady process of weathering and wear-and-tear set-in. The longer in traffic, whether cleaned regularly or not, the darker and less

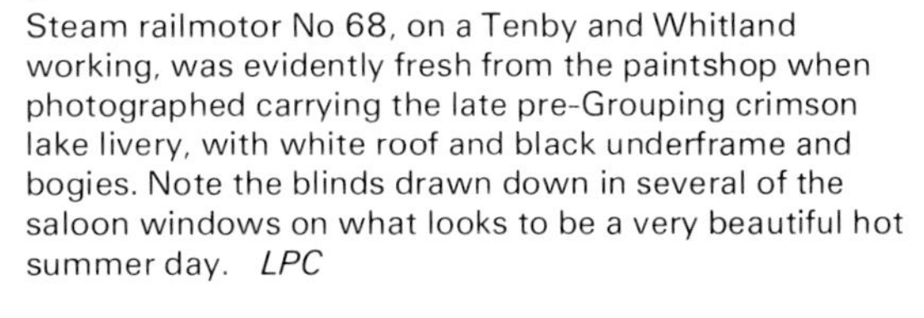

3
Steam railmotor No 68, on a Tenby and Whitland working, was evidently fresh from the paintshop when photographed carrying the late pre-Grouping crimson lake livery, with white roof and black underframe and bogies. Note the blinds drawn down in several of the saloon windows on what looks to be a very beautiful hot summer day. *LPC*

4
'Photographic' or works grey finish, seen here on the first of Collett's celebrated 'Castle' class 4-6-0s, No 4073 *Caerphilly Castle*, posed for the official camera when just completed at Swindon, on 1 August 1923. This finish gave excellent monochromatic rendering, and allowed the mechanical detail to be accurately recorded. However the tonality was completely false — with some 'dark' areas appearing light, and vice versa. The lining out, and the bright metal finishes were painted in black and white to provide maximum contrast and avoid shine. Features of interest in this photograph are the bogie brakes (fitted to first 10 of class) and narrow outside steampipe to the cylinders; also the diagonal rainstrip on the cab roof. With his new 'Castles' Collett reintroduced full lining-out for GWR express passenger locomotives. Note the 'garter' coat of arms on the tender sides, and the style of lining for the outside cylinders. *Ian Allan Library*

▲
3

4

contrasting became the individual colours. Painted lining-out and numerals, and gilt transfers of lettering or insignia, also darkened-down with time. A remarkable fact of some GWR steam locomotives was the length of time sometimes ensuing between repainting. Intermediate repairs would perhaps involve partial repaint, or 'touching-up', but such was the quality of the original paintwork that a complete repaint was not deemed necessary. Thus some engines still carried their pre-World War 2 liveries when the GWR was nationalised in 1948 and in some instances continued to carry them for a few more years!

A particular feature of Swindon practice was that the final painting, lettering and varnishing all took place in the locomotive erecting shop, and not in a special paint shop as in the majority of cases in British locomotive workshop practice. This meant that the painters and liners had to work alongside mechanics and fitters — not the most ideal conditions for achieving a quality finish, free from dust! Nevertheless the Swindon painters had a reputation for the consistently high standard of finish they bestowed upon the engines that passed through their hands. Lining-out, in particular, requires a skill and concentration which soon separates the craftsman from the amateur, and it was always a pleasure to watch the delicate procedure of applying the fine chrome-orange and broad black lining to the boiler bands or cabside. The Swindon painters were true artists in this respect.

The GWR is certainly the best represented of all Britain's former steam railways in the present-day

5

5
Light repairs or intermediate overhauls did not necessarily see any attention to livery detail, and sometimes the engine was returned to traffic with just a little necessary 'touching-up'. Here 'Manor' class 4-6-0 No 7812 *Erlestoke Manor*, has received attention at Newton Abbot works and sports a freshly painted smokebox and chimney; all else is very grimy indeed. *Ian Allan Library*

6
Sometimes a GWR engine ran for many years without receiving a full repaint. Quite remarkable is this Class 58xx 0-4-2T No 5809, photographed at Bristol on 5 March 1950. The insignia carried on the tankside, 'Great Western', dates back to the day it was built in 1933, before the adoption of the monogram; some 16 or more years previously. *R. H. G. Simpson*

6

preservation societies and operating private railways. This is scarcely surprising in view of the great affection and esteem which it gained during its existence, and there are many beautifully restored items for the public to admire. There is a great deal of accuracy in the liveries of many of these, and the temptation exists of illustrate this book with these contemporary restored examples. However this would defeat the object to a great extent, because the main purpose is to review the liveries and practices of each railway company as it existed *at the time*. I have therefore restricted the illustrations to actual contemporary records. As such they sometimes do not have the technical brilliance of today's photographers, and in one or two instances they have been oft-reproduced before. I ask my readers to be a little indulgent, in the hope that the overall picture presented benefits from complete authenticity.

A particular problem exists when illustrating the liveries of the GWR in its final years. Particularly during World War 2 and to a lesser extent in the period 1945-47 the standard of cleanliness suffered very considerably, and many otherwise interesting photographs show scarcely any livery detail because it has been submerged by coats of grime. Again and again I have rejected pictures because the chocolate and cream of the coaches is scarcely evident, whilst the insignia on the locomotives are barely visible to the eye even on the original photograph, and certainly would not reproduce. I can vividly recall the GWR main line at Old Oak Common in 1947/48 when I made numerous 'spotting' expeditions to the embankment in the vicinity of Old Oak Lane overbridge; a favourite location. Many trains of empty carriage stock passed before our eyes at a snail's pace, and the very dirty condition of many of the chocolate and cream carriages left a lasting impression. (There were also quite a few all-chocolate wartime painted carriages still to be seen). These begrimed carriages were always emphasised when a newly painted vehicle was included in the rake, showing the chocolate and cream in all its glory! I sometimes feel that today's enthusiasts have a false picture of the GWR in its final days. Certainly it was cleaner and more colourful than either the LNER or the LMSR at this time, but it still left a lot to be desired when compared to the prewar years. Freight stock in particular had a very run down appearance and paint was scarcely applied at all; many wagons had repairs done with bare wood except for a patch of paint where the lettering and other details had to be applied. Generally speaking the GWR still managed to keep its top link locomotives presentably clean, but many lesser types were only given the occasional wipe with an oily rag. It was not a happy period in British railway history.

The aim of this series of books on British Railway liveries, past and present, is to create a balanced overall picture of this fascinating aspect of railway progress; a picture which has been comparatively neglected by many railway historians who have a bias towards mechanical engineering or day-to-day performance on the road. It is the livery of a railway which identifies it to the public at large, and which makes a considerable and sometimes colourful contribution to the everyday environment in which it operates. I wonder how many people who are not railway enthusiasts nevertheless cherish childhood memories of the GWR and of holiday resorts; of sparkling copper and brass, and of polished deep green; of chocolate and cream carriages, and of smart uniformed staff with a certain feeling of pride in the job? These outward manifestations of this great railway company — its livery — reflected the magnificent traditions and loyalties it could boast.

A very great deal of literature has already been produced upon the subject of the GWR and this has included two excellent publications in recent times by the Historical Model Railway Society* which has dealt with the livery aspect in considerable detail. Far more detail indeed than I wish to encompass within the span of this present series, which is for more general reference and reading. I heartily commend the serious student to these two books, and also to the now famous series of partworks produced by the Railway Correspondence & Travel Society, entitled *The Locomotives of the Great Western Railway*. Only one comprehensive book has been produced on the whole subject of liveries,

* (i) *A Livery Register of the Historical Model Railway Society. No 2 The Great Western Railway. Locomotives, Carriages Vans, Wagons, Buildings and Signals 1835-1947* (HMRS).
(ii) *Great Western Way* J. N. Slinn (HMRS).

7

Still carrying the prewar style of circular monogram when photographed on 17 June 1951, former Weston, Clevedon & Portishead Light Railway 0-6-0T No 5 *Portishead* is seen here stored in Swindon stock shed. No 5 (and sister engine No 6) were originally built for the London Brighton & South Coast Railway in 1877/75 respectively, and were members of Stroudley's famous 'Terrier' class; subsequently passing into the ownership of the Weston, Clevedon & Portishead Light Railway, which was absorbed by the GWR in 1940.
R. H. G. Simpson

8

Locomotives constructed or repaired at Swindon received their final paintwork and livery details in the erecting shop. 'Bulldog' '3300' class 4-4-0 No 3438 is seen prior to repainting; undergoing overhaul. Standard style numerals on bufferbeam. *C. R. L. Coles*

entitled *Britain's Railway Liveries 1825-1948* by Ernest F. Carter and published by Harold Starke Limited. I have already referred to this book earlier because it contains a colour chart that must be regarded as the most accurate and comprehensive guide to British railway livery colours that exists. Throughout this book I shall refer to this chart, as well as supplying my own set of colour guides. Thus a particular colour reference which can be matched to Mr Carter's book is referred to by the prefix C followed by the number given on his chart. In this particular instance the GWR standard locomotive green — middle chrome green — is C19. My own reference is GW1 and earlier pre-Grouping shades will be described as GW2 onwards in due course. Thus throughout this present book the reference of the GWR standard green livery is C19/GW1. (Wherever Mr Carter does not supply a colour sample I will of course endeavour during this series to add the missing detail, if reliable evidence can be found.) For certain subsidiary colours, on carriages, or wagons, either Mr Carter's chart will supply the shade or else a careful written description must suffice. This is due to colour printing limitations.

It is of course not just the livery of locomotives and rolling stock that create the corporate image of a railway. There are other important visual aspects, such as symbols or coats-of-arms, uniform designs, publicity material, and colour schemes for architecture; even lettering styles are important. In this series I include a survey of these features to help create a picture. On the GWR a particularly important event was the adoption of a monogram of the letters GWR enclosed in a circle; introduced in 1934. This was a serious attempt by the company to produce a 'modern' symbol, more in keeping with that used by London Transport for example, which would be used on all aspects of their services instead of the coat-of arms or the full title. This monogram worked well when used on printed publicity and on some architectural items, but sad to relate it looked decidedly weak when placed upon the tender or tank sides of a locomotive (perhaps because it was too small) and only marginally better on the sides of passenger carriages. For some odd reason it worked better on the AEC diesel railcars and the road vehicles. Although abandoned by F. W. Hawksworth during the war years it was still in evidence in many instances when the GWR was nationalised in 1948. Readers may judge its effectiveness for themselves from study of the illustrations.

A deliberate omission in this book concerns signals. Although an important visual element in the railway landscape, their colours were so strictly functional as to hardly warrant a description as par of the livery. I think scope exists for a comprehensive book upon which the subject of signal styles and colour schemes, but it lies beyonc my present researches. Perhaps someone would like to take up the gauntlet? In passing, one must remark that on the GWR in particular the stylish lower quadrant signals gave an added character to an already extremely characterful railway.

9
The Swindon painters putting the finishing touches to the tender of 'Dean Goods' 0-6-0 No 2516, whilst this was being prepared as an exhibit for the Swindon Railway Museum in March 1962. Transfer lettering being applied with fine chalk line as a guide. Tender finished in plain standard green with black beading and underframes, etc. *M. Edwards*

9

1: The Collett Years 1923–1941

When the new and greater Great Western Railway was created on 1 January 1923, C. B. Collett the recently-appointed Chief Mechanical Engineer of the previous company of the same name, was again appointed to the post. Under Collett some important locomotive developments were destined to take place, keeping the GWR and Swindon in the forefront of British Steam Locomotive practice until the late 1930s. This was also a period which saw a considerable brightening-up of the GWR livery, a move which had already been commenced by Collett in 1922 when he decided to revert the coaching-stock to the traditional chocolate (C46) and cream. With the introduction of the first of his now legendary 'Castle' class 4-6-0s in 1923, Collett re-introduced the attractive fully-lined livery for important passenger locomotives. Lesser types and tank engines however, never reverted to lining-out. (It was ironically left to BR to re-apply this feature!) It is convenient to illustrate the Collett years in two phases, to clarify the livery developments. Phase one was the restoration of pre-World War 1 standards; albeit somewhat modified. Phase two was the introduction of 'GWR Modern' complete with the monogram, in 1934. This second phase lasted until the beginning of World War 2. When C. B. Collett retired in 1941 it was left to his successor F. W. Hawksworth, to tackle the problems of locomotive and rolling stock liveries in the midst of war; a problem previously faced by G. J. Churchward during World War 1. Collett did a great deal to revive the GWR image, and the popularity of the railway was undoubtedly stimulated by the sparkling presentation of his express passenger engines and by the modern rakes of chocolate and cream express carriages; not to forget the pioneer diesel railcars with their streamlined bodywork.

The broad specification throughout was as follows:

Locomotives

Express passenger livery: Basic body colour of middle chrome green (C19/GW1), including cab fronts, splasher fronts and rear of tender. Black smokebox, underframes and wheels. Orange chrome lining on either side of a 1in wide black band, separated by a ½in band of the green each side (making a 2¼in band of lining). A single orange chrome line on the edge of the running plates, footsteps and edge of tender side frames. Double orange lining to form a panel on cylinder sides with a single line to front and rear edges. Buffer beams signal red with a single orange chrome line to the edge, and on outer end of shanks, with gilt numerals shaded black.

The tender had the outer beading of the top painted black, the flared plated coal rails were panelled with the 2¼in orange chrome/green/black/green/orange chrome lining, and the tender body proper was panelled in the same style to the sides and rear. The letters 'Great' and 'Western' were in black shaded gold and red Egyptian slab serif letterforms applied as transfers and between these was a transfer of the GWR 'Garter' coat-or-arms. This coat-of-arms was replaced by a new simplified coat-of-arms in 1926, on express passenger locomotives with lining-out. Polished copper chimney cap and polished brass safely valve casing and trim details. Nameplates and numberplates polished brass, black background, with a single orange line on number plates.

Other tender and tank engines: Basic body colour of middle chrome green (C19/GW1) including cab fronts; tank fronts; tender or bunker rear; dome cover and/or safety valve casing. Black chimney top and smokebox, running plates, wheels, frames, tender beading, etc.

The letters 'Great' and 'Western' were applied as transfers in same style as express passenger engines (see above) and sufficient space was left between the words for a coat-of-arms to be added, but this was never done. Buffer beams signal red with gilt numerals shaded black. Standard numberplates with raised brass numerals on a black background. No lining-out.

Variations: When introduced in 1927 the 'King' class 4-6-0s had the black leading bogie side frames and front guard irons lined in an orange chrome line. The guard irons were lined-out on the first few 'Castles', but later this ceased. Some diligent enginemen, or shed staff, sometimes scraped the green paint off safety-valve casings and restored them to polished brass, if the official livery was to paint them; a few copper chimney tops were likewise restored. In September 1934 the lettering and crest on tender and tanks sides was replaced by the new circular GWR monogram, in gold with a fine black line to the edges.

Goods Engines: Unlike the LNER, LMSR and SR which generally favoured black for their goods engines, the GWR did not differentiate between types and gave these the unlined green livery, although a few elderly 0-6-0s were painted black in their final years, during the 1920s, and photographic evidence exists that some ROD 2-8-0s ran in black livery as late as the mid-1930s. Black appeared again during World War 2 (see later).

Rolling Stock

Passenger stock: The 1922 decision to revert to chocolate (C46) and cream was perpetuated by the new Company. The lower panels of bodysides and the roof gutters were chocolate, and above the waist was cream. Lining-out to panelling was in gold and black. Ends, window surrounds underframes and bogies and buffers and drawgear were black and roofs were white. This was basically the specification, to which was added Indian red (or mahogany) for droplight surrounds.

Lettering and numerals were in gold transfers with black shading. Detail changes were frequent until 1927, and during the period 1923-1927 steel-panelled stock was being introduced. To begin with Swindon painted the flush sides of this stock in the same elaborately panelled style as wood-panelled coaches! Apart from being a costly practice this denied the carriages their more modern appearance, and in 1927 the GWR made a drastic change to the lining-out style for all carriages. The carriage sides became the plain two colour chocolate and cream, with a yellow or gold line between the two (originally no line was applied). The following year the garter coat-of-arms and flanking crests were replaced by the new coat-of-arms, which was already carried by express passenger locomotives. In 1929-30 new rolling stock for the 'Cornish Riviera' and Torbay trains had double waist lining reintroduced and this became the norm for the best express stock, but lesser types retained the single lining-out, a black edge being added to the gold line. Droplights and moulded window surrounds were still in mahogany. From 1927 modern oil axleboxes had the top half of their covers painted bright blue for identification. In 1934 the circular monogram was used instead of the letters GWR and the coat-of-arms; lasting until the end of the Collett era. Some old suburban and local train carriages were painted in all-over chocolate brown in the 1930s.

Other stock: Auto-trailers; vans used in the important passenger trains; travelling post offices (TPOs); Ocean Mails vans and special saloons all carried the full passenger livery, but in the early 1930s the majority of passenger luggage vans reverted to all-brown livery, but with lettering and crest in passenger carriage style.

Diesel Railcars: These were finished in the chocolate and cream livery, with gold and black lining. Later examples appeared new with the monogram on nose ends and sides.

Freight Stock

Goods wagons: The basic livery colour was a dark grey, including the underframes. Roofs (where carried) were white and lettering and numerals were white. The initials GW were to begin with on existing stock usually in 25in letters in white (smaller when the wagon side could not carry them). Wheels, buffers, drawgears and brakegear were black. But since 1920 the large letters had been steadily replaced by a 16in version. In the mid-1930s these were abandoned in favour of 5in initials above the weight and running number on the lower left hand portion of the sides. Vans for express fish or milk traffic and other vans and wagons frequently used in passenger trains were painted chocolate brown, as were Horse boxes, with yellow ochre (to simulate gold) lettering and numerals. The brown vehicles carried the circular monogram from 1934 onwards, but the grey stock never had this feature for some odd reason. Some MICA meat vans and special insulated/refrigerated vans carried white livery with red lettering. Goods brake vans had the dark grey, as did shunting trucks. Handrails and brake levers were white. Engineers' Dept and Loco Dept wagons were black, with white lettering.

Containers: The development of the road/rail container was enthusiastically pursued by the GWR and the first examples coincided with Collett's appointment. These were painted in chocolate and cream complete with the coat of arms on the chocolate and the full company title; they were used for furniture carrying. Before long they became all-chocolate, together with a variety of other types that were introduced for general merchandise. The initials GWR replaced the earlier style and then the full title once again. Slogan s such as 'Door to Door' and 'Saves Handling' were painted on the sides for publicity purposes. In 1934 the circular monogram was applied and use of this on containers carried on until nationalisation. The insulated meat containers were painted white, with black lettering.

10

The garter crest had been in use for locomotives and carriages since 1903 (modified slightly as seen here, in 1912) and was retained by Collett at the Grouping, until 1928. On carriages it was flanked by the two shields of London and Bristol but locomotives did not carry this feature. (Although commonly described as coats-of-arms, or crests, the devices used by railway companies as part of their livery were rarely correct heraldic practice.) *Author's Collection*

10

11

Collett's magnificent 'King' class 4-6-0 design which appeared in 1927 featured the garter crest on the first batch built, as seen here, flanked by the letters 'Great' and 'Western'. Full orange chrome and black lining-out, and polished brass trim; copper chimney cap; burnished steel wheel rims and handrails. Commemorative brass bell carried on top of front buffer beam following the visit of this particular locomotive to the USA for the Baltimore & Ohio Railroad Centenary Exhibition in August 1927. No 6000 *King George V* is seen soon after its return, at Old Oak Common. Medals awarded by B&ORR Co, carried above cabside numberplate; twin red route restriction discs painted below. *LPC*

11

12

12

For all types of locomotive other than the latest express passenger and more important tender engines, the Collett livery specified unlined middle chrome green, and black. Chimney caps and safety valve casings were supposed to be painted-over, but sometimes a locomotive retained one or both of these features in polished state as seen here on 'Bulldog' class 4-4-0 No 3322 *Eclipse*. This locomotive is of additional interest in showing the large non-standard oval combined name, number and worksplate that featured on some engines built around the turn of the century. Note that the lettering 'Great' and 'Western' on the tender is sufficiently widely spaced to allow room for a coat of arms; not applied. *LPC*

13

13

A feature of some tank engines during Churchward's regime had been the placing of the standard brass numberplate centrally on the tank sides. In this state they did not carry either the crest or the words 'Great Western'. Collett ordered that numberplates should be moved to the bunkersides and that the 'Great Western' transfer letters should be applied to the tanksides; without a crest. In this picture of Class 4500 2-6-2T No 4516 the location of the original numberplate is still clearly visible on the tankside (this was previously No 2177 and was built at Wolverhampton). Chimney and safety valve casing both painted over. *Ian Allan Library*

14

15

14

For the locomotives inherited from the absorbed companies, the standard middle chrome green and black livery was applied as they were shopped. All evidence of previous ownership was deleted and standard brass numberplates attached. These had the additional feature of the initials GWR immediately above the numerals, in small sans serif letters. This picture of a former Barry Railway 0-6-0T, repainted in green and renumbered 782 in the GWR list, shows clearly the marks where the Barry Railway oval brass numberplate had been carried previously; to the left of the GWR plate. Polished brass Hudswell Clarke & Co worksplate retained on cabside. *Ian Allan Library*

15

The simplified coat-of-arms introduced in 1928, without the garter surround and with the two crests placed above. This final design was used on locomotives and tenders until 1934, and then again from 1942-1947. *Author's Collection*

16

16
Fine orange chrome lining was applied to the bogie frames on the 'King' class 4-6-0s, and a burnished steel finish was given to the piston valve and cylinder end covers. Few engines in British railway history have achieved the high standard of finish and livery that Collett bestowed upon these, and upon his 'Castle' class. No 6011 *King James 1* is seen at Old Oak Common, with the final design of coat-of-arms on the tender. The newly out-shopped carriages in the background are in Collett's simplified chocolate and cream livery, devoid of panelling and lining. *LPC*

17
This superb official photograph of 'Castle' class 4-6-0 No 5028 *Llantilio Castle* serves to demonstrate the Collett express passenger livery in all its glory; pictured here at Swindon in 1934 when the engine had just been constructed. *British Rail*

17

18
Detail of front buffer beam, footplating and outside cylinder, showing fine orange chrome lining-out on the black. *British Rail*

19
Detail of cab and firebox, showing lining-out. The cab roof area was black. Note polished brass trim to front and rear edge of cabside, and brass side window frame and splasher beadings. Whistles, numberplate and nameplate also in polished brass. *Real Photographs collection*

18

19

20

21

20
Standard locomotive numberplate with raised beading and numerals. The background was black and also the outer edge to the beading.

21
Cabside numberplate on 'King' class 4-6-0 No 6021 *King Richard II*, showing the fine orange chrome lining, inside the outer raised beading, on the black background. A feature only applied to the green engines with lining-out *C. C. B. Herbert*

22
Standard numerals for brass cabside numberplates, 5¾in high. *British Rail*

23
Standard letters for engine nameplates. Drawing dated December 1937 but almost certainly a tracing of an earlier one. Note method of fixing the brass letters to the backing plate. *British Rail*

22
23
FULL SIZE
KING GEORGE VI
- G.W.R. -
STANDARD LETTERS FOR ENGINE NAMEPLATES
- SWINDON. DECEMBER. 1937 -

24

25

6"

5600

24
'Castle' class nameplate of No 5076 *Gladiator*; with class name incorporated. *Alec Swain*

25
Sans serif numerals, in gilt or yellow, shaded black to the right were used throughout from 1923-1947 on locomotive bufferbeams.

27

26
For all types of locomotive that did not carry the lining-out and the coat-of-arms, the standard plain green finish, with black, was embellished simply by the use of the words 'Great Western' applied as transfers (see photo 9). These had lettering in similar style to the nameplates and had red shading picked out in white, and black countershading. Note the painted safety valve casing and handrails, on this class 5700 pannier No 9716.
Real Photos

27
The wide spacing of the lettering on both tender and tank sides allowed room for a coat-of-arms to be added in the centre, but presumably for reasons of economy this feature was not applied. Class 7200 No 7200 displays its massive form, in October 1934. *Real Photos*

28
Standard tender numberplate of the Collett era, located on the centre rear, and painted green with the raised lettering and numerals in white. Seen is No 3002 on the tender of Class 2251 0-6-0 No 3205 *K. P. Lawrence*

29
When John Fowler & Co of Leeds delivered the first 0-4-0 diesel-mechanical shunter to the GWR in 1933 they gave it fully lined green livery and a copper-capped chimney! No 1 was a service department locomotive and lasted until 1940. The lettering 'Great Western' was hand painted and very elaborately shaded but not countershaded with black. Fine orange chrome lining on the wheel centres, frames and buffer beams.
Ian Allan Library

28

29

30

30
The GWR monogram, or totem, was introduced in late 1934 for widespread application, including rolling stock. On locomotives it was in gilt with a fine black outline.

31
The 'modern' phase of Collett's livery adopted the monogram in place of the coat-of-arms or the 'Great Western' lettering. Sadly, on locomotives the monogram was so small as to be insignificant, and the gilt finish did not show up at all well, even when newly applied. Needless to say it soon virtually disappeared when weathered and worn! 'Castle' class 4-6-0 No 5083 *Bath Abbey* is seen here in Swindon running shed (having just been outshopped after rebuilding from 'Star' class 4-6-0 No 4063,) in 1937. The monogram is faintly discernible on the tender side, just to the left of the bucket hanging on the rear of the pannier tank (right). *C. R. L. Coles*

31

32
For his new 'Grange' class 4-6-0s, Collett relented a little, and although they carried no lining-out, he re-introduced the copper-cap chimney and polished brass safety valve casing; also adding brass beading to the splashers. No 6800 *Arlington Grange* is seen in new condition at Swindon in August 1936. *Real Photos*

33

34

35

33
Class 8100 2-6-2T No 8106, outshopped at Swindon in 1939 in plain green livery, with monogram. Painted safety valve casing, but copper chimney cap (not polished) left unpainted. Black cab roof. *C. R. L. Coles*

34
Photographed in June 1925, this three-car articulated dining set epitomises the first Collett style of livery for chocolate and cream rolling stock; in effect a modified revival of pre-World War 1 styling, as had been applied to wooden-panelled carriages. These new carriages were however of flush-steel panelling and the elaborate panelwork at waist level and above was all an illusion created by the skill of the painters! Garter coat-of-arms carried flanked by the two crests of London and Bristol.

35
Detail of the nearest carriage, No 10004 of the three car set, showing lining-out and lettering styles, in gold and black, and garter coat-of-arms and crests. The roofboards were in white, with red lettering in this instance. Black surrounds to windows, edged wtih gold. *Real Photos*

36

37

36
This interesting study of the connection between a slip coach (left) and the main train (right) also shows the livery in some detail. The slip coach No 7688, is of wood-panelled construction and the panelling is emphasised by the colour scheme and lining. The carriage on the right, No 4915, is a new steel-panelled one, but the livery has created a panelled effect, to match the older stock. Lettering and numerals on bodysides in gold shaded black; subsidiary lettering on frames and ends, white on black. *Ian Allan Library*

37
A second view of carriage No 4915, showing the flexible connections for releasing the slip coach at speed, suspended by chains after the slipping has been effected. Complete end of carriage painted black, also underframes and bogies. This angle emphasises the flush bodyside panels of Collett's new rolling stock.
Ian Allan Library

38
In 1927 a dramatic change of policy swept away all the elaborate painting and lining of panelwork (both real and illusory) and instituted a completely simple livery scheme of chocolate brown below the waist and cream above. The garter crest was then quickly replaced by the new simplified coat-of-arms, and there was no lining-out to begin with. Composite first and third class Restaurant car No 9582 displays the new scheme. Roofboard destination in black on white; blue tops to axlebox covers. *Ian Allan Library*

39
Evidently the complete lack of lining was considered to be too austere and a single gold (or yellow) line, edged with black was soon re-introduced, at waist level, as seen here on standard third class corridor coach No 5776; note coat-of-arms with letters GWR above. No class designation, for third class carriages. *Ian Allan Library*

40
The next move was that the more important main line corridor stock had double lining-out at waist level restored, as seen here on first class special saloon No 9005; photographed in July 1930. First class designation retained. *Ian Allan Library*

41
'Super Saloon' No 9111 *King George* (the GWR's answer to the Pullman car luxury image) in original livery, with double waist lining and two coats-of-arms. The name was in gold, shaded black. *LPC*

38
CORNISH RIVIERA EXPRESS
THIRD CLASS
G W R
RESTAURANT CAR
FIRST CLASS
39
40
41
KING GEORGE

42

43

42
The 'modern' phase, with the use of the monogram, coincided with a more modern appearance for new carriages, which had full depth bodyside windows, without toplights. On the new Buffet Cars these windows were however of reduced depth compared to most other new stock. A double lined panelled area below them had a central cream panel with gold lettering, edged with black. No 9632 is illustrated, photographed in July 1934.

43
Bodyside detail of Buffet Car No 9632. Note that the lettering and monogram were hand-painted, and the style of letters in the monogram GWR are not strictly correct, having semi-serifs. *Ian Allan Library*

44
New excursion train stock (of saloon layout with 'Art Deco' furnishings) appeared in 1935 and carried the standard livery, with single lining-out at waist level and the monogram, in gilt on the chocolate brown. No third class designation. *Ian Allan Library*

44

45

46

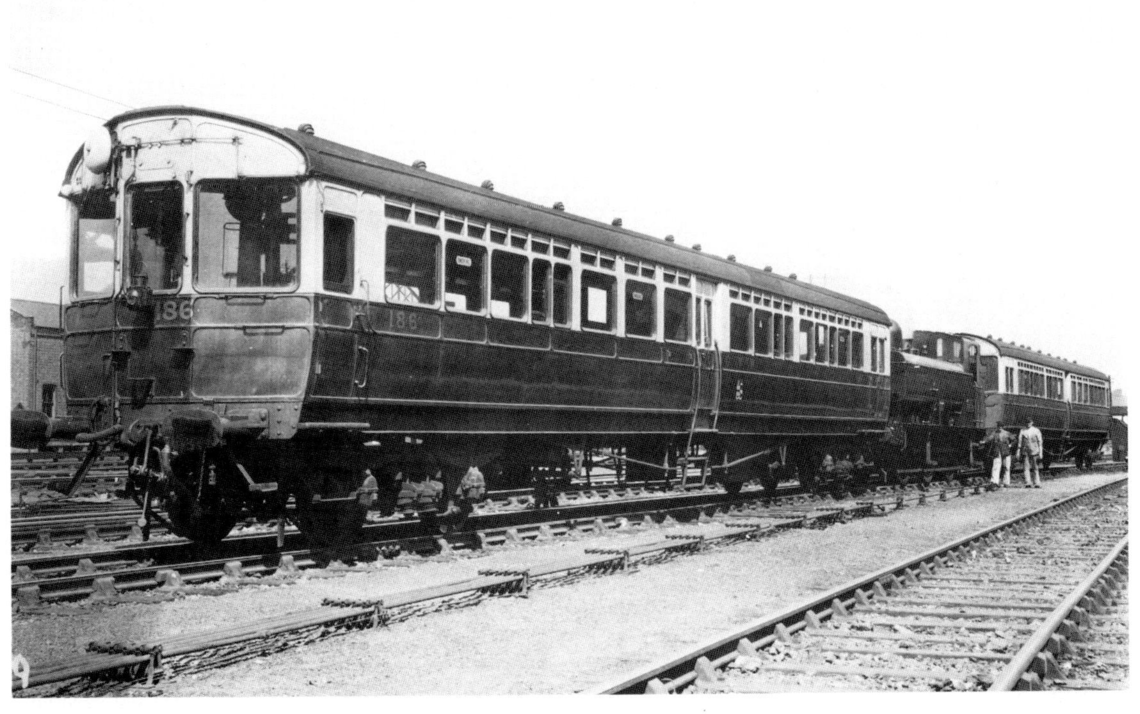

45
The magnificent new rolling stock produced for the 'Cornish Riviera Express' in the GWR Centenary year 1935 was sumptuous and comfortable indeed. Utilising the generous loading gauge inherited from Brunel these carriages had restrictions over certain other routes and this was painted in white upon the black underframe (just to left of the nearest wheel in this picture.) Third class designation painted at waist level on this restaurant car, No 9637. Blue painted axlebox covers and suspension detail. The deep gutter between roof and bodyside was in chocolate brown with a black line to the lower edge.
Ian Allan Library

46
Collett restored chocolate and cream livery to the auto-trailers, and gave them double lining-out at waist level. The colours were extended around both ends. Numerals were larger than standard and in gilt shaded black, being on each end and twice on each side near the end. The letters GWR (larger to match the numerals) were placed at waist level, with the coat-of-arms below. *LPC*

47
The GWR's 'modern image' first took on a real meaning with the appearance of the first of the streamlined AEC diesel railcars, in October 1933, (actually pre-dating the introduction of the monogram). This sleek machine, No 1, was in beautifully finished chocolate and cream, and carried the coat-of-arms on each nose end, but not on the sides. Black and gold lining-out. *Modern Transport*

48
A second view of railcar No 1, taken at Southall station in October 1933. Built by AEC at their Southall works with bodywork by Park Royal Coachworks it featured many lessons learned from road vehicle and bus construction. Standard transfer 'Great Western' locomotive lettering, either side of the central doors. *Modern Transport*

48

49

50

49
By the time railcar No 4 appeared, the monogram had replaced the coat-of-arms; it was used on the sides as well as the nose ends. *British Rail*

50
Railcar No 18 was designed to draw a tail load of 60ton and had standard railway type buffers and drawgear. Built by the Gloucester Railway Carriage & Wagon Co it was delivered to service in January 1937. Control equipment housed in the centre of the nose end meant that the monogram had to be put to one side, and to balance this, presumably, the number was put to the other side. No 18 is seen hauling an auto-trailer. *Modern Transport*

51
Swindon carriage works built the body of No 19 in June 1940 and it (and following railcars) featured a considerably more angular front end design. The basic livery remained the same however, although the monogram was low down on the nose, beneath a central tail light. *British Rail*

51

52

53

54

52
A 20ton mineral wagon, with end tipping and one door each side, produced 1924/25 and finished in the standard dark grey livery; including underframes, etc. White 16in 'GW' letters and characteristic italic script writing for weight details. White end to handbrake lever. Note the 'Return to GWR. Not common user' sign below the 'W'. *LPC*

53
A very characteristic open wagon of the 1920/30 period, of 12ton, with side planking including one deeper than the rest (second from bottom). 16in lettering; grey livery.
British Rail

54
Four ton open goods wagon on the narrow gauge Vale of Rheidol section; standard livery, scaled down.
LPC

55
Some categories of non-passenger carrying stock, such as for milk or fish traffic, which nevertheless could be found attached to passenger trains, were painted in all-over chocolate brown, with black bogies and underframes and white roof (above the curved gutter line), and these had yellow ochre lettering and numerals (to simulate gold). The ends were sometimes painted brown as well. 'Siphon J' bogie van No 1219 shows this livery. It carries the branding 'To work between Carmarthen and Paddington with Milk Traffic only'. 'Siphon J' was the telegraphic code for this type of vehicle. *LPC*

55

56
'Mica B' was the telegraphic code for Refrigerated Meat Vans. These were painted white, with red lettering. Note the number painted on the ends as well as sides. The underframes, etc, were nominally dark grey, but this example appears to have them painted black. *British Rail*

57
A characteristic feature of the GW scene was the 20ton brake van, with only one large open verandah. These were allocated to specific goods yards and carried the name of the yard, in this case 'Saltney', on the sides. Grey livery; white lettering and handrails. *British Rail*

56

57

58

58
The late 1930s witnessed a simplified livery for goods wagons, due mainly to the need to economise. The 16in letters were abandoned and replaced by 5in 'GW' on the left hand lower portions of wagons and vans. The italic script was also replaced, with sans-serif letters to match the rest. No numerals on wagon ends (a practice actually dropped some years earlier.) Grey livery retained. Illustrated is a prototype 12ton shock-absorbing van, built 1938. *British Rail*

59

59
Wagons for departmental use, for example pw work or locomotive coal and ash carrying, were painted overall black with white lettering. This 20ton hopper wagon for loco coal shows the 16in lettering and end numerals, so the picture dates from the late 1920s/early 1930s period. *LPC*

60
The drawing depicts a typical 4ton container (in this case for bicycles) mounted upon a four-wheel 'Conflat' wagon, as running in the early 1930s. The containers were in chocolate brown livery with white lettering in this period. The 'Conflat' would be in the dark grey, however.

60

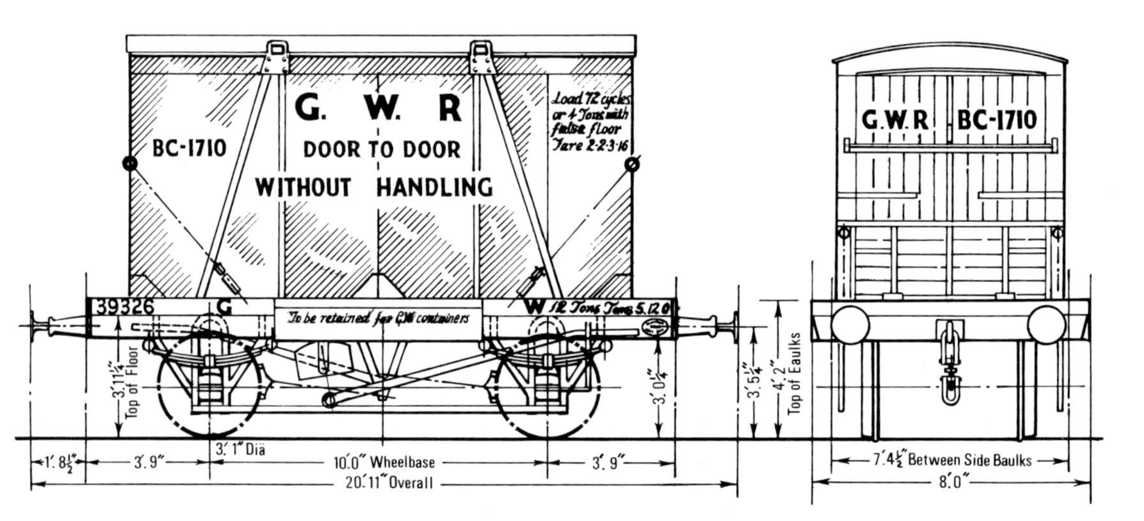

2: The Hawksworth Years 1941–1947

World War 2

The outbreak of World War 2 affected C. B. Collett's final period in office and by the time he retired in July 1941 all normal locomotive development work, and repair and maintenance schedules, had been completely disrupted by the emergency. Painting of locomotives and rolling stock was a quick candidate for economic restraint, plus there was a real problem in obtaining supplies of paint to the required shades and specifications. It should be remarked here that a considerable number of locomotives and carriages ran the entire war years without seeing a paintbrush, and still had their prewar finish in 1945; albeit hard to decipher beneath the grime. For those locomotives that were repainted, some were merely 'touched-up' where necessary, but some were completely painted as part of a general overhaul. For these, overall plain black was the livery for all locomotives except the 'King' and 'Castle' Class 4-6-0s some of which were repainted in unlined green. (Early on in the war some 'Kings' and 'Castles' were still receiving full lining out.) In view of the fact that locomotive cleaners were virtually non-existent the black livery was quite appropriate, and apparently at one stage even a few passenger carriages received it as well. Perhaps to alleviate the gloom, Hawksworth decided to do-away with the GWR monogram in 1942 (except for non-passenger brown stock; road vehicles and containers) and he re-introduced the full coat-of-arms, flanked by the initials 'G' and 'W' for the more important locomotives. Lesser types carried the letters GWR widely spaced, in black shaded gold and red Egyptian slab-serif transfer letters. Some tank locomotives repaired in Wales, in particular, carried the initials GWR in unshaded sans-serif style, in pale ochre or white. All brasswork and copper was painted-over and the glass of side window cabs was replaced by sheet metal as an air-raid and blackout precaution. Tarpaulin sheeting was introduced between the cab roof and the front of the tender to reduce the glare from an open firebox door at nighttime. These tarpaulins were stencilled with the GWR monogram.

The emergency livery was extended to carriages and wagons, using brown, because for some reason stocks of brown paint were easier to come by. Many vehicles ran the war years without repainting, but in late 1941 all-chocolate brown became the standard for repaints (except special saloons and the Centenary stock — probably mostly in store and still in prewar colours in any case.) The diesel railcars remained in chocolate and cream. The use of white for coach roofs was very wisely abandoned and dark brown was often used. Some coaches were in what was described as a reddish-brown overall. By 1942 chocolate brown overall with a single orange line was being used for wooden-bodied stock, and with a gold line for steel panelled stock, later also changed to orange. July 1942 saw a newly out-shopped set of carriages produced for the Cornish Riviera service in all-chocolate with an orange line at waist level. With this Hawksworth re-introduced the GWR coat-of-arms as a transfer, to match the locos, and the initials GWR were placed above.

As the war dragged-on many lesser vehicles for local or suburban use were simply painted plain brown overall, including auto-trailers, but in 1943 Hawksworth began to re-introduce chocolate and cream for the corridor stock used on the principal passenger services only, with a single gold line (bronze according to one eye-witness) edged with black, at waist level. Brown with an orange line remained in use for non-corridor stock and all older passenger vehicles. Vans in brown livery, for luggage, newspapers, etc still carried the old monogram. Roofs were now painted black on some carriages.

For goods wagons, vans and containers (except the white insulated and ventilated meat wagons and containers) a reddish-brown (red-oxide) colour replaced the dark grey. Open wagons were scarcely painted at all but a reddish-brown patch on the bottom left-hand corner of each side carried the lettering and numerals in white. Some goods brake vans were in brown.

It must be emphasised that for carriages and vans in a great many instances a partial repaint took place, perhaps retaining the best of the existing brown portions and replacing the cream and the prewar insignia and monogram. The style of lettering was changed in 1943 to unshaded gold sans-serif with a thin black outline. Possibly some of the Saloons and Centenary stock were retouched and revarnished during this period; keeping their excellent prewar finish a little longer.

The Postwar Recovery 1945-1947

Clearly, the liveries of wartime were not the

product of any planned or consistent policy but simply the outcome of expediency. If one colour was not available, another had to suffice. In fact, one is hardly talking of colour at all, because the range was reduced to brown and black, with occasional touches of green, orange or red, and the general finish can only be described as austere in the extreme.

F. W. Hawksworth was fortunately a devoted Swindon man and he lost no time in deciding to present a brighter image of GWR locomotives and rolling-stock once hostilities had ceased. In this respect both the GWR, and the SR under O. V. S Bulleid, were more progressive than the LNER and LMSR, both of which had quickly decided that lack of cleaners prevented any immediate return to prewar livery styles. The GWR, it seems in retrospect, decided that if its locomotives and carriages were repainted in decisive and attractive colour schemes, then the cleaners would appear!

Miracles do happen, but it has to be observed that even Hawksworth's newest locos and carriages often ran in a filthy state; due entirely to lack of cleaners. It was a national problem; men returning from war were reluctant to take on dirty jobs with little reward. Yet to come was the era of the mechanical washing plant and detergent.

The broad specification for Hawksworth's postwar livery was as follows:

Locomotives

Express Passenger Livery: From 1945 onwards the basic body colour remained the middle chrome green (C19/GW1) of prewar days, although due to inferior paint quality and poor finishes this often appeared to be very drab and yellow in character, inclining towards olive green. As better paint became available it took on a richer and bluer shade, nearer to the colour of mature Holly leaves; eventually achieving the original shade! The standard orange chrome and black lining-out was restored to the principal express passenger classes, but only on the green portions. One engine, the prototype Hawksworth 'County' class 4-6-0 No 1000 *County of Middlesex*, introduced in 1945 had the full prewar lining-out, with orange chrome on the black cylinder covers, tender side frames, footsteps, etc and the buffer beam was lined. However, the standard livery dispensed with these features and all black areas were unlined. Copper chimney caps and brass safety valve casings were reintroduced. The insignia of wartime was retained, with the letters 'G' and 'W' flanking the coat of arms.

Other tender and tank engines: All lesser types and tank engines were in unlined green, with black and carried the initials GWR widely spaced. Chimneys were black and safety valve casings painted green.

General details: For all types of engine the lettering on the bufferbeam retained the standard sans-serif style and name and numberplates remained to prewar specification except that the 'County' class had horizontal plates to suit the driving wheel splashers.

Passenger Stock

Passenger stock: Chocolate (C46) and cream was retained and with the introduction of the new Hawksworth steel carriages the double waist lining was reintroduced for the more important rolling stock. The roof on these coaches was now either black or dark grey. The initials GWR were replaced by the words 'Great' and 'Western' in a sans-serif letterform with a black outline to the gold, flanking the coat-of-arms on the chocolate area below waist level. Lesser types of stock retained the single waist line.

Other Stock: Auto-trailers were restored to chocolate and cream, and on these the colours were carried around the body ends. TPOs, Ocean Mails, vans and special saloons all received full passenger livery, but lesser types of van used in passenger trains remained in chocolate brown overall, but roofs were grey or black instead of white. The monogram was painted-over during repairs and the letters GW appeared on the left hand end of each side, low down on the body.

Diesel Railcars: These retained their chocolate and cream livery but the monogram was replaced by the coat-of-arms on the nose ends. During the late war years the initials GWR were carried but in postwar days the final style on the bodysides was the same as for the main line coaches, ie 'Great' and 'Western' flanking the coat of arms; nothing on the nose ends.

Freight Stock

Goods wagons: Although a return to the dark grey was begun, in particular for brake vans, many wagons received only patch-painting and ran with bare planks after repairs. Lettering was in white, with the use of the small initials GW. Steel wagons were painted grey including underframes. Engineer's vehicles were black.

General Note

Hawksworth's efforts to restore colour to the monogram and were in plain chocolate livery, with white lettering.

Hawksworth's efforts to restore colour to the GWR were overtaken by events; the company was nationalised in 1948 and the new BR liveries soon began to replace the traditional colours; not by any means for the better!

61

61
The first of the Hawksworth 'Modified Hall' class 4-6-0s, completed\at Swindon in August 1944 and liveried in overall plain black. No cabside window and no nameplates fitted but safety valve casing in brass finish. The words 'Hall Class' were painted in very small white letters on the centre splasher. The tender carries the revised arrangement of lettering 'G' and 'W' flanking the coat-of-arms, which Hawksworth reintroduced in place of the monogram for larger types of passenger engine. 'SDN' Swindon shedcode stencilled just behind bufferbeam on running plate valance. *British Rail*

62
Recently out-shopped in a fresh coat of overall wartime black, 'Grange' class 4-6-0 No 6821 *Leaton Grange* is seen on a running-in turn at Reading West Junction. Copper chimney cap and brass safety valve casing both painted black. Note the deplorable condition of the carriages. The nearest is in wartime overall brown; the rear three show vestiges of prewar chocolate and cream beneath the grime. *M. W. Earley*

62

63
Between 1942 and 1945 some tank engines were outshopped carrying sans-serif style lettering 'GWR'. It is believed that these were mostly done at works other than Swindon and that it was a lack of the new transfers that resulted in these simple hand-painted letters, which were not unlike those used on prewar road goods vehicles. 0-4-0T No 1104 displays this style, in black livery. *F. W. Day*

63

64

64
For all tender and tank engines other than the most important types (which carried the letters 'GW' and the coat-of-arms), Hawksworth introduced the bold shaded lettering 'GWR' for use on the plain green livery. These are seen here on the tender of an oil-burning 'Hall' class, No 5955 *Garth Hall*, the first GWR passenger engine to be converted to burn oil fuel during the abortive postwar scheme sponsored by the Government. *British Rail*

65
Evidently photographed on the occasion of an enthusiast's outing, (there are so many people on the footplate that the fireman is riding on the running plate *outside* the cab!) this 'Dean Goods' 0-6-0 displays the 'GWR' lettering on the tender sides. On the rear of the tender the large original numberplate has been lovingly restored to its brass finish. *Ian Allan Library*

65

66

67

66
For the first of his new 'County' class 4-6-0s, built at Swindon in 1945, Hawksworth applied the fully lined-out green livery of prewar days, but with his revised lettering and crest upon the tender. No 1000 *County of Middlesex* was the only engine in the postwar era to have the orange chrome lining on the black cylinders, footplate valances and tender frame valances, and the footsteps. The bufferbeam, however, was *not* lined. No 1000 sports its original copper-capped double chimney, and shows the distinctive horizontal nameplates used to match the single elongated driving wheel splasher. *Real Photos*

67
'King' class No 6018 *King Henry VI* is seen here in May 1948, five months after nationalisation, carrying the final version of the express passenger engine livery, with all areas below the running plates in unlined black. (The rear of the tender was finished in green with lining-out.) The engine was photographed in foreign territory, leaving Wakefield with a Kings Cross-Leeds-Bradford express during the historic locomotive exchange trials. *Overend Press Agency*

68

68
Also photographed during the exchange trials of the spring of 1948, Class 2800 2-8-0 No 3803 is seen here passing New Southgate on an up Peterborough-Hornsey freight train. Final GWR livery for all locomotives except express passenger types — plain overall green and black; letters GWR on tender; standard numerals on bufferbeam. Safety valve casing painted green.
F. R. Hebron

69

70

71

72

73

74

69
Photographed leaving Reading West station, this Reading-Newbury autotrain, being propelled by an 0-6-0PT, is composed of two trailers in the overall brown livery used during World War 2. Although the coat-of-arms is visible on both carriages, the closest examination of the original photograph has failed to reveal any other lettering or numerals on the carriage sides!
M. W. Earley

70
Hawksworth restored the full chocolate and cream livery to the autotrailers in postwar days, complete with double lining-out around the waist. The lettering and numerals were in unshaded gold sans-serif edged with black. The coat-of-arms was carried with the letters 'Great' and 'Western' flanking it, in the final sans-serif style. Grey roof, black underframe and bogies. Class 1400 0-4-2T No 1462 is seen here attached to trailer No 190.
P. Ransome-Wallis

71
The final main line carriage livery of the GWR is seen here on one of Hawksworth's postwar carriages, in chocolate and cream with double waist lining; coat-of-arms with sans-serif 'Great Western' lettering. Note the sans-serif black on white letters of the roofboard, 'Cornish Riviera Express'. (The position of the roofboard was lowered on Hawksworth's design to below the gutter line; above windows.) The down train is seen passing Reading engine sheds, with 'King' class 4-6-0 No 6020 *King Henry IV* in charge. Although the engine is in lined green livery, the tender is lettered 'British Railways' (in GWR style) as this engine was repainted in the first months of nationalisation — prior to the introduction of the new BR liveries. *M. W. Earley*

72
Postwar chocolate and cream livery for the narrow gauge Vale of Rheidol Section coaching stock, with single black and gold waist line, sans-serif initials 'GWR' above the coat-of-arms, and retaining white roof. Photographed at Devil's Bridge in August 1948. *H. C. Casserley*

73
Diesel railcars Nos 35 and 36, with a trailer coach sandwiched between, seen on the Reading-Newbury service. Built at Swindon in 1941/42 they nevertheless carried the prewar chocolate and cream livery, and had probably not been repainted since building when this postwar picture was taken. Note the coat-of-arms on the nose end with the letters GWR in shaded serifs above. Coat-of-arms repeated on bodysides, including trailer coach. *M. W. Earley*

74
Seen here standing at Swansea High Street station in July 1947, one of the original AEC railcars, No 4, displays the final GWR livery; note also the portions of bodyside valance removed to expose the bogies. No coat-of-arms on nose ends; only on bodyside and flanked by sans-serif 'Great Western' lettering. Sans-serif numerals; grey roof. *H. C. Casserley*

75

75
An iron-bodied goods van, No 47305, dating from Edwardian times was given a new role as a wartime Salvage Van; painted in chocolate brown livery. Photographed in November 1940 the 10ton van has two GWR monograms in ochre and the slogan lettering in white; also a white roof. These vans went from station to station encouraging people to donate salvage.
Ian Allan Library

76

76
Postwar lettering style for goods wagons, seen here on a demonstration 13ton open, carrying an open steel bulk container. The container still features the monogram. Photographed June 1947. *Ian Allan Library*

77
In the very last month of its existence (December 1947) the GWR placed this special six-wheeled vehicle in service, for the conveyance of demountable containers of liquid paints and varnish in bulk, from ICI Slough to various industrial centres. The lettering and numerals have had to be elongated slightly to fit the narrow sideraves. Note the very wide spacing of the letters G and W. *Modern Transport*

77

3: Stations and Buildings

It is difficult to suggest too many hard and fast rules for the colour schemes applied by the GWR to its stations and buildings, but some basic colours and applications can be described. Study of contemporary photographs soon reveals many variations upon the theme; this was because much was left to the discretion of the painters on the site.

The basic colours used were light and dark stone, maroon brown and white. The light and dark stone could vary in shade because they were mixed 'on site' using tints in a white base. The maroon brown appears to have been favoured in place of chocolate, probably because it had better wearing characteristics. (Study of the chocolate used by BR Western Region after 1948 shows that it deteriorated to a very shabby brown quite quickly). The maroon brown was often used instead of the dark stone.

Depending upon the architectural character of the station, the colours either predominated (on timber buildings) or merely enhanced the appearance. The use of stone or brick for buildings, left in their natural finish, was of course commonplace. Signalboxes were predominantly wooden, but it was a common practice to use corrugated iron for waiting rooms (Pagodas) and secondary structures in station yards and goods yards. Grounded railway carriage and van bodies were sometimes used to provide accommodation either as waiting rooms for passengers, or as staff amenities or stores.

For guidance, the basic applications of the colours were as follows:

Timber buildings: Walls, recessed door panels and barge boards in light stone. Outer frames of building, raised door panels and jambs and window frames, window sills and surrounds, gutters and drainpipes in dark stone. Window sashes or casements and glazing bars were white.

Stone or brick buildings: Door panels (recessed), window frames, sills and mullions, barge boards in light stone. Gutters, drainpipes, door frames and raised door panels, ironwork on windows, and wooden structural features on exterior of building and wooden plinths at ground level, in dark stone. White was used for window sashes or casements and glazing bars. Where the maroon brown replaced the dark stone it seems to have been for areas receiving particularly heavy wear or exposure to the elements. It was used mainly for raised areas of doors in early colour schemes, but seems to have been common on signalboxes throughout.

Other details were broadly as follows:

Lamp posts, nameboard posts (plain): either light or dark stone.

Lamp posts, nameboard posts (decorated): would be in light stone with the decoration around the base or the top of the post in dark stone. The metalwork of the lamp head was black.

Signs and nameboards (cast): were black with white lettering, however there were many enamelled nameboards and signs with white lettering on a dark blue background; mostly dating from pre-Grouping days when such signs were much in vogue for some time; as advertisements also.

Timber battens on walls: dark stone, or maroon brown.

Awnings: horizontals in dark stone, valancing (early) alternate light/dark strips; (later) light stone only steel framed awnings dark stone.

Poster Boards: frame dark stone; board black.

Ridges/chimneys: light stone. (Metal stovepipes, black).

Canopy columns: Same treatment as nameboard posts (above).

Pagodas (corrugated iron): Light stone, black roof, dark stone doors and white windows.

Firebuckets: Signal red with black lettering GWR.

These basic colour schemes also applied to signalboxes, goods sheds and other buildings in non-passenger areas.

The standard GWR colours were replaced in early BR days by chocolate and cream; thereby creating a false impression in many people's minds that the GWR employed this scheme for buildings as well as carriages. This was never the case. The GWR did however make one or two experiments with alternative colours to the light and dark stone, and of particular interest was the used of green and white on the Cambrian section immediately prior to World War 2, and just after the war ended a bluish-green and cream scheme was tried-out on the Yarnton-Eynsham (Witney) line. One or two other stations appeared in non-standard colours at the request of local interested parties.

78

79

78
AEC railcar No 25 (note coat-of-arms and initials GWR on nose) stands at Monmouth Troy station, having just arrived from Chepstow, on 12 September 1949. On the adjacent line the 6.05pm autotrain for Ross-on-Wye can be seen. Large station nameboard in black and white; supports and fencing in light stone. Lamp post in dark stone (base), light stone (upper main portion of column), and black (lamp head.) Window frames in buildings white; natural stone finish to buildings; roof awnings light stone with a dark stone (or possibly maroon brown) upper trim; black top to roof of buildings and bridge. Main areas of the bridge in light stone with structural supports to ironwork in dark stone. Station seat in dark stone (base) and light stone (wooden planks.)
R. J. Buckley

79
Pontsticill Junction, photographed on 3 May 1951 after nationalisation, but still in GWR colours. An autotrain for Merthyr stands in the bay on the left. Basically wooden buildings, but stone base to the signalbox. Nameboards in black and white with light stone surround and supports; base of supports dark stone. Buildings dark stone to mid height; light stone above. Horizontal timber board at base of signalbox wooden structure in dark stone with the signalbox nameboard upon it. Whitewashed edges to platforms and foot crossing in foreground. *R. C. Riley*

80

80
A Vale of Rheidol train standing at Aberystwyth, with locomotive No 9 at the head. (Throughout the Grouping days the locomotive livery for these narrow gauge engines followed standard GWR practice for tank engines; plain green and black.) In the background the canopy ends of the main line station show how the wooden mouldings were sometimes picked out in dark stone upon the light stone finish. *P. Ransome-Wallis*

81
The station at Devil's Bridge on the narrow gauge Vale of Rheidol section. Timber and corrugated iron structure with simple finish in light and dark stone. Roof probably black, soon weathering to grey. Red firebuckets prominently displayed. *Ian Allan Library*

81

82
PADDINGTON
1B13
83
CORYATES HALT
84
PARCELS AND CLOAK
ROSS-ON-WYE
WAY OUT
OFFICE
REFRESHMENT ROOM
LADIES ROOM

85

86

82
A feature of the robust GWR station nameboards has been their longevity in service; in fact some still exist in BR use today! This Paddington sign was photographed in May 1971 and although the concrete supports are somewhat the worse for wear, the board itself was still reasonably presentable. The WR had repainted it in the original black and white. *Michael H. C. Baker*

83
Coryates Halt, seen on 1 March 1952. 'Pagoda' iron shelter in light stone finish; nameboard in black and white with rail supports painted dark stone. *O. H. Prosser*

84
Although photographed after repainting by BR in chocolate and cream colours, this view of the down platform at Ross-on-Wye is included because it shows a variety of standard GWR signs (all except the station name sign, which is BR enamel), and also shows such characteristic touches as the attractive iron work, the glazed clerestory roof, and the flowers in hanging baskets. *Ian Allan Library*

85
During its '1930s Modern' phase the GWR rebuilt or modernised some important stations. The railway architects found expression by using steel and glass and glazed tiling and brickwork. This sign at Bristol Temple Meads dates from this period and is in brown and cream tiles. Still extant, and photographed in May 1980. *C. G. Maggs*

86
Quite a common feature was the promotion of the railway's own services, on the sides of prominently sited warehouses and other buildings along the lineside. This example was at Stroud, in an old loading bay, and was still perfectly legible when photographed in February 1971. *P. J. Fowler*

87

88

87
Big bold image of the 'modern' phase! The sign posting for Paddington station, high up on the Chief Goods Managers Offices. Photographed in July 1946.
Ian Allan Library

88
All that is modern is not beautiful — nevertheless this overbridge entrance to Parson Street station in Bristol is of interest in showing metal lettering fixed to stone, and the use of the initials 'GW' only. Photographed in 1967 with posterboards and other signs in BR style brown and cream enamel. *P. J. Fowler*

4: Road Vehicles

Buses

The GWR were pioneers in the use of regular bus services, to connect its trains to important town centres, hotels or resorts, which were some distance from their nearest station. They commenced in 1903 with a service between Helston and The Lizard, worked by some Milnes-Daimler motor wagonettes (open-sided above waist level, but roofed-over,) which had first been worked by Sir George Newnes in connection with the Lynton and Barnstaple Railway.

For the first 10 years of its existence as a Grouping company the GWR continued to operate feeder bus services, then these were handed-over to a private operator. In this final period the buses received chocolate and cream livery, to match the trains, having previously run in all-brown since 1908.

The broad specification for the GWR motor bus livery in the period 1923-33 was as follows:

Bodywork below waist, and sometimes roof above gutter: chocolate brown.

Window area, above waist level, sometimes including top of bonnet or rear windows, sometimes only on the sides: cream.

Wheel centres: chocolate brown with black trim.

Lining-out (1923 specification) was a single thin gold line, emphasising panelwork at waist level; by the 1930s this had given way to a black line (thicker) usually on the mouldings at waist level, separating the two colours.

Lettering GWR was gold in bold sans serif style, with red shading picked out in white to the left of the gold block letters and countershaded to the right with black.

Goods vehicles

The GWR operated horse-drawn goods vehicles until the last year of its existence; these were in chocolate brown and had black canvas trim. Some received cream panels on the sides in the late 1930s, with the lettering upon them. A pleasing feature was the polished harness and traditional horse brasses carried by these hard-working horses. However, this review is more concerned with the motorised lorries and vans, which of course steadily replaced the faithful horse.

The Grouping coincided with an improved design of bodywork for covered vans, whereby the traditional canvas finish was replaced by solid bodywork. This covered area above the waist level was then given the cream livery, with the remainder of the bodywork in chocolate.

The broad specification for motor vehicles was as follows:

Covered vans: Chocolate brown except for the panel above waist level. On the cream panel the lettering GWR was in unshaded block serifs, in brown. Various slogans such as 'Express Cartage Services' appeared below this. The letters GWR appeared in the same style, but in cream upon chocolate on the front of the dashboard area. In 1927 this feature was replaced by a cast metal plate with the letters GWR which was fixed to the radiator or cab front. In 1934 the new circular monogram was introduced and applied to road vehicles; the cast plates being removed. Space was then provided for posters to be carried on the sides of covered vans and for this purpose a grey panel was painted on, outlined in black. Generally speaking there was no lining-out on road vehicles but an interesting variation was the use of the monogram in either brown on cream or vice versa. With the former it was customary to enlarge the cream circle to outline the monogram — certainly making it eyecatching! Roofs were medium grey or cream and light grey also appears to have been used sometimes for wheel centres, with black trim, in the final years.

Open lorries and trailers: Originally these were in all-over chocolate brown with cream lettering in similar style to the vans, but the cream was soon applied as a narrow panel along the lower side of the bodywork, or on the raves. This panel had the full lettering, 'Great Western Railway' in chocolate, or sometimes as applied metal plates. Tarpaulins carried the large initials GWR in white on black. The circular monogram appeared on these vehicles in 1934, and remained in use for the rest of the company's years. One interesting feature was the use of the telegraphic code names on trailers, which were all-over chocolate brown except for those used for express cartage service which had a similar treatment to the vans, with cream on their side planking.

89

A GWR bus for the Oxford-Cheltenham coach service; a 15-seat charabanc-type Thornycroft-built vehicle. The livery of chocolate and cream interestingly has the chocolate brown carried right up the back and on to the rear fixed portion of the roof. Forward of this is the demountable canvas roof. Black tarpaulin provided to cover the luggage rack on the rear top of the roof. Cream limited to window areas above the waist. Standard gold shaded block serif lettering on sides and rear.
Modern Transport

89

90

Of particular interest is this 1929 Guy with Duple bodywork, introduced for an inter-station bus service between Paddington and Victoria, as part of a new GWR/SR through Contintental Service (note the route panel on the roof.) Standard livery and lettering with black lining on moulding separating the chocolate and cream. Roof either silver or pale grey. *Modern Transport*

90

91

A 10ton rigid six-wheeled, hinged-sided lorry, supplied by Thornycroft and known as their 'J. C. Forward' type. Photographed in 1929, in brown livery with white lettering. Cast metal GWR plate above cab windows. Note that the maximum speed was a mere 20mph!
Modern Transport

91

92

92
A 1934-built Thornycroft lorry with tipper-type body, finished in chocolate brown overall, and white lettering, but with black wheel centres. *Modern Transport*

93
These Thornycroft delivery vans featured chocolate and cream livery; photographed in 1934. Note the cast metal GWR plates on the radiators and also the legend Great Western Railway in cast metal plates with a cream surround, on the sides. Black tarpaulin with large GWR letters in white. *Ian Allan Library*

93

94

94
A Brush 'Brush-Bred' electric express cartage delivery van; delivered in 1947. Chocolate and cream bodywork with grey panel for advertisements; grey roof and wheel centres. Use of GWR monogram perpetuated long after it had ceased to be used for railway locomotives or carriages. Of interest is the cream circle for the monograms on the front of the vehicle. Note the single headlamp! *Brush Co. Ltd*

95
A 1947 demonstration vehicle; comprising a Bedford Scammel articulated lorry with hydraulic tipping gear. The driving cab is in cream overall above waist level, the main body and the lorry portion are in chocolate brown. Black mudguards and grey wheel centres with black trim. Telegraphic code 'Jason F' carried and GWR monogram retained. *Ian Allan Library*

95

5: Miscellany

It was the GWR General Manager, Sir Felix Pole, who encouraged the return to prewar colours for the new company, and C. B. Collett lost no time in following his lead for locomotives and rolling stock. As we have just seen, the road vehicles also benefited from the restoration of the chocolate and cream. These improvements were a major element in restoring the GWR to the forefront of the public's mind and creating a lasting loyalty and pride. There were, however other aspects of the day to day operations that also helped to build this pride in the job. One aspect was the characteristic GWR attention to detail.

On rolling stock for example, the locomotives carried the 'visual symbols' of the GWR to the very end; namely the characteristic brass safety valve casing (albeit sometimes painted-over) and the beautiful brass numberplates and nameplates. The copper chimney cap was another symbol on the foremost types. Details such as route restrictions and shed allocations were clearly and cleverly displayed in codes, and painted telegraphic codes were a common feature of the goods wagon fleet. Legends for operating purposes (such as 'Return to Paddington' etc) were standardised and very readable. On the wagon fleet the use of italic script writing for some loading and dimensional details was a tradition unchanged for over half a century. It all added-up to a sense of order and efficiency. The carriages carried clear destination roof boards with labelling in black upon white, whilst as an aid to the signalmen the use of large black and white reporting numbers, carried on the smokebox door of the locomotive in a special frame, was introduced in 1934.

The GWR Publicity Department was very go-ahead and during the 1920s and 1930s it was well to the fore in producing poster designs which

96

In 1934 large train description numbers were introduced as an aid to the signalmen. These had 16in white letters on black and were of metal; carried in a frame 3ft wide, attached to the locomotive smokebox. Numbers from 100-799 were allocated to all main routes; special trains and boat trains had OXX, such as seen here (the nought is missing!) on an up train at Twyford hauled by 'Grange' class 4-6-0 No 6822 *Manton Grange*; circa 1947.
E. C. Ive

96

were of considerable artistic merit as well as being eye-catching. A famous series of books 'For boys of all ages' written by W. G. Chapman had a great following, and gave detailed lists, photographs and details of the GWR locomotive fleet. There were also special books, such as *Track Topics* and *The 10.30 Limited*, the story of particular locomotives such as *'Caerphilly Castle'* and *The 'King' of Railway Locomotives* Even jigsaw puzzles were produced and sold!

The introduction of the GWR monogram in 1934 gave a new unity to printed matter of all sorts. The monogram also featured on fabrics, furniture and cutlery, as well of course as being applied to locomotives, rolling stock and road vehicles, and as lapel badges for uniforms. Staff uniforms did not change much over the years (it was left to BR to make such changes in the 1960s!) but perhaps this only added to the great sense of tradition and pride that existed. It was commonplace to see train guards and station staff wearing flowers in their buttonholes, and they kept their uniforms well-pressed and smart.

The Great Western Railway officially ceased to exist on 31 December 1947, at midnight; in reality it still lives on!

97

97
Throughout the Grouping period the GWR used carriage destination roofboards painted white with black lettering, (an exception was the new articulated dining car set, which used red lettering). These letters were of three distinct styles, depending upon the number of words needed; the longer legends having more 'condensed' letters; closely spaced. In postwar years the serifs were replaced by block letters. This 'Paddington, Birmingham and Wolverhampton' example is very typical of the prewar period. The photograph is of additional interest because it shows 'King' class 4-6-0 No 6014 *King Henry VII* in the semi-streamlined form it was given in 1935. Note the single horizontal splasher and nameplate to match, and the streamlined fairings behind the chimney and safety valve casing. *C. R. L. Coles*

98

99

98
Until the arrival of the infamous monogram in 1934 the GWR publicity department was not particularly strict about lettering styles for its name or initials, and these were often left to the fancy of the individual artist. In this 1920s poster for Oxford, the artist Fred Taylor has drawn Roman style lettering to suit the classical subject.
Author's Collection

99
Although dating from the same period, this poster by Brian Ll. Davies had fanciful lettering to match the overall style, and used the full name of the railway.
Author's collection

100
Applications of the new monogram were many and varied and it was a bold feature of the interior of the 1935 'Centenary' stock. The anti-macassars, the carpets and even the cutlery and tableware featured it!
British Rail

101

102

101
The monogram worked quite well in stencil-form as seen on this wartime blackout curtaining applied to the cab of 'Castle' class 4-6-0 No 4096 *Highclere Castle*; photographed in 1940. Glass removed from cabside window, but lining-out retained for the time being. Well illustrated is the route restriction colour code painted above the numberplate; in this instance D, Red.
British Rail

102
A long-lasting application of the GWR monogram was to prove to be its use in cast iron form as part of the base on platform seats. Many of these still exist today. They were usually painted maroon brown or dark stone in GWR days. A youthful train-spotter of the 1970s poses at Swindon on an example which was still in everyday use then. *T. G. Flinders*

103
Enginemen's uniforms varied very little during the Grouping years, but a feature was the use of the monogram in woven form as cap and lapel badges. The fireman of this 'King' class 4-6-0 No 6021 *King Richard II* has the cap badge. *C. C. B. Herbert*

103

104

104
Railwaymen's uniforms had to be particularly robust and protective in the steam era. This GWR guard wins few marks for style, but the heavyweight material was well-suited to the bleak task of working brake vans in all weathers and hours of the day. Typical touches are the polished metal buttons on the waistcoat and heavy watch chain. The peak cap has the legend 'Guard' woven in gold italic on the band above the peak.
Author's Collection

105

105
The ships of the GWR fleet were characterised by a red funnel with a black top. The hull was black and the upperparts of the superstructure and bridge front were white. The house flag was white with a red stripe along top and bottom edges, with the coat-of-arms of London and Bristol in the centre, with the words 'Great Western Railway Company' in black on yellow surrounding them. Pictured here is the steamship *St Patrick* built in 1930 for the Fishguard-Rosslare service; she was torpedoed and sunk whilst on this run in June 1941.
Ian Allan Library

LONDON MIDLAND & SCOTTISH RAILWAY COMPANY.
LONDON
MIDLAND &
SCOTTISH
RAILWAY

Previous page (inset)
The coat of arms, or crest, of the London Midland & Scottish Railway Company in the form applied to rolling stock and some road vehicles and publicity. *British Rail*

1 Below:
Crossing the Border. The up 'Coronation Scot' express at speed near Gretna Green, hauled by Class 7P Pacific No 6223 *Princess Alice*, in the 1937 livery of blue and silver. *W. Hubert Foster*

Introduction

The LMSR Image

It was called the 'LMS', but the full title of 'London Midland & Scottish Railway' was LMSR in abbreviated form. And as such I will refer to it in this text; otherwise I will find myself writing about the 'GW', the 'LNE' — both plausible — and the S — quite ridiculous!

The LMSR was a huge railway; the biggest of the 'Big Four' created in 1923 and it took time to weld the various constituents of the new company into a cohesive whole. One of the most important contributions towards creating a corporate image was the adoption of a recognisable LMSR livery, which would replace the various colour schemes of the absorbed pre-Grouping companies. Perhaps the LMSR directors were aware that the other three of the 'Big Four' were selecting green, of differing shades, for their locomotives, or perhaps it really was an all-powerful Midland Railway bias, that led them to select the MR crimson lake as their colour scheme — not only for locomotives but for carriages as well.

Many myths and legends attend the early days of the LMSR, and their choice of a livery is no exception. In particular it has been alleged by many writers that the former LNWR Crewe works did not like the idea of painting its locomotives in MR colours. This was not really the case, and there is ample proof that Crewe was actually quick to paint some of its more important express passenger locomotives, as well as some smaller types in the new colours. The reason that so many ex-LNWR types retained their black livery during the 1920s was the method employed by Crewe for repair work, which had become highly organised and efficient, partly under the guidance of H. P. Beames. Locomotives receiving intermediate repair, or specific alterations, or collision damage repair were not necessarily repainted; but 'patch painted' where necessary. Black it should be emphasised is the easiest of all to 'patch-paint'. It was both effective and economical. By way of contrast, to change the complete livery of a locomotive from black to crimson lake took time, and was more expensive, and was thus restricted by Crewe to major overhauls, or new construction, which included a period of days in the paintshop. Locomotives receiving light repairs at other workshops on the system, such as Rugby or Bow, were not repainted, although sometimes the existing insignia was retouched.

Indeed the cost of applying the crimson lake complete with lining-out and final varnishing evidently worried the LMSR directors, because after some six years it was decided to use the colour only for the more important passenger types and to replace it with varnished black with a single red line for 'intermediate' or as we nowadays call them, 'mixed traffic' types. Goods engines were in plain black throughout from 1923 to 1947.

The colour, crimson lake was the same shade as that used on the former MR, and indeed to begin with the same style of gilt and black numerals and gilt shade of lining was employed. During the latter part of the 1930s, when the lining had been changed to chrome yellow and the lettering was often in chrome yellow shaded red, it was suggested that the crimson lake *appeared* to be darker, but to some extent this may simply have been an optical effect created by the brighter numerals and lining.

There is another possible explanation for this suggestion that the crimson was darker. By good fortune some colour film was taken of LMSR locomotives in the late 1930s, and even allowing for fading and weak colour rendering, which makes some of them unsuitable for reproduction, these authentic photographs show the crimson lake to have a definite tendency to darken and blacken after some time in service; especially on those areas exposed to heat. No doubt locomotives were not so frequently and meticulously polished as had been the case in MR days, so the blackening effect steadily built-up, in particular on the boilers and fireboxes. There is no reliable evidence to show that the LMSR ever changed the shade of the crimson lake in prewar days, but this blackening effect may well have led to the suggestion that a darker shade was being used.

Until the outbreak of World War 2 the LMSR had a very strong and attractive image, with the added colour and appeal of the recently introduced streamlined express trains. The latest Stanier Pacifics graced the most important duties and the Stanier rolling stock was modern and comfortable. The initials 'LMS' were recognised by the public immediately, although the company also put its full title on many poster boards and station signs, and it used the circular coat-of-arms or crest on a wide variety of applications, from carriage sides to posters.

3
The prewar LMSR scene in its heyday, when all the locomotives and rolling stock were liveried to a basically uniform style. The date is 22 September 1938, and the location is Camden Bank, outside Euston. Fowler 'Patriot' Class 5XP 4-6-0 No 5525 *Colwyn Bay* climbs the incline with the 4.35pm express to Birmingham and Wolverhampton whilst in the background a Euston-bound suburban electric train waits at signals. All the rolling stock in the picture and the locomotive itself are finished in the crimson lake livery. The destination boards on the main line carriages are white, with black lettering. *E. R. Wethersett*

3

The war years had a particularly severe effect upon the LMSR, due partially to the important bomb targets of the industrial areas it served, and the system was in decidedly poor shape when peace was restored, with a huge backlog of repairs and maintenance for locomotives and rolling stock and track, and a surprising amount of bomb-damage to repair on its buildings and structures. The directors abandoned all hope of a quick return to prewar speeds and schedules and as a result, the 'Coronation Scot' streamlined train was never reinstated. During the war the crimson lake had been abandoned for locomotives, to be replaced by overall plain black, whilst carriages only retained the crimson lake if 'patch-painted' (which most were) otherwise they were given a plain *maroon* finish. This maroon *appeared* to be of a bluer shade — ie more purple — than the true Midland crimson lake, and it was more opaque in quality because probably a single coat had to suffice; this could have been achieved by the addition of a little white. Locomotives did not receive it, except a few 'patch-painted' examples where areas such as the cabside were dealt with; some even lasting into early BR days and carrying BR numbers; the last one recorded being Compound 4-4-0 No 40934 still in crimson lake until September 1951. Only *one* locomotive was officially repainted maroon after the war, as an experiment, and this will be described later.

The name maroon is therefore I suggest appropriate to the paint used in the later war years and afterwards and which was almost certainly of different quality and manufacture to the fine shade, known as 'Midland Red' (the crimson lake) of prewar days. What is not 100% certain is whether

4

4
The postwar LMSR scene, by contrast, was typified by black locomotives and even the streamlined 'Pacifics' were given this drab finish, as seen here on Class 7P 4-6-2 No 6243 *City of Lancaster*, photographed on a Perth-Euston express approaching Leighton Buzzard tunnel. This locomotive was destined to be the last to remain in service with a streamlined casing, being rebuilt in June 1949, by which time it was running with the BR No 46243 but still in LMSR black livery. *W. S. Garth*

5
A very early suggestion for a new company livery for the LMSR, tried-out on a Hughes ex L&Y 4-6-0 No 1670 and photographed in full 'photographic grey' treatment. The lining style was pure L&Y but the letters LMS in simple sans serif form upon the tender were new. The locomotive retains its 'Horwich 1923' combined numberplate and worksplate on the cabside. The basic livery would presumably have been black. *British Rail*

the actual shade was deliberately altered to look 'bluer', or whether it was *intended* to be the same colour. What caused the change of shade was probably simply the requirements dictated by wartime shortages and economies, namely that carriages and locomotives no longer received such careful preparation and undercoating as had been the prewar practice. The opaque maroon allowed quick top coating, whereas the prewar paint was more translucent and relied to an extent upon the colour of the final undercoat to give it its intensity. In 1946 the LMSR started to use the name maroon officially, for carriages and for the lining on locomotives, and BR perpetuated this name.

My own personal recollections and observations of the LMSR commence with the middle war years of my childhood and result from almost daily 'train-watching' from a convenient lineside recreation ground near Kenton on the ex-LNWR main line. The later streamlined Pacifics made a lasting impression, with glimpses of their crimson and gold colours sometimes showing through the grime that seemed to cover everything. Particularly impressive to my young eyes was the bright shade of vermilion red applied to the bufferbeams of the recently repainted black locomotives — it seemed almost orange, and was certainly more visible than the 'signal red' that BR adopted in its place. I was also fortunate enough to see the last 'Claughton' 4-6-0 No 6004, still in shabby vestiges of prewar crimson lake, and working freight trains from Willesden. Also recalled are a number 'Royal Scots' and 'Jubilees' in similar condition; normally only recognisable as such by their hastily cleaned numerals and lettering (a common practice was to clean just the cabsides) which revealed the crimson lake beneath the grime. But the vast amount of locomotives that powered their way past were in black, and filthy dirty towards the end of the war. About this time my 'spotting' expeditions took on a double role, watching the skies for flying-bombs ('doodlebugs'), as well as the trains!

The final years of the LMSR are portrayed in part two, including the 1946 livery experiments which resulted in the decision to retain black for locomotives. This was a sad choice which reflected the mood of these austere times, and it was with some pleasure that I observed the various shades of blue and green that BR experimented with in 1948/49.

This book is written with the model maker very much in mind. Within this format it is not possible to go into exhaustive and minute detail about specific livery applications; the aim is to present a broad but concisive description of the livery applications and policy changes of each railway, thus enabling the reader to research still further if so desired, armed I hope with sufficient background information.

Because space does not permit there are some omissions which should perhaps at least be mentioned here. In particular, I have not described the rolling stock of the narrow gauge Leek & Manifold Light Railway, which the LMSR took over from the North Staffordshire. This, and the LMSR's two tramway systems — the Wolverton & Stony Stratford Tramway and the Burton & Ashby Light Railway — did not survive very long. In at least two cases, the Leek & Manifold and the Wolverton & Stony Stratford, the stock (or some) received crimson lake livery. Also worthy of mention is the Manchester South Junction & Altrincham electric rolling stock, which was of LMSR design but which had a *green* livery (fully lined) because it was a line jointly owned with the LNER. Also for space reasons I have not described the special liveries applied by the LMSR to post office sorting carriages, with their large 'Royal Mail' lettering, and the remarkable insulated 'sausage vans' operated for Palethorpes. The sight of one of these, with the huge slogan 'Palethorpes Royal Cambridge' along the length of the crimson lake bodysides, and with a highly realistic picture in full colour of a pack of sausages, (about 4ft×4ft 6in) was one not easily

5

6

6
The first year or so of the Grouping witnessed some curious hybrid liveries such as the one carried on this former North London Railway 4-4-0T, which became LMS No 6466. In LNWR black, with full lining-out, Bow Works has simply removed the cast numberplate from the centre of the sidetank and applied the Midland Railway style numerals, in unshaded pale yellow, or gilt. No LMSR coat of arms, or company initials were carried. *Ian Allan Library*

forgotten! These special vehicles are all described in *The LMS Coach 1923-1957*; a book referred to later.

The practice of putting the locomotive power classification on the locomotive cabside should be mentioned. This was derived from MR days when brass numerals were used. In the LMSR period the style of painted or transfer numerals and letters, eg 5XP or 4F, followed the style of the main insignia as a rule. Two other details, the cast iron smokebox numberplates and the oval cast iron shedplates were also very characteristic touches; their style and location being readily deduced from photographs, as they were usually picked-out in white paint, and I have not included detailed close-ups of these features.

In the Preface to this book, I have given the reader a basic introduction to the subject and to the problems which exist in any attempt to describe livery schemes of the past. In this third book of the series I feel it necessary to repeat some of these observations, and I beg the indulgence of those readers who have already encountered them.

Although the emphasis of both text and illustrations is understandably upon the liveries of the locomotives and rolling stock — the figureheads of the railways — there are other aspects which help to create a wider spectrum and I have decided to include architecture (mainly stations), road vehicles, publicity and some other elements to a degree at least offering a general idea of what occurred at any given period. The specialist in search of deeper knowledge of these associated elements is referred to the excellent work being done by the members of many societies at the present time. In particular I would mention the Historical Model Railway Society and the Railway Correspondence & Travel Society, both of whom publish very detailed information upon railways, their stock and their liveries, from time to time. In this instance, the LMSR has also been remarkably well researched and documented in recent years by members of the LMS Society and by two noted experts in the field. Information in great detail is contained in their two books which are thoroughly recommended to the reader: D. Jenkinson's *Locomotive Liveries of the LMS* (Roundhouse Books/Ian Allan) and R. J. Essery and D. Jenkinson's *The LMS Coach 1923-1957* (Ian Allan) already mentioned. On the specialist subject of goods vehicles a recent book by R. J. Essery and K. R. Morgan, *The LMS Wagon* (David & Charles) gives much useful detail.

Finally, a word on the subject of colour illustrations. With so many preserved railways in existence today, and with an array of operational rolling-stock restored to what purports to be its original livery, or style, a strong temptation existed to take a camera and record these in colour for use throughout the series. For two basic reasons I have decided not to do this. One is that wherever contemporary evidence of a livery exists, I prefer to use it, as it is of course completely authentic even allowing for the known vagaries of film emulsions and suchlike. The other reason is that, sad to say in a fair number of cases, what is otherwise truly

7

7
Crewe Works locomotive maintenance policy whilst under the guidance of H. P. M. Beames was extremely efficient and well organised and no time was lost in repairing locomotives and returning them to revenue-earning service. One aspect of this was that many locomotives and tenders would go through the overhaul without complete repaint — particularly the black engines — and a patch-painting policy was adopted. This led to such mixed images as this one, where the tender of 'Rebuilt Claughton' 4-6-0 No 5953 *Buckingham* still has LNWR lining-out, despite the date of the photograph, 1928, by which time the second LMS livery style, had been applied with the initials LMS replacing the numerals on the tender, and these numerals painted on the cabsides. *Ian Allan Library*

8
Another example of Crewe's thrifty painting policy is seen on 'Rebuilt Experiment' 4-6-0 No 5554 *Prospero*, photographed at Coventry about 1929. In plain black livery, (there are some faint traces of LNWR lining on the tender, in the original photograph) the locomotive carries an LMS standard smokebox numberplate and the numerals are painted on the cab sidesheets. The tender however clearly shows a blank patch in the centre, where the numerals were previously located, and which have simply been obliterated with black paint. *A. Flowers*

8

excellent restoration work is spoiled by inaccurate livery details — perhaps due to lack of professional painters, or lack of proper lining-out and final varnishing. In the worst instances some of these preserved items are in the wrong colour, or shade, for the period which identifies the mechanical condition of the locomotive or carriage concerned. There is no point in perpetuating errors or omissions of this kind. Happily there are a good many really authentic museum-restored pre-Grouping locomotives and rolling stock in existence, and for this period, prior to the availability of colour film, I will be making some use of them. For the Grouping (certainly from mid-1930 onwards) a considerable amount of original colour material has been unearthed in recent years, in particular by the diligent efforts of Ron White of 'Colour-Rail', and by the now defunct 'Steam & Sail', and wherever possible I will use this rare and interesting collection. Some of these early colour photographs have faded, some have the blues and magentas too evident, but even allowing for this they bear the stamp of authenticity and carry with them a fine air of nostalgia.

9

A clear example of patch-painting, or more accurately, 'retouching' is shown by the numerals and lettering on Class 2F 0-6-0T 'Dock Tank' No 7166. The existing letters and numbers have been retouched to make them more visible; the locomotive itself has not been repainted. This was a very common sight on the LMSR from the war years onwards, and certainly existed long before then; being basically a Crewe practice. This detail is from a photograph of the mid-1940s.
Ian Allan Library

SOUTHERN 759

SOUTHERN 123

Top to bottom: Lettering as used on coaching stock, 1923-38.

'Schools' class nameplate.

Locomotive lettering style, 1923-39.

Locomotive lettering style, 1936-41.

Locomotive lettering style, 1941-48, as used on black engines.

Locomotive lettering style, 1941-48, as used on green engines.

The Maunsell Years 1923-1937

Above: SR1/C21 Urie sage green (LSWR).

Below: SR2/C20 Maunsell green.

Below: Class D No 1092, standing in Ashford shed yard in ex-works condition, in September 1937. Maunsell green livery, with white lining edged with black. *Colour-Rail/J. P. Mullett*

Below: Ex-SECR Class F1 4-4-0 No 1043 standing in Ashford works in September 1937. It awaits its tender, which is still in the paintshop. This pristine finish and clear lighting gives a good idea of the richness of the Maunsell green when freshly applied. *Colour-Rail*

Below:'King Arthur' class 4-6-0 No 742 *Camelot*, in Maunsell green livery, standing at Oxford with a Birkenhead-Bournemouth through train, in April 1939. The train is composed of SR and GWR stock. *Colour-Rail*

The Bulleid Years, 1937-1947

Above: SR3/C12 Maunsell experimental light olive.

Below: In experimental light olive green livery, with white lining and black edging 'King Arthur' class 4-6-0 No 789 *Sir Guy* is seen standing at Templecombe with an up express. The new sans-serif gilt lettering with inner green line is seen on the tender and the numerals, in shaded gilt, are on the cab side. Photographed in 1939. *Colour-Rail/S. C. Townroe*

Below: SR4/C14 Bulleid malachite green.

Below: Class M7 No 51 in spotless Maunsell green livery, with black and white lining; standing at Bournemouth shed in 1939. In the background can be seen a portion of a 'Lord Nelson' tender, in Maunsell green, but with new style lettering applied by Bulleid. (This was No 864). *Colour-Rail/S. C. Townroe*

Below: Class H2 ex-LBSCR Atlantic No 2425 *Trevose Head*, in malachite green livery at Newhaven shed in June 1949. *Colour-Rail/W. H. G. Boot*

Above; Bulleid's postwar malachite green livery sits prettily upon the lines of ex-LBSCR Class J2 4-6-2T No 2326, photographed at Tunbridge Wells in September 1947. Note the bufferbeam numerals, unusually placed to the left of the centre coupling. *Colour-Rail/J. M. Jarvis*

Above: Bulleid 'Merchant Navy' class Pacific No 21C12 *United States Lines*, in malachite green livery, at Nine Elms shed in April 1947. *Colour-Rail/H. N. James*

Above: GW1/C19 standard GWR middle chrome green, as used 1923-47.

Below: 'Castle' class 4-6-0 No 4073 *Caerphilly Castle* stands outside Swindon works in November 1937, following a general overhaul. The locomotive has the GWR mongram on its tender and standard fully-lined passenger green livery. *Colour-Rail/J. P. Mullett*

Above: 'Saint' class 4-6-0 No 2937 *Clevedon Court* is seen standing at Birmingham Snow Hill in April 1939, in fully-lined passenger green livery. GWR brake van in standard dark grey livery, and suburban carriage in single-lined chocolate and cream with monogram, are to be seen in the background on the right. *Colour-Rail*

Above: After some time in service, the middle chrome green weathered to an almost black appearance, despite (or perhaps partly because of) cleaning by shed staff. A rich patina of oil and soot was basically the cause. 'Duke' class 4-4-0 No 3256 *Guinevere* was photographed at Newbury in April 1939 at the head of a stopping train to Southampton. In the left-hand background is AEC railcar No 18. The clerestory carriage behind the tender carries the 1934 mongram, but the tender has the earlier lettering style. *Colour-Rail*

Below: In immaculate ex-works green and black livery, Class 4200 2-8-0T No 4283 was photographed outside Swindon works in November 1937. Note the painted safety valve casing. *Colour-Rail/J. P. Mullett*

Right: In April 1947 'King' class 4-6-0 No 6010 *King Charles 1* heads 14 coaches at the western end of Reading station, on an up fast Plymouth train; about to 'slip' a carriage without stopping. Autotrailer No 179 stands on the right. The engine is in Hawksworth's lined-out postwar livery. *Colour-Rail/H. N. James*

Right: The same train as in the preceding picture, photographed again first as the slip carriage is detached at the rear. Note the station sign in standard black and white. *Colour-Rail/H. N. James*

Above: A rare colour picture indeed! 'Castle' class 4-6-0 No 100 *A1 Lloyds* is seen at Reading with an up express in April 1947. The engine is converted to oil-burning; note the fuel tank in the tender and sliding cab shutter. Postwar Hawksworth express passenger green livery, with coat of arms and initials G and W on tender.
Colour-Rail/H. N. James

Above: Also photographed at Reading in April 1947, this rear-threequarter view of Class 9300 Mogul No 9303, seen taking water, shows the final GWR lettering style on plain green engines. *Colour-Rail/H. N. James*

Above: A beautiful study of 'Castle' class 4-6-0 No 5007 *Rougemont Castle* nearing Reading with an up Swansea express, in really immaculate condition; photographed in August 1947. *Colour-Rail/H. N. James*

Above: Passing Severn Tunnel Junction, 'Castle' class 4-6-0 No 5054 *Earl of Ducie* heads for London on an up express. Note the standard black and white station nameboard in the background. *Colour-Rail/H. N. James*

Left: LM1/C28 LMSR crimson lake.

Below: 'Princess Coronation' 4-6-2 No 6224 *Princess Alexandra* in blue and silver livery, at Shrewsbury in 1938. Taking water whilst on a 'run-in' turn from Crewe. *Colour-Rail/P. B. Whithouse*

Above: The non-streamlined version of the 'Princess Coronation' class (the 'Duchess') had a de-luxe finish to their crimson lake livery; illustrated is No 6232 *Duchess of Montrose* on a Crewe local at Shrewsbury in 1938. The locomotive is in original condition with single chimney, and before the addition of smoke deflectors.
Colour-Rail/P. B. Whitehouse

Above: Stanier Class 2P 2-6-2T No 91 in ex-works condition in the lined black 'intermediate passenger livery', with red shaded gilt numerals and lettering. Photographed at Derby in July 1938. *Colour-Rail*

Below: Class 4P compound 4-4-0 No 1111 in standard 1930s crimson lake livery; featuring 'countershaded' insignia. *Steam & Sail*

Below: A wartime photograph taken on the Cromford and High Peak line, showing ex-NLR 0-6-0T No 27527 at Middleton in September 1943. Note the closely spaced plain gilt letters and numerals! Plain black goods engine livery, with freshly painted smokebox. *Colour-Rail*

Below: Ex-CR 4-6-0 No 14622 standing at Oban shed in 1938. 'Intermediate' lined black livery and gilt insignia with vermillion shading. Note how the red lining has all but disappeared on parts of the engine (splashers and running plate in particular). *Colour-Rail*

Above: 'Cauliflower' goods 0-6-0 No 8592 standing by the coal stage at Bletchley in June 1938; plain gilt lettering, with white outline evident. *Colour-Rail/L. Hanson*

Below: Class B3 4-6-0 No 6166 *Earl Haig* in grass green livery, is seen leaving Aylesbury with an up Manchester express; photographed in December 1938. The teak carriages carry white destination boards. *Colour-Rail*

Below: Class A3 Pacific No 2548 *Galtee More* stands by the coaling plant at York shed, in 1937, in full prewar passenger green livery. *Colour-Rail*

Below: LNE1/C10 standard grass green.

Below: LNE3 standard garter blue for the streamlined express passenger locomotives.

Below: Robinson Class C4 Atlantic No 5262 in the fully lined black livery, showing how colourful this finish could be if kept clean. *Colour-Rail*

Below: Class B1 4-6-0 No 1134 displays the final postwar grass green livery, with Gill Sans letters and numbers; photographed at Elgin in 1946. (Note the highly polished valve motion.) *Colour-Rail/J. M. Jarvis*

Left: A postwar repaint but in full prewar style, complete with shaded letters and numerals. Class B12 4-6-0 No 1543 presents an immaculate picture at Kittybrewster in 1948. *Colour-Rail/J. M. Jarvis*

Below: Class A4 Pacific No 11 *Empire of India* at Newcastle Central in August 1947, in postwar condition with the valence removed; garter blue livery restored, with stainless steel Gill Sans letters and numerals. In the right-hand background is a Tyneside-electric train. The Pacific is heading the down 'Flying Scotsman' composed of new steel-panelled carriages in imitation teak livery. *Colour-Rail/H. N. James*

Below: A special livery, in grass green complete with Gill Sans letters and numerals was given to Class D3 4-4-0 No 2000 (with side-window cab) because the engine was used to haul the Director's saloon in postwar days. The LNER coat of arms was featured on the tender sides. No 2000 is seen here at Grantham in 1948. *Colour-Rail/J. M. Jarvis*

Below: Gresley Class A4 Pacific No 2509 *Silver Link* in the silver-grey livery first adopted in Silver Jubilee year. No 2509 is seen at Grantham with the 'Flying Scotsman' in June 1937. A Gresley full brake in teak is the leading vehicle. *Colour-Rail/J. A. Whaley*

1: The Prewar Years 1923-1939

It was in October 1923 that the directors of the newly formed London Midland & Scottish Railway Company announced that they had decided to paint all its locomotives (except goods engines) in the crimson lake livery of the former Midland Railway. The goods engines were to be plain black. The first locomotives to appear in the 'Midland Red', or crimson lake (LM1/C28) were reported to be an ex-LNWR 4-6-0 'Claughton', an ex-LYR 4-6-0 and an ex-LYR 4-4-0.

Prior to this decision a few tentative experiments had been made, using either the new initials in full — LM&SR — or in the abbreviated form — LMS — on locomotives retaining their pre-Grouping livery colours. To further confuse things some locomotives appeared carrying their new LMSR numbers but without any evidence of ownership whatsoever. However, once the decision was taken, the application of crimson lake was made with remarkable alacrity, in particular in Scotland, where the new colour scheme seemed to give added character to many of the varied and aged types of locomotive that the LMSR had, in some cases, reluctantly inherited! At this time pre-Grouping loyalties were naturally very strong, but the new livery seems to have been generally well received — despite latter-day stories about the reluctance of Crewe in particular to paint its locomotives in Midland colours — a myth I have already challenged in the Introduction.

Passenger carrying rolling stock, and non-passenger carrying stock that nevertheless ran in passenger trains were given crimson lake livery, generally following the former MR style, and it was not surprising that the goods wagons were basically in MR grey livery too!

The prewar years can be conveniently divided into two main livery styles for locomotives: 1923-1927, 1928-1939, plus one short-lived variant (1936) and two 'special' liveries, for streamlined locomotives. Perhaps the prewar period could conveniently be described as 'the red years', whereas what followed was *black*, in more senses than one!

Although in this series, I try to give a broad specification for each livery period or style, in this case the prewar locomotive livery underwent some changes that require more detailed description, as follows:

Locomotives

Passenger livery; first period, 1923-1927

Ex-MR crimson lake, or 'Midland Red' (LM1/C28) for bodywork (ie boiler barrel, cab side sheets, footplate valances and running plates, cylinder covers, footsteps, tender sidesheets and rear, and tender underframes). Only one pale yellow line was applied to the boiler, on the band between the smokebox and the barrel. All lining was in pale yellow, with black edging and this was a shade of yellow chosen to match the gold (gilt) transfers edged with a fine white line and shaded black, which were used for the large numerals. This yellow lining edged the crimson lake on all areas where it was bordered by black, except on cylinder covers where it was not always applied. Many locomotives appear to have had a yellow line on the wheel rims close to the outer ends of the spokes; the wheels themselves being painted black. Black was also used for the smokebox, footplate and splasher tops and most upper surfaces, including the top of the cab (above gutter level) and the tops of tenders and tanks. Buffer beams were in vermilion red with pale yellow lining edged in black.

To begin with, the letters 'LMS' appeared in small serif characters on cab sidesheets or bunker sides, with the large gold (gilt) numerals on the tender, or tankside. These initials were replaced in 1927 by the circular crest. The engine number was also applied in polished numerals on a black painted iron casting on the front of the smokebox, following former MR practice; (this also applied to goods engines).

Goods livery; first period, 1923-1927

The goods engines were painted in unlined black, with vermilion red buffer beams and shanks, without lining. The numerals were in the same gold (gilt) shade, style and location as for the passenger engines, but had only the fine white line (on the right hand and lower edges — as a highlight) to separate them from the black background; being in all probability the same *black-shaded* transfers as were used on the crimson lake engines. A few black locomotives carried the circular LMS crest, and some the initials 'LMS' as on the earliest crimson lake examples, but the standard style was a gold bordered vermilion red panel on the bunkerside or cabside, with the letters 'LMS' in gold, shaded black (see drawing). There were two different styles of panel over the period, with the second version having a more modern appearance. Cast iron numberplates were specified for the top of the smokebox door, as on passenger engines.

Passenger livery; Second period 1928-1939 (except 1936/7)

The main body colour remained the same (LM1/C28) but the number of locomotive types using it was now restricted to the more important and modern.* A major alteration was the use of the letters 'LMS' in shaded serif form on tender and tank sides, instead of the circular crest, and the relocation of the locomotive running number on the cabside of the engine portion of tender locomotives, and on the bunkersides of tank locomotives. The chief consideration was the need to avoid the confusion that had arisen from the 1923 livery style where the *tender* carried the *locomotive* number. Changes of tender sometimes occurred in the course of workshop overhaul, or through an emergency in day to day running, and it was not uncommon to see locomotives carrying one number on the smokebox door numberplate and another, quite different, on the tender. By placing the running numbers on the engines themselves, and simply the initials 'LMS' on the tender, this allowed tender changes to be made without problems (except that sometimes a black tender became attached to a red engine, or vice-versa!). At the same time the practice of placing the number on the smokebox door, as a cast iron plate, was apparently eased somewhat for older types of locomotive, although all *new* locomotives continued to feature it. Tenders now had their own numbering scheme; with a cast rectangular metal plate applied to the rear of the tender superstructure.

The style of application of the crimson lake livery itself remained basically the same, except that the covers of outside cylinders were now definitely specified for yellow lining to the front and back edges. The yellow line sometimes put on the black wheels was not applied (officially) after the mid 1930s. The insignia varied a good deal in this second period livery, and there were serif gold letters shaded black, serif gold letters shaded red, and serif chrome yellow letters shaded red. The pale yellow lining, to imitate gold, was changed to a richer chrome yellow in the mid-1930s. The buffer beam style was not altered, except to receive the richer yellow line. A feature of new locomotives built in the Stanier régime was the bright metal finish given to the valve motion, cylinder ends, buffer heads, wheel rims and bosses and handrails. In certain instances (see illustrations) chromium plate was even specified.

**The locomotives selected were the non-streamlined 4-6-2s, 'Royal Scots', 'Patriots', 'Jubilees', 'Claughtons', ex-LYR (Hughes) 4-6-0s and ex-MR Compound 4-4-0s.*

Mixed Traffic livery; second period 1928-1939 (except 1936/7)

Because the crimson lake livery was henceforth only applied to select passenger classes, 'intermediate passenger' classes (mixed traffic types) were accordingly specified for a new varnished black livery, with single vermilion red lining. The letters 'LMS' and the numbers were applied as just described for the post 1927 passenger locomotives, and cast iron smokebox numberplates were still applied to new locomotives, although some older ones seem to have had them removed, once the numbers were on the engine cabside instead of the tender.

Basically the single red line was applied to the same format as the yellow one on crimson lake engines; there were however variations, as can best be deduced by study of contemporary photographs. The bufferbeams were the same vermilion red, *without* lining; edged black. On new Stanier mixed traffic types the same bright metal finish was given to the valve motion and wheel rims, etc, as has been described above for crimson lake engines.

The lettering and numerals on the lined black locomotives were in vermilion red-shaded gold (gilt) serif characters. To begin with these were in a new style which had the red shading *countershaded* with lake and white to produce a more three-dimensioned effect. (There is little doubt that this version was produced specifically for the lined black locomotives, but it did find its way on to some crimson lake and plain black examples as well.) There were also some with plain gold (gilt) transfers (actually *black* shaded!) and finally in the later 1930s a chrome yellow version was favoured, with vermilion red shading.

Goods livery; second period, 1928-1939 (except 1936/7)

Virtually no change, except that the all-black livery had bright metal motion parts etc, on newly-built Stanier locomotives. The revised arrangement for cabside numerals and tender lettering was adopted. In the case of tank engines, the numerals were now normally on the bunkersides and the letters 'LMS' on the tanksides. Plain vermilion red was used for bufferbeams and shanks. The colour of the insignia varied, as with the lined black mixed traffic locomotives, being in turn gold (gilt) shaded red or plain gold, then chrome yellow shaded red, or in some instances plain yellow. (Probably hand-painted retouching produced this latter type.)

The 1936/7 livery variant

This was a shortlived attempt to change the style of the lettering and numerals, on all types of locomotive, to a more up-to-date sans-serif form (somewhat similar to the LNER 'Gill sans' style). First of all a 'Compound' 4-4-0 No 1099 was repainted in November 1935 with plain gold sans-serif insignia; then No 1094 of the same class was given a black shaded version, but what actually appeared on most new locomotives, and some repainted ones, during 1936/7, was in gold shaded in vermilion red (see illustrations). The locomotive colour schemes were not altered, ie crimson lake engines remained crimson lake, etc, but there were a few goods engines finished in plain black with plain yellow (or perhaps gold) insignia — most however, had the red shading. The cast iron smokebox numberplates were altered to the new style numerals, and being very durable they continued in use until the last days of the LMSR in some cases, whereas the transfers (or perhaps hand-painted) insignia reverted to the earlier serif style from late 1937, early 1938 onwards.

The special streamlined liveries; 1937/1939

The 'Coronation Scot' express train of 1937 for which the first of William Stanier's classic new 'Princess Coronation' Pacifics were specially built in streamlined form, featured a livery of Caledonian blue (Carter calls it Royal blue; his chart reference is C24) which was applied overall to locomotive and tender, and the carriage sides. A darker, Prussian or perhaps Navy blue, was used for the locomotive driving wheels and as a background colour to the chromium plated nameplates, and as lining to the edges of the silver (aluminium paint) broad bands which ran horizontally along the length of the locomotive and train, commencing in a vee-shape on the front of the engine. The style of insignia was basically the 1936 sans-serif, but without shading. Only the first five locomotives, Nos 6220-6224 received the blue livery.

When five further streamlined 'Pacifics' were delivered the livery was changed to the standard crimson lake and with horizontal gold bands instead of silver, edged with a fine vermilion line and a bolder black border; still using the sans-serif insignia. This was the intended livery for the new 1939 'Coronation Scot' train, which was exhibited in America (complete with No 6229 *Duchess of Hamilton* masquerading as No 6220 *Coronation*) and which was stranded there by the outbreak of World War 2; of which more anon.

Passenger Stock

Unlike the locomotive stock, where economies reduced the number of types carrying crimson lake livery, the passenger carriages retained this colour scheme throughout the prewar years; only the style of lining and some insignia detailing was changed.

The broad specification was as follows:

From 1923 until late 1933/early 1934

Crimson lake (LM1/C28) bodysides and ends. Gold (corridor stock) or pale yellow (non corridor stock) lining each side of a black band on the raised beadings of wooden-panelled stock; a fine vermilion red line separating the crimson lake. The same livery was applied to flush-sided steel-panelled stock; giving an impression of panelling.
Black underframes and bogies
Black roof between rainstrip and cantrail; grey above rainstrip.
Letters 'LMS' and descriptions, ie 'Sleeping Car' in 4in high elongated serif letters in gold, with countershaded red to the left and black to the right. It is interesting to note that the red shading for the lettering on carriages was on the *opposite* side of the letterform to that applied to locomotives, and had an additional *black countershading* which was not used on locomotives at any time.

From 1934 until 1939

Crimson lake (LM1/C28) for bodysides; the ends also until 1936, when they became black.

Simplified lining with two single yellow lines between cantrail and windows and a single black band edged each side with a yellow line just below the windows. The yellow being a darker chrome, on corridor and non-corridor stock.
Black underframes and bogies, and ends after 1936. Roof in aluminium metallic finish; or grey.

Running numbers in sans serif shaded numerals; other insignia unchanged.

The 'Coronation Scot' trains, 1937/39

The 1937 train was finished to match the streamlined Pacifics, in Caledonian (or Royal) blue (C24). Sans serif silver insignia with a dark blue outline was used, but the train name was carried in black on white on the carriage roofboards. The 1939 train was in crimson lake and gold, this time with the train name painted in gold outlined in black above the windows. (See the locomotive descriptions for further details of the lining, etc which was carried along the carriage sides to match the locomotive.)

Railcars and multiple-unit electrics

Normally these were in the standard crimson lake, but sometimes lined in special fashion (see photo of the Leyland railbus, for example). Electric stock followed the styles adopted for non-corridor locomotive-hauled carriages. The exception was the diesel three-coach articulated railcar set introduced in 1939, which had a bright red and cream livery, with silver roof.

Other Stock

Passenger brake vans, milk vans, fish vans, horse boxes and other specialised non-passenger carrying stock

All stock that was permitted to run in passenger train consists, received full crimson lake livery from 1923 to 1933/4, complete with pale yellow lining-out. Then when the simplified passenger carriage livery was introduced, all these vehicles (except passenger brake vans) received plain crimson lake, devoid of lining but retaining the shaded serif letters for the LMS insignia, and for special descriptions such as 'Milk Van'. The numerals were in unshaded sans serif style.

Goods wagons; from 1923-1936/7

Light to mid grey, bodywork sides and ends, and solebars and headstocks.
Black running gear and buffer heads and shanks and all details below solebar.
White unshaded sans serif numerals and lettering.

Goods wagons; from 1936/7-1939

Bauxite brown (or red) bodywork sides and ends, solebars and headstocks and sometimes roof; otherwise aluminium or grey was used for the roof.
Black running gear and buffer heads and shanks and all details below solebar.
White unshaded sans serif numerals and lettering, all details being in small characters grouped at the lower left-hand end of the bodyside.

Service vehicles

Loco coal wagons, some crane match wagons and the plough brake vehicles used in engineers' trains appear to have followed much the same style as revenue-earning wagons except for the insignia carried. However ballast and sleeper wagons were in red oxide and some crane match wagons were painted black.

Containers

Open type containers carried the wagon livery; ie grey from 1923-1936/7 and bauxite afterwards. Ordinary covered containers were in crimson lake with yellow lettering, and sometimes the LMSR crest was applied. For insulated types (such as for meat traffic) there was a special white livery with black lettering, etc. Slogans were carried for publicity purposes on many types; in particular furniture containers.

10

10
Looking quite splendid, groomed to haul the Royal Train, 'Claughton' class 4-6-0 No 5944 was photographed on Bushey water troughs on 15 August 1925, with the 11.00am Royal special from Euston. The locomotive is in the new crimson lake livery, complete with numberplate on the smokebox door, and the cab sidesheet carries the initials LMS, a short-lived idea prior to using the new coat of arms. Until World War 2 the Royal Train continued to carry the livery of the former LNWR, known unofficially as 'plum and spilt milk', at the specific request of the late King George V, who apparently preferred it to the LMSR crimson lake scheme.
F. R. Hebron/Rail Archive Stephenson

11
The Midland Railway-inspired crimson lake livery with pale yellow and black lining and edging, sat very happily upon the standard 4-4-0 'Compounds', which were to carry Derby practice to most corners of the LMSR system; becoming known as the 'Crimson Ramblers' as a result. No 1115 depicts the standard livery for passenger locomotives of the 1923-1928 period, with the LMSR coat of arms, or crest, upon the cabside and the locomotive number on the tender; plus a MR style cast numberplate on the smokebox door. *LPC*

12
The locomotives of the Scottish constituents of the LMSR seemed to carry the crimson lake livery exceptionally well. It certainly suited the ex-HR 'Clan' class 4-6-0s, as No 14768 *Clan Mackenzie* shows, in this official broadside view. In the first version standard crimson lake livery from 1923-1928 the numerals were on the tender, or on the tank sides, and the locomotive carried the coat-of-arms on the cab sides. The lettering was in gold leaf with black shading, including the name whenever (as in this case) it was applied hand-painted, and not as a cast plate. This style of lettering was exactly as used previously by the MR. *Ian Allan Library*

11

12

13

Fowler's 'Royal Scot' class 4-6-0, in its original form was very obviously Derby-inspired in appearance, and the livery emphasised this! Features to note on the 1923-1928 crimson lake engines are the MR style numerals and the lack of lining for boiler bands except at the edges adjacent to the smokebox and cab front; the pale yellow lining out on footsteps on engine and tender; lining out on the black-painted wheels immediately adjacent to the outer ends of the spokes, and the lining with black edging to the outer edges of the bright vermilion bufferbeam and buffer shanks. On some classes including the 'Scots' there was a band of crimson lake above the vermilion area; as seen here on No 6110 *Grenadier Guardsman*, photographed at Camden. *LPC*

13

14
Goods engines in the 1923-1928 period were painted plain black, with gold leaf numerals and vermilion bufferbeams; without lining. On the cabsides a panel of vermilion carried the initials LMS, with the lettering and edging in gold leaf, shaded black. Two versions of this panel were produced (see drawing 16) and the first version is seen here on ex CR McIntosh '179' class 4-6-0 goods engine No 17909. *Ian Allan Library*

14

15

15
Standard Fowler Class 3 0-6-0T No 16624, photographed at Forres on 16 May 1928, when newly delivered from Beardmore's. Plain black livery with gold leaf numerals and second version of the 'LMS' vermilion and gold panel with rounded corners, on the bunkerside. *H. C. Casserley*

16
Left: The elegant numeral style of the 1923-1928 livery, based upon MR practice, in gold leaf with black shading; plain gold leaf on black engines. Two sizes of numerals were used, 18in and 14in high. The 14in style differed in being slightly more condensed.
Right: Lettering style on black engines for the cabside, or bunkerside, panels. The first version was replaced by the second in 1926. Background colour was vermilion, and the letters and border were in gold leaf, shaded black.

16

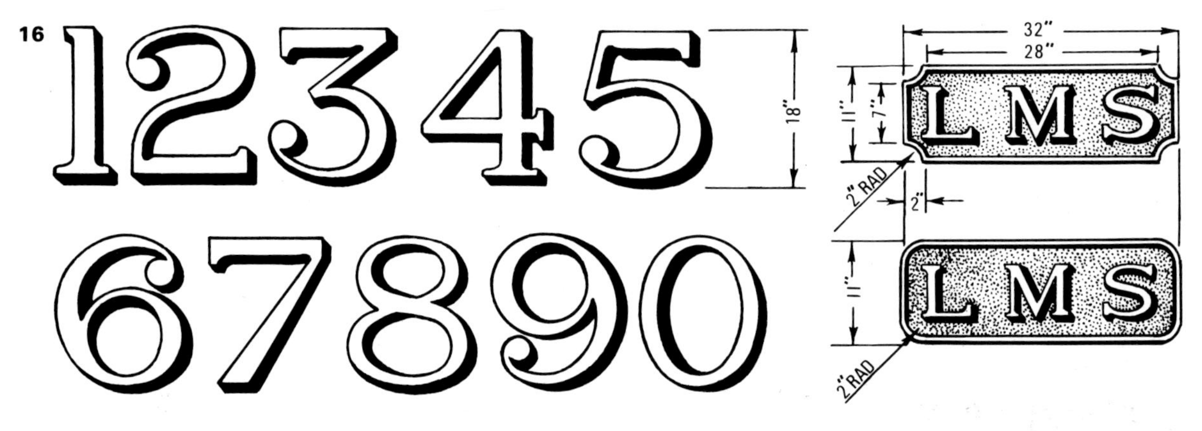

17

17
In 1928 a revised standard livery was introduced, retaining the same livery colours, but placing the locomotive number on the cabside of tender engines and replacing the coat-of-arms, or crest, with the initials LMS on the tender. 'Royal Scot' class 4-6-0 No 6149 *Lady of the Lake* (later renamed *The Middlesex Regiment*) displays the revised scheme to perfection in this photograph taken at Crewe North. The large cabside numerals were shaded black and were in the traditional Derby style (see drawing) and were 14in high. No lining-out to boiler band except for a single yellow line adjacent to the smokebox. No lining on the wheels. The crimson lake was carried up to the gutter line above the cab; above the roof was black. The small brass oval below the nameplate depicted the LNWR locomotive of the same name. *T. G. Hepburn/Rail Archive Stephenson*

18

18
In the revised livery, tank engines carried the initials LMS on the tanksides, and the numerals on the bunkersides. Crimson lake was still applied at first to some selected passenger tank engines, as seen here on the first of the Fowler Class 4P 2-6-4Ts, No 2300, photographed at St Albans on a St Pancras suburban working. It was however not long before black with red lining was substituted for the crimson lake, but over half of the first 25 engines of this class were delivered in crimson lake. One example, No 2313 carried the name *The Prince* painted above the initials on the tanksides, from 1928-1933, to celebrate the visit of the Prince of Wales (later the Duke of Windsor) to Derby Works in February 1928, when the engine was nearing completion. Note the standard cast iron numberplate fitted to the smokebox door, and the shallow vermilion red buffer beam area with a band of crimson lake above it. The ex MR 0-4-4T in the righthand background is still in the first version of the crimson lake passenger livery for tank engines, with the LMSR crest on the bunkerside. No 2300 has the small 10in high numerals, shaded black. *LPC*

19
In 1933 the express passenger engine, 'Royal Scot' class 4-6-0 No 6100 *Royal Scot* was sent to North America by the LMSR for exhibition purposes. For this it was fitted with an electric headlight and warning bell, and the smokebox numberplate was replaced by a polished metal plate carrying the name of the train 'The Royal Scot', (*not* the name of the locomotive, which was simply *Royal Scot* on the nameplates). Although specially finished for this event, the burnished steel buffer heads, and the outer ring and hinges to the smokebox door were a feature often found on other examples of this class running on the LMSR (and on the smaller 'Patriots' and Compound 4-4-0s). The shallow vermilion red area on the buffer beam is well depicted, with the yellow and black surround; above it was painted crimson lake. Smoke deflectors were added to the front end. The headlight was removed when the locomotive returned to Britain, but the nameplate and bell were retained as a souvenir of the visit. *British Rail*

19

20

20
When William Stanier, (later Sir) took over LMSR locomotive affairs he did not alter the existing livery schemes (unlike many CMEs in the past) and the crimson lake scheme suited his new express passenger locomotives admirably; as portrayed by the superb 'Princess Royal' class Pacific No 6201 *Princess Elizabeth* in this official broadside of the locomotive when new. Original Derby-style tender, with an additional lined-out crimson lake panel at the footplate end. Polished wheel bosses and rims, valve motion and spring details, and cylinder end covers. *LPC*

21
In original condition, with domeless boiler, Stanier's Class 5XP 'Jubilees' were extremely elegant locomotives, with polished wheel bosses and rims, motion, and metal fittings including the handrails, and reversing lever. The cylinder end covers were in bright metal, and these details gave the crimson lake livery the finishing touch. No 5564 is illustrated, brand new and not yet carrying the name *New South Wales*. Note the low placing of the 12in cabside numerals, in line at their base with the lining on the running plate above the driving wheels; whereas the initials LMS were carried centrally on the tender sides. *British Rail*

21

22
In honour of the Silver Jubilee of King George V and Queen Mary in 1935, the 'Jubilee' Class 5XP 4-6-0 No 5642 was taken into works and given a special black and chromium plate finish, at the same time exchanging name and number with the existing No 5552 *Silver Jubilee*, which became No 5642 *Boscawen*. The new No 5552 had a very glossy black paint finish and the numerals and lettering were in polished relief metal, in bold 'Grotesque' sans-serif style. The smokebox numberplate was also in a particularly neat sans serif style; unique to this locomotive. All the boiler bands, and the top feed cover (again in a style unique to this locomotive), the outside steampipes, the entire cylinder ends, the handrails and sundry other external fittings, were given a chromium-plated finish. Before going into normal revenue-earning service, the locomotive went on an exhibition tour of the LMSR system. Photographed at Camden shed. *P. Ransome-Wallis*

23
Fowler 'Royal Scot' class 4-6-0 No 6160 *Queen Victoria's Rifleman* with Stanier tender and smoke-deflectors added, in correct early to mid-1930s crimson lake livery, with black shading to the 14in numerals, and the tender lettering. The power classification, 6P, is placed above the numerals on the cabside; previously it had been higher, between the cab window and the rear cutaway. Comparison with photo 17 shows the difference in appearance created by the larger Stanier tender and the smoke deflectors. *British Rail*

22

23

24

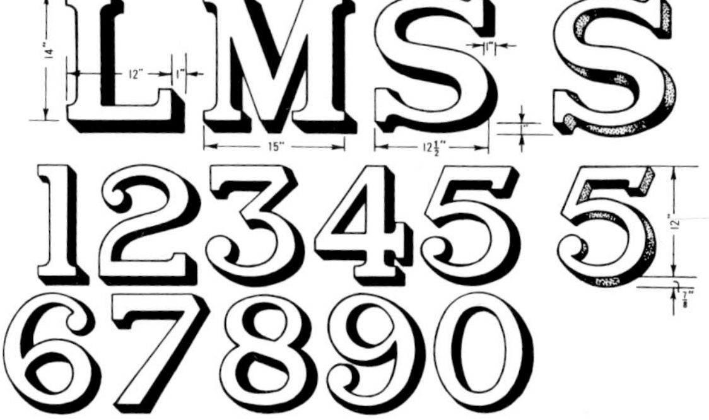

24
The lettering and numerals of the revised livery, introduced in 1927 and used until 1947 (with exceptions, as described later). There were three sizes of numerals: the existing 14in plus new style 12in and 10in. The 14in letters for 'LMS' were applied in gold leaf shaded black; in gold leaf with vermilion red shading, or with blended red to white countershading; in plain gold, plain yellow and (in latter days) plain yellow with red shading. There were similar colour variations for the numerals.

25
The nameplate of 'Royal Scot' class 4-6-0 No 6118 *Royal Welch Fusilier*, with cast gun-metal regimental crest carried below. This picture shows well the bold lining style applied to the crimson lake engines. The ½in yellow line was pale (straw) until 1935 when it was changed to a richer yellow, more like 'old gold'. Nameplates were normally in polished brass, with a black background. *Ian Allan Library*

26
Evidently someone on the LMSR, in authority, wanted a more 'modern' style of lettering and numerals for locomotives, and in 1936 (March, to be precise) a 4-4-0 'Compound' No 1094 was repainted with bold sans serif numerals in yellow shaded black. This cabside detail also shows the style of lining-out for locomotives with Derby-style cabs, and power classification '4P'. *British Rail*

26

25

27

28

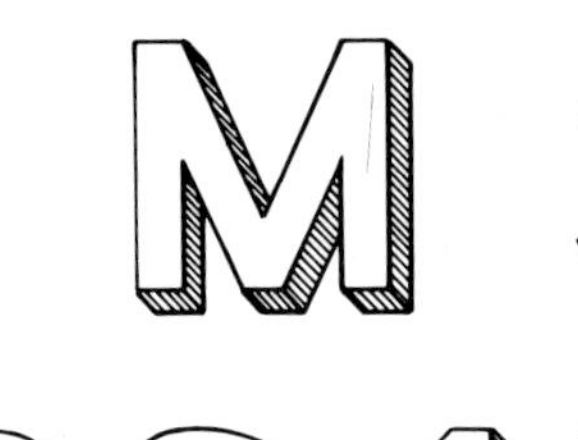

67890

27
The sans serif style began to appear on some repainted and some new locomotives, but the black shading was replaced by vermilion red and the yellow by gold leaf. 'Patriot' Class 5XP 4-6-0 No 5502 *Royal Naval Division* demonstrates the style, sometimes referred to as the '1936 style'. *British Rail*

28
The '1936 style' sans serif alphabet. The letters 'LMS' were in 14in high characters and the numerals were 10in high. Smokebox numberplates were also produced to this style.

29

The magnificent streamlined 'Princess Coronation' Pacifics, introduced by Stanier in 1937 specifically to haul the new 'Coronation Scot' train, were strikingly finished. The basic livery was intended to be a match of the Prussian blue of the former Caledonian Railway (and appears to have been an accurate one). To this was added silver for the lettering and numerals and for the bold stripes, or 'cheat lines' which commenced at a point low down on the nose, just above the coupling, and then widened to run along the entire side of the locomotive and tender; being continued along the carriage sides of the train itself. The numerals and lettering were basically to the '1936 style', but without shading. No 6222 *Queen Mary* is illustrated. External metal details, such as handrails, were given a chromium-plated finish. Photographed in August 1937. *British Rail*

29

30

30

Left: The nameplate of the first of the 'Princess Coronation' class, No 6220 *Coronation*, which was chromium-plated and had a dark blue background. The same dark blue (navy blue) was used as a fine $\frac{1}{4}$in lining to each side of the silver stripes (actually aluminium paint was used). Note the chromium finish to the handrail at the top of the picture, and to the sandbox filler cap, and the Crown in polished relief metal finish

Below: Drawing of 'Princess Coronation' nameplate.

British Rail

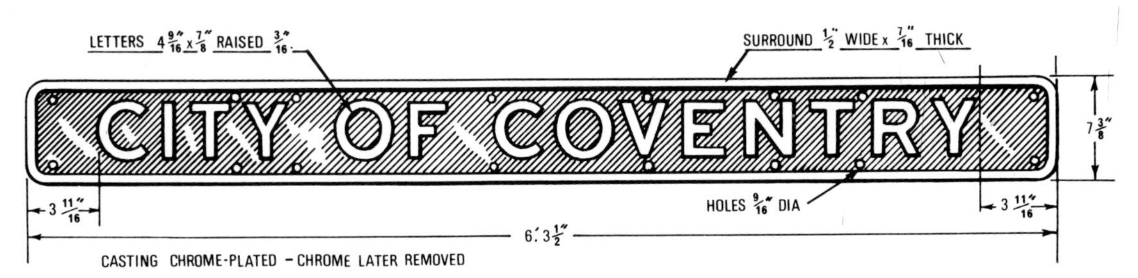

31

In 1935 Stanier had rebuilt the experimental Fowler high-pressure 4-6-0 No 6399 *Fury* into a taper-boilered version of the 'Royal Scot' class, renumbered No 6170 and named *British Legion*. This was the only taper-boilered 'Royal Scot' to carry a single chimney (later replaced by a double), and the only one to carry LMSR crimson lake livery; all subsequent rebuilds appearing in black, as described later. No 6170 was a most handsome machine, as can be seen in this picture of the locomotive heading the up 'Mancunian' passing Crewe. Shallow vermilion red panel to the bufferbeam, with crimson lake band above. *Real Photos*

31

32

A special high-quality crimson lake livery finish was bestowed by Stanier upon his five superb non-streamlined 'Princess Coronation' (or 'Duchess') class 4-6-2s Nos 6230-6234. Here No 6231 *Duchess of Atholl* is seen on shed, with the chromium-plated handrails to cab and tender well depicted. The lining-out was gold, instead of yellow, with a fine red line to each side of it, and the 12in numerals and 14in lettering reverted to the pre-1936 pattern, but in gold leaf shaded with vermilion. The nameplates were in polished chrome with black background, and certain other small external fittings (such as sandbox filler caps) were also chromium-plated. *P. Ransome-Wallis*

33

34

33
The abandonment of the '1936-style' sans serif characters (except on the streamlined-engines) was decided upon only some two years after their introduction! In their place, the 1927-style characters were again used, but the gold finish was replaced by yellow (except on Nos 6230-6234) and vermilion red shading replaced the black, on many repainted engines. These bright and contrasting colours had the effect of making the crimson lake itself look darker in tone. 'Royal Scot' class 4-6-0 No 6139 *The Welch Regiment* was photographed at Crewe in 1939. Note the blank backing-plate above the nameplate, ready for the cast gun-metal regimental crest; not fitted.

34
Only the first five streamlined 'Princess Coronation' Pacifics were given the Caledonian blue livery, and then the standard crimson lake was substituted. The bold stripes were applied in gold paint with a fine ⅛in vermilion line to each side, with a black line (somewhat thicker) separating it from the crimson lake. Lettering and numerals were in gold to match; external metal details were still chromium plated, including the nameplates which had a black background. In 1939 a new 'Coronation Scot' train was constructed, and prior to use in this country it was sent on an American Tour (see also photo 50). The locomotive and train were both finished in the crimson lake and gold livery. No 6220 *Coronation* (in reality No 6229 *Duchess of Hamilton*, which exchanged identities to become No 6220 for the duration of the Tour, being a newer locomotive), is seen here on the Baltimore & Ohio RR, complete with headlight and bell, to conform with American Railroad regulations.
Ian Allan Library

35

35
Cabside detail of No 6220 (actually No 6229) in the crimson lake and gold livery scheme with '1936-style' numerals, but without shading and outlined in black. Note the power classification '7P' placed *below* the numbers. Fireman J. Carswell and Driver F. C. Bishop, both seen here, were the men that took the locomotive to America, but Bishop fell ill and R. A. Riddles (later destined to be the last cme of BR steam) did most of the driving on the Tour.
Crown Copyright, National Railway Museum, York

36

36
Former Caledonian Railway mixed traffic 4-6-0 No 14800 (ex No 956), photographed in May 1929 in lined black, following the decision to restrict the use of the crimson lake, circa 1928. The new livery for mixed traffic locomotives (or as they were sometimes called 'intermediate passenger locomotives') was black with red lining. This replaced the crimson lake at first applied by the LMSR to many pre-Grouping types in this category.
Crown Copyright, National Railway Museum, York

37
New mixed traffic locomotives were delivered in the lined black livery, and foremost amongst these were the classic 'Black Fives' (or 'Black Staniers') which of course gained their nickname from this livery, thereby segregating them from the outwardly very similar Stanier 'Jubilees', which were in crimson lake. Class 5 4-6-0 No 5157 *The Glasgow Highlander* (one of only four of the class named in LMSR days) displays the lined black livery to perfection, and shows the gold lettering and numerals with red countershading that were introduced for this livery. 5P5F power classification on cabside below windows, and tablet catcher on cabside adjacent to the figure 7, which it partially obscures. Note the polished steel cylinder end covers, wheel rims and bosses and valve motion.

38
Stanier Class 4P 2-6-4T No 2629 in lined black livery; photographed in September 1938. The smokebox door numberplate is in the '1936-style' sans serif numerals whereas the tank and bunkerside carry the yellow, shaded red, characters which replaced the sans serif style in that year. The vermilion red bufferbeam has a narrow black border around it. No lining on cylinder covers or along the running plate. *British Rail*

37

38

39

40

39
The prewar film has failed to render the red lining in this photograph of Fowler 2-6-4T Class 4P No 2341, but close inspection of the original print shows it to be there (but faded). It is included here to show the use of unshaded insignia on a black engine, sometimes resulting from the use of *black* shaded transfers, presumably done for expediency in the workshops!
P. Ransome-Wallis

40
The goods engine livery was unlined black, with vermilion red bufferbeam and shanks, throughout from 1923-1947; only the styles and location of insignia varied, and these changes followed the same pattern as those made to the passenger and mixed traffic types. The lettering and numerals were in unshaded gold to begin with, but from about 1929 onwards red shading was sometimes used. This Beyer-Garratt, No 4994, photographed north of Elstree in a down empty wagon train, carries the plain gold version. The letters LMS were closely spaced to fit the cabside on this particular class.
F. R. Hebron/Rail Archive Stephenson

41
The '1936-style' insignia was applied *unshaded* to a few of the new Stanier 2-8-0s then being built by Vulcan Foundry in the period 1936/37, as seen here on No 8042 in glossy black livery, with polished metal wheel rims, bosses and motion. These were an exception, however, because the majority of locomotives which received this style of insignia had them in gold shaded red.
British Rail

41

42

The '1936-style' was also applied to smokebox numberplates, and examples of these lasted considerably longer in service (even after the locomotive had been repainted and had lost the sans serif on the cabsides, etc). These numberplates were very legible, as is demonstrated by Stanier 8F 2-8-0 No 8207, photographed pounding along on an up goods train near Elstree.
E. R. Wethersett

42

43

Although the design of this Class 0F 0-4-0ST has sometimes been ascribed to Stanier, it is doubtful if he had much to do with them; being basically a Kitson-type industrial design, introduced in 1932. No 1540 displays the plain gold insignia, and small 10in numerals on the plain black livery. *LPC*

43

44

A non-standard, but very attractive livery was bestowed by the makers upon Sentinel 0-4-0T shunter No 7164. The engine is in glossy black with a gold line and a thinner red one inside it. The lettering and numerals are in gold, boldly countershaded to give a relief effect. A most attractive and simple machine for the modelmaker! *LPC*

44

45
From 1923 until the end of 1933/early 1934 all the LMSR passenger carriages were painted in what was virtually the style of the former Midland Railway, with fully lined crimson lake livery; only the crest and insignia being changed to suit the new company. The crimson lake was also applied to the carriage ends, but without the elaborate black and gold, or yellow lining with vermilion edging. This lining was on the beading of the panelwork (stock being basically of wooden construction above the underframes, with mahogany or steel panelling) and the effect was to emphasise the panelwork, in a most attractive way. The LMS crest was carried on the lower bodyside with the initials above in gold, shaded left in graduated lake, or red and countershaded right in black. The roof was black between rainstrip and cantrail and grey above the rainstrip. Bogies, underframes and all detail below the body, buffers and end beading and fittings were all black. Note the elaborate etched-glass toilet window in the centre of this elegant semi-open first class carriage No 15933 of circa 1930. *Ian Allan Library*

45

46

47

46
The LMSR introduced steel panelling for its carriage construction during the 1920s, and also purchased a quantity of all-steel carriages from outside builders. To begin with the livery style of the wooden panelled stock was retained and 'pseudo' panelling was painted upon the steel sides! Illustrated is an all-steel brake third open, No 7670 built by the Leeds Forge Co in 1926. Note the riveted steel roof. *British Rail*

47
All-steel third open built by Cammell/Laird in 1925/26, with revised livery style, simplified to avoid vertical waist and eaves panel divisions; giving a more modern appearance. *British Rail*

48

49

48
A Stanier design combined kitchen and third class dining car, on six-wheel bogies, in steel-panelled form with flush surfaces but retaining traditional lining-out to simulate beading. Roof finished in aluminium/silver paint. No 102 also shows the attractive style of lettering used for the words 'Dining Car' and the sans serif numerals for the running numbers. *Ian Allan Library*

49
Third class open of 1938 Stanier-build, with the revised and simplified style adopted, devoid of panelling and certainly more suitable for modern flush-surfaced rolling stock. Two fine yellow (instead of gold) lines above window level and a black line edged with yellow lines along the waist. Grey roof and black carriage ends.
Ian Allan Library

50
Top: The previous year, 1937, witnessed the introduction of the 'Coronation Scot' express train, between London and Glasgow. For this a special livery of Caledonian blue and silver was applied (see photo 29) and the lettering and numerals were in silver sans-serif. Illustrated is Kitchen car No 30089 of the 1937 train.

Bottom: In 1939 Stanier introduced a completely new train set for the 'Coronation Scot' service. This purpose-built set was finished in crimson lake and gold livery (see also photo 34) and the horizontal gold stripes were carried round to the rear of the end brake vehicle, as seen here. This brake was part of an articulated twin with first class accommodation, Nos 56000/1. The brake end had no gangway vestibule connection. The name 'The Coronation Scot' was painted in gold sans serif lettering on the carriage sides above the windows, whereas the 1937 train had carried normal black on white roofboards. Note the flush steel valances carried down between the bogies. This train was sent to North America for a Tour in 1939, where it was marooned by the outbreak of World War 2, and it spent the entire war years there in use as an officers' mess in a military camp! It never ran as a complete luxury passenger-carrying set in Britain, because the LMSR decided not to reintroduce the train in the difficult immediate postwar period. Note the oval buffers fitted to this train.
Crown Copyright, National Railway Museum, York

50

52

51

The livery for non-corridor passenger stock followed the same style as the corridor stock and the use of 'pseudo-panelling' was a feature of early steel panelled construction, being emphasised even more by the more numerous doors and windows! This attractive view of 'Push and Pull' brake third No 24404 also shows well the 'LMS' insignia. Yellow was used instead of gold for the lining-out on non-corridor stock, but otherwise the application was the same and included plain crimson lake ends (until 1936, when only 'Push and Pull' carriages retained the crimson lake ends, as seen here, all others being painted black). A small destination board is fitted above the windows near the centre of the carriage; in this case reading 'Pye Bridge' in black lettering on white. The locomotive is former MR Class 1P 0-4-4T No 1340, in black livery with red lining. *British Rail*

53

52

Sentinel-Cammell steam rail motor-car No 4151 built 1926/27, with third class accommodation only. The engine unit, nearest the camera, is articulated with the passenger saloon, which had 44 seats. One of 14 steam rail-motors that the LMSR operated for about 10 years. The crimson lake livery had the beading picked-out in yellow and black, including the driving ends.
Ian Allan Library

53

Electric rolling stock followed the standard livery pattern, and the same 'pseudo-panelling' was painted on the flush steel sides to begin with, later being simplified. The driving ends were plain crimson lake by way of contrast and the bufferbeam and shanks were in bright vermilion red. Note that there is no LMSR crest on the sides of this motor brake third No 8881, built in 1927.
Modern Transport

54

The electric stock constructed during the Stanier period was considerably more up-to-date in concept, and it looked extremely smart in the simplified crimson lake livery, with sans serif numerals and black and yellow waist lining and the LMSR crest. No 29287 is the leading car of a three-car set on a Liverpool Central-West Kirby working, photographed at Birkenhead North. Earlier types of electric rolling stock also received the simplified livery in the late 1930s. *W. Hubert Foster*

54

55

55

Leyland diesel railcar No 29950, one of three four-wheeled vehicles delivered in 1934, and basically of bus-type construction. These 40 seat third class only railcars were in crimson lake livery, complete with the LMSR crest on the centre doors. No accurate record has come to light concerning the colour of the two light bands around the waist and skirt, but it is assumed that they were either pale grey or cream. No lining-out was applied, and these vehicles presented a very modern appearance for their time. *LPC*

56

A remarkable train produced by Stanier was the three-car diesel set, introduced in 1939 and unfortunately overtaken by the outbreak of war, which did not favour such experiments. It had an articulated layout and fully streamlined nose ends (reminiscent of German high-speed railcars) and the livery was bright red and cream with black waist line and thin black lining to the upper band of red, with silver roof. Lettering and numerals were in sans serif cream, and no LMSR crest was applied. Nos 80000/1/2 (the latter is nearest in this picture) were stored during the war years and afterwards rebuilt as a maintenance unit for the MSJA electric line; being reduced to two cars in the process. A sad end to a fine experiment! *LPC*

56

57

Non-passenger carrying rolling-stock which nonetheless was hauled attached to passenger carriages was accorded full crimson lake livery, complete with yellow and black, or plain yellow lining, until the introduction of the simplified livery scheme for passenger carriages, when all lining-out was abandoned (see photo 59). On modern steel panelled stock, such as this early Stanier (1932) designed six-wheeled passenger brake van, No 2860, the 'pseudo-panelling' was applied to match the rest of the train. The legend 'To carry 6 tons' was painted in yellow italic script on the lower right hand corner, below the number and a grey panel was painted above (at waist level) for chalked inscriptions. *Real Photos collection*

57

58

Wooden-bodied stock, such as horse boxes and fish vans, which could run in passenger trains, received the crimson lake livery, but the style of application of the yellow and black lining depended upon the form of construction. On this fish van, No 7674, only yellow lining was applied and this was restricted in use to the edges of the raised framing. *Real Photos collection*

58

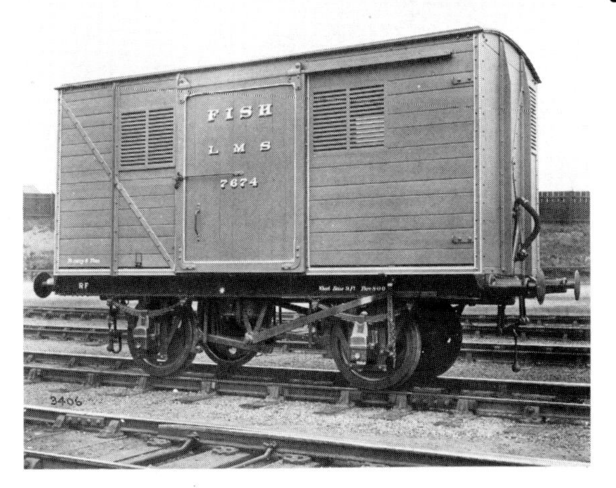

59

When Stanier introduced the simplified lining for passenger carriages, the non-passenger stock in the lined crimson lake livery (except passenger brake vans) was henceforth painted without any lining-out, and with sans serif unshaded numerals. The 'LMS' insignia however, and special inscriptions such as 'Insulated Milk Van', as seen here, retained the shaded serif characters. No 38551 was a new-type insulated milk van designed to carry milk in churns, and was built at Derby works in 1935. *Modern Transport*

59

60
The LMSR wagon livery was basically a perpetuation of MR practice, with a grey finish for bodywork and solebars, with white lettering and numerals, and black for running gear, buffers and all details below the solebars. The exact shade of grey appears to have varied somewhat, but newly painted stock (see next photo) was in a light shade. This delightful picture shows tractors being loaded on to a special train composed of medium open goods wagons. *Ian Allan Library*

61
A publicity pose for a complete train of cattle wagons and brake van, all in fresh light grey livery. The brake van has the number in white upon a black panel; all other lettering and numerals being in white on grey. Note that the solebars are all grey and also the rear bufferbeam of the van. An ex MR 0-6-0 goods engine is just visible at the head of the train, which was photographed in 1923. The cattle wagons carry the letters LMS to the left of the centre doors, and the inscription 'Large' to the right.
Crown Copyright, National Railway Museum, York

60

61

62

62
The size of the letters 'LMS' varied considerably, and being hand-painted it also varied slightly in style (particularly the drawing of the letter 'S') and in thickness. This 'Bulk grain' hopper wagon, photographed in grey livery in 1936, has quite small and 'bold' letters. Note the patch of black paint on the solebar, to carry the oiling date and district number.
Crown Copyright, National Railway Museum, York

63

63
Also photographed in grey livery in 1936, this 20ton brake van makes an interesting comparison with the one depicted in photo 61. In particular the change of style and location for the running number. Note that the handrails were all painted white. The roof on covered vans was grey, but aluminium was specified in later years (1936).
Crown Copyright, National Railway Museum, York

64

64
An insulated meat container, in white livery with glossy black lettering, detail and roof. The colour of containers was grey for open containers (changed to bauxite after 1936) and for covered containers either crimson lake see photo 101, or white (for insulated types). The flat wagon is in grey livery. *Ian Allan Library*

65
In 1936/37 the livery for goods wagons was changed from grey to bauxite brown (or red, being an indecisive shade between red and brown). At the same time the use of the large letters LMS was abandoned and these appeared at the left hand end of the body in small characters, painted white together with the running number and other details. This 12T shock absorbing wagon is in the bauxite livery (including solebars and headstocks and buffer shanks) and has three vertical white stripes to denote its special type; note the exposed control springs on the underframe.
Crown Copyright, National Railway Museum, York

65

2: War and Postwar 1939-1947

I have already discussed the effects of the war years upon the LMSR in the Introduction, and the photographs that follow tell their own story. Basically it was a period of 'make-do and mend'. The crimson lake livery was abandoned for locomotives and replaced by plain black, either with the existing insignia retouched, or in new transfers of yellow, shaded red. The carriages received plain maroon if repainted, devoid of lining; and I have expressed my belief that this maroon was the result of wartime shortages both of top quality paint and of manhours to apply it. This state of affairs was most evident in the case of goods wagons, which scarcely saw a paint brush! Wartime wooden-bodied wagons had bare planks, with just patches of bauxite where white lettering was needed. If there was a standard livery for the LMSR when the war ended it could perhaps be summed-up as overall grime with glimpses of black and maroon!

In the winter of 1945/6 the LMSR directors evidently began to consider the livery to be applied for their weary postwar railway system. Quite apart from an appalling backlog of repairs and maintenance, they were faced with chronic staff shortages — personages such as engine and carriage cleaners were virtually non-existent because the normally dirty environment of many depots had been dramatically worsened by bomb-damage and lack of repair and they were *not* inviting places for work — hence staff-recruitment was a major problem. Obviously it was pointless to consider a return to the red and gold of the final prewar streamliners, if no-one cleaned it!

A large drawing was first of all produced (fortunately it has survived and is now in the National Railway Museum's collection), showing the side elevation of a non-streamlined 'Princess Coronation' Pacific. This was to portray the proposed livery for express passenger engines, and the basic colour was a dark blue/grey similar to that used by the RAF for their road vehicles. This blue/grey was embellished with wide maroon boiler bands, maroon and straw yellow lining out and straw yellow, (to match gold) insignia. To assess the likely effect of the proposed lining and insignia Pacific No 6235 was decked-out in photographic grey (without the boiler bands painted) at Crewe, when de-streamlined. Evidently there was then some internal dispute, with some directors preferring a return to the 'Midland Red' — or more accurately, maroon — and the next stage was the granting of authority to paint three locomotives in March 1946 in full experimental livery schemes, for comparison. Details of these were as follows:

'Jubilee' class 4-6-0 No 5573 *Newfoundland*:
Blue/grey livery with full lining out in prewar style, but using maroon instead of black for the edging, with straw yellow lining and sans-serif insignia.
'Jubilee' class 4-6-0 No 5594 *Bhopal*:
Maroon livery, with one side lined in black and straw yellow, the other having plain maroon with only a single straw yellow line along the running plate. Splashers were plain maroon on both sides. Straw yellow sans serif insignia, without shading.
'Princess Coronation' class 4-6-2 No 6234 *Duchess of Abercorn*:
A *lighter* shade of blue/grey, with maroon edging and straw yellow lining and insignia. One side was more fully lined than the other, as in the case of *Bhopal*. The nameplate had a maroon background with the lettering picked out in straw yellow.

Two locomotives, Nos 5594 and 6234 were brought to Euston for official inspection, being housed overnight at Willesden roundhouse on 23 March 1946, where the well known photographer H. C. Casserley was fortunate to record them. These pictures appear as Plates 33b and 33c of D. Jenkinson's book *Locomotive Liveries of the LMS*, and he also reproduces an excellent colour sample of the blue/grey, complete with lining-out. Unfortunately Mr Jenkinson is mistaken in describing No 6234 as having a 'half and half' paint finish to the rear of the tender; what is seen in Mr Casserley's photograph is a trick of light showing the reflection of the roundhouse windows! I saw both locomotives some months afterwards, in general service, by which time a goodly layer of dirt had all but disguised their novel colour schemes.

One influential board member at this period of LMSR affairs was R. A. Riddles, then the vice-president for engineering, and he has since personally told the author of his stated preference for black as a locomotive livery; on more than one occasion. Perhaps it was Riddles' persuasion, or perhaps just an act of bowing to the inevitable that led to the final choice of black as the postwar locomotive livery, commencing in the early summer of 1946.

The broad specification was as follows:

Locomotives

Passenger livery

Overall glossy (varnished) black finish, with maroon* edging and single straw yellow lining. To begin with (1946), the insignia were in plain straw yellow bold — 'grotesque' — sans-serif; hand painted. Bufferbeams were vermilion red, without lining. The nameplate was *painted*, with a maroon background and straw yellow letters and border. (Note that the sans serif letters and numerals were *not* Gill sans, as has been frequently mis-stated, but 'grotesque', which is a sans serif variant.)

Within a few months, two changes were made to this scheme. One was that on the running plate valance, from front to rear, the maroon was lined on *both* sides with straw yellow (forming a bold band of colour) and two boiler bands were painted to match — the one nearest the smokebox and the one nearest the firebox, plus the band where the firebox met the cab front. The other change involved the insignia, which had a fine maroon line added within the straw yellow, (see illustrations). Some smokebox numberplates were still produced in the '1936-style' sans serif form for this livery, but the majority had serifs.

Mixed traffic and goods engines

With the exception of all the Stanier 'Princess Royal' and 'Princess Coronation' 4-6-2s, the 'Royal Scots', 'Patriots' and 'Jubilees' (in rebuilt and original forms), and the solitary, unique 'Turbomotive', *all* locomotives were to be in plain black, with a vermilion red bufferbeam without lining; which meant that there was no longer any differentiation between mixed traffic and goods types, in so far as their livery was concerned. The same style of lettering and numerals, in straw yellow with inner maroon line, was used as on the express passenger engines, with a smaller size of numerals for some types.

It should be emphasised that comparatively few locomotives in this lesser category received the new livery prior to nationalisation. The most numerous being the new mixed traffic Class 4 and 2 2-6-0s and the Class 2 2-6-2Ts constructed to H. G. Ivatt's design during 1947/early 1948.

**I have not given a separate colour sample for maroon in this book, because no official statement that it was meant to differ from the crimson lake has been discovered. Personally I think it was more purple, or bluer; a matter of opinion.*

Diesel locomotives

Plain glossy black with aluminium/silver insignia and trim; aluminium paint for bogies and roof for main line types.
Plain black with straw/maroon insignia for shunters.
Vermilion red bufferbeams on the latter.

Passenger Stock

Maroon.
Straw yellow lining, with straw/black/straw at waist (late prewar style). Grey roof.
Black ends, bogies, underframes, etc.
Electric stock was in similar livery, but in some cases only lined with a straw/black/straw line at waist level.

Other Stock

Most non-passenger carrying stock capable of working in passenger train consists was painted in plain maroon (as the late prewar style) but some passenger brake vans had lining to match the carriages. Roof and other details as above.

Goods Wagons

The wartime austerity scheme was for the most part continued, with the minimum of bauxite paint on wooden construction. No basic change from the late 1930 livery style for repainted or new vans.

66
The outbreak of World War 2 put paid to the LMSR streamlined trains and later also to the crimson lake livery. Overall black became the order of the day, and the streamlined casings that were to have graced the new Stanier Pacifics Nos 6249-6252 built in 1944 at Crewe were abandoned, but not before the tenders for them had received their streamlined fairings! Previously Nos 6245-6248, built at Crewe in 1943 had been delivered in streamlined form but painted plain black. No 6252 *City of Leicester* shows the wartime livery, devoid of all lining-out and with yellow and red numerals and insignia, and vermilion red bufferbeam. It has been stated that these engines had red backgrounds to their polished brass nameplates, but this photograph clearly shows a black background. The boilerside handrail has been left in polished steel; all others being painted black.
British Rail

67

68

67
The Stanier '8F' 2-8-0 was chosen by the War Department for quantity construction, for use overseas and on the home railways, and the workshops of the LNER, SR and GWR all constructed batches, as well as the LMSR and outside contractors. The plain black livery was in effect the same as the prewar goods engine livery, and was relieved only by the yellow and red numerals and insignia, as seen here on No 8400, the first example built at the Swindon Works of the GWR, in 1943.
British Rail

68
The wartime livery was perpetuated for some time after the restoration of peace, and No 2242, a Fairburn version of Stanier's Class 4P 2-6-4T, built at Derby in 1946 shows it well. Of interest is the smokebox numberplate, in the 1936 style! The Scottish enginemen have groomed their locomotive to perfection, with pale blue background to numerplate and shedplate and silver paint embellishments to the smokebox door and pony truck guardirons. A black engine *could* look beautiful! No 2242 was photographed at Glasgow Central in April 1948.
H. C. Casserley

69

69
The postwar LMSR livery experiments are described in some detail in the text, and I hope that some of the confusion relating to this photograph in particular has now been clarified. This picture purports to depict Stanier Pacific No 6235 *City of Birmingham* in de-streamlined condition and in photographic grey paint. It must be emphasised that it *never ran* like this, in particular without a new casting for the double chimney; what is seen here is the crude casting which existing streamliners had *beneath* the outer sheet metal casing. Coincidental to the decision to remove the streamlined casings from the Pacifics, the LMSR was seeking a new postwar livery style; the colour probably to be either crimson lake or a blue/grey shade, with simplified sans serif numerals and insignia, and lining. This picture shows one proposal with a fully lined and edged bufferbeam, but with no lined boiler bands and only a single yellow (pale straw) line along the running plate (see also next photo) and with yellow and black edging to cab and tender; a scheme suitable for either livery colour. In fact, it was No 6234 *Duchess of Abercorn* that was actually painted in the blue/grey, in March 1946.
Crown Copyright, National Railway Museum, York

70
Two 'Jubilee' class 4-6-0s featured in the 1946 livery experiments: No 5573 *Newfoundland* which ran in the blue/grey colour, with full prewar style lining-out in pale straw yellow and black but with unshaded sans serif numerals and insignia, and No 5594 *Bhopal*, seen here, which was in maroon. On this side of No 5594 only a single straw yellow line was applied, from end to end of the running plate. The other side was more fully lined for comparison, (but there was no lining on the splashers or boiler bands). The insignia and numerals were in bold sans serif straw yellow; note the close spacing for 'LMS' on the tender, and no lining on bufferbeam. *J. H. Platts*

70

71
The outcome of the livery experiments was a decision to retain black! A glossy finish was favoured, with straw yellow and *maroon* (this was the official description), lining and edging was adopted for express passenger locomotives. At first the lettering and numerals were in plain straw yellow, but an inner maroon line was soon added, (see drawing). 'Royal Scot' class 4-6-0 No 6134 *The Cheshire Regiment* displays the new livery in this official broadside. Note that all the handrails, the wheel rims and bosses were painted black; only the valve motion and nameplates had a polished metal finish. The new livery soon included the addition of lining to the boiler bands at each extremity and to the firebox next to the cab. *British Rail*

71

72
This view of the unique Stanier 'Turbomotive' 4-6-2 No 6202, seen leaving Crewe with the 8.30am Euston-Liverpool train on 14 June 1947, shows that the rear of the tender was in plain black. Another feature of the postwar black livery was that the power classification was placed *below* the number on the cabsides on the larger types of locomotive. *H. C. Casserley*

73
H. G. Ivatt continued Stanier's policy of rebuilding the Fowler express passenger 4-6-0s with taper-boilers, and both the 'Royal Scot' and some of the 'Patriot' class were so altered in the final LMSR days (and afterwards by BR). The lined black livery sat quite smartly on these excellent machines, as is shown in this view of 'Rebuilt Patriot' 4-6-0 No 5526 *Morecambe and Heysham*; photographed in 1947 at Camden shed. In the lefthand background a portion of the cabside of 'Princess Coronation' class 4-6-2 No 6223 *Princess Alice* can be seen, with the numerals in plain straw yellow, ie without the maroon inner line. The nameplate on No 5526 has a maroon background to the polished brass.
P. Ransome-Wallis

74
Photographed on the occasion of the naming ceremony in his honour — 17 December 1947 — Sir William A. Stanier FRS is seen at the controls of No 6256, one of the two final 'Princess Coronation' Pacifics introduced by H. G. Ivatt, with certain modifications. The cabside numerals are well illustrated in their sans serif 'grotesque' style (*not* 'Gill sans') showing the maroon inner line on the straw yellow. Also evident is the maroon edging to the cabside, separated from the black by a straw yellow line. *British Rail*

72

73

74

75

76

75
For mixed traffic locomotives, Ivatt retained a plain black livery overall, but with the maroon inner line added to the straw yellow sans serif lettering. His new Class 4F 2-6-0 No 3001 was photographed at Bletchley in April 1948, complete with the hideous original double chimney. Note that the power classification '4F' is carried *above* the numbers in this instance. *P. Ransome-Wallis*

76
No 6419 of the smaller Ivatt mixed traffic 2-6-0 design, the Class '2F' is seen here, at Manchester Victoria & Exchange station on 24 April 1947, in the plain black livery with new insignia. One curiosity was that the larger 4F design had '1936-style' sans serif smokebox numberplates, whereas these smaller engines had the normal serif version. *H. C. Casserley*

77
Perhaps Ivatt had memories of No 5552 *Silver Jubilee* in the special black and chromium livery, (see photo 22) when he chose the striking black and silver (aluminium) livery for his first main line diesel-electric locomotive No 10000, which appeared in December 1947, just three weeks before the LMSR became a part of the new nationalised 'British Railways'. The lettering and numerals and the line around the body at waist level were in relief polished aluminium, and the roof and bogies were painted to match. White headcode discs were carried instead of oil lamps during daytime. No 10000 is seen here soon after entry into service, heading a Midland line express. *E. R. Wethersett*

78
Diesel shunting locomotives were always in plain black livery, to begin with yellow and red lettering and numerals were applied but under the postwar livery scheme they were intended to receive the straw and maroon sans serif characters. No 7080 is seen however in the livery it received in 1939; when delivered to traffic. *Ian Allan Library*

77

78

79

12½"

LMS

10"

12345
67890

79
The 1946 insignia, destined to last only 18 months, until the LMSR was nationalised; a bold sans serif style in pale yellow (straw) with an inset line of maroon, except for some early examples which were in plain straw. The height varied from 12½in (as shown) to 14ins, for the letters, and from 10in to 12in for the numerals.

80

80
The crimson lake livery of prewar days, with the simplified lining style was restored for postwar construction, with straw yellow replacing the chrome yellow; also on routine repaints. The roof was grey and the carriage ends were black, together with the underframe, bogies and buffers. Two small detail changes should be noted (compared with photo 49): the third class designation has a redrawn 3 with flat top, and the running numbers were in serif style, to match the 'LMS' insignia. It is interesting to note that the circular crest was used throughout from 1923-1947 on some types of main line passenger stock. Illustrated is third open No 27106. *British Rail*

81
First class kitchen/dining car No 43, of prewar build, was refurbished in 1946 with a modern interior. At the same time it received a modified livery, retaining the crimson lake (or maroon) but with straw yellow and black lining and straw yellow sans serif letters and numerals. These were clearly intended to match the new black locomotive livery, but only a few examples were so painted before nationalisation. The crest had straw yellow instead of chrome yellow for the letters and surround. Note the change of title to 'Restaurant Car', instead of 'Dining Car'. *British Rail*

81

82

83

82
During the war period all lining-out was discontinued if a carriage received a full repaint (most it seems were only patch-painted, for economy) and this Southport-Liverpool train of compartment stock, seen near Seaforth, is in the plain maroon livery. The later style of flat-topped 3 is used on the doors; the buffer beam on the motor coach was in vermilion red. *W. Hubert Foster*

83
The postwar livery for electric rolling stock had the simplified lining, in this instance the carriage sides have a single broad band of black along the waistline beading, edged by straw yellow lines. No crest is carried and buffer beam area is black on this type of stock. Photographed at Manchester Victoria. *W. Hubert Foster*

84

84
The war brought about an austere livery change for wooden-bodied goods wagons. New construction had virtually no paintwork on the wooden portions, with just patches of bauxite where white lettering was needed. Metal details remained in bauxite, including the solebars, buffer shanks and headstocks. Wheels and other details below the solebar were black. Note the very small lettering for LMS on the top example a 13ton open with steel ends, whilst the lower one is an engineer's departmental wagon, with 'Stoke' district, but not marked LMS.
Crown Copyright, National Railway Museum, York

3: Stations and Buildings

Unlike the GWR and the SR, where the civil engineers had early on prepared a fairly rigid specification for the colours to be used in painting stations and buildings, the LMSR seem to have retained the varied schemes of their pre-Grouping constituents for the first decade or so, although the new namestyle 'London Midland and Scottish Railway' appeared on signs, and poster boards; usually in black and white. Perhaps this was because the various colour schemes were actually quite similar, or perhaps it was a matter of economy; using-up existing paint stocks. However, in the mid-1930s a list of colours was decided upon, but its exact application to each structure still seems to have been vague, and left to the discretion of the local engineer, or the foreman painter. The basic rule seems to have been to 'pair' the colours, one light with one dark. The dark colours generally being on the lower portions of structures, cast iron columns, doors, ironwork of seats, etc. (Black was sometimes substituted on small items of ironwork.) Above the dark colour, the lighter one was used for the upper part of wooden wall surfaces, roof and awnings and upper part of some columns, also window frames and sashes if these were not white. The listed colours for stations were as follows:

Dark: Middle brown/Venetian red/Mid-Brunswick green
Light: Deep cream/Portland stone.

Use of the green appears to have been limited to the more rural stations, and what scant contemporary colour photographic evidence the writer has unearthed shows the venetian red and deep cream as favoured for larger stations and the buildings in important goods yards, etc. For stations on electrified lines a Golden brown colour was sometimes applied in order to mask the effects of the brakedust from these trains. This was either used alone, or with deep cream. Poster boards, signs and nameboards were basically white on black, using raised letters (many dating to pre-Grouping days) except for the warning signs which had black letters on white, as a rule, although red on white was to be found on some trespass signs and some public crossings; certainly in postwar days.

In the 1930s the LMSR produced a new design of station nameboard known as the 'Hawkseye' target type (see drawing) and at the same time the small signs hung adjacent to lamps were in black letters on yellow enamel. In the postwar period some stations received a new style of sign, with white Gill sans on a maroon enamel background (pre-dating the very similar BR type!) and one of these is seen in the photograph of Watford

85

85
Until the mid 1930s the LMSR seems to have been content to retain many of the pre-Grouping colours and station signs and furniture that it had inherited. Thus this scene at Crewe differs but little from LNWR days, although the hanging signs have been freshly painted in white on black. The letters, numerals and the 'pointing finger' direction sign are all in raised characters, screwed to the wooden backing frame. 'Royal Scot' class 4-6-0 No 6146 *Jenny Lind* is seen arriving, on an evidently well patronised express duty.
Real Photos

Junction (photo 92). This was probably a future standard type.

A more rigid painting specification existed from 1931 onwards for signalboxes, using light stone and dark brown, as follows:

Dark brown: Doors, staircases, guttering pipes and facia boards, barge boards, bottom sills, corner posts and window cleaning stage.
Light stone: All other areas of woodwork except window frames and sashes which were white.
The signalbox name was specified to be in white letters on black; firebuckets in red.

It has been recorded that signalboxes on the Central Wales line were painted green and cream in 1937; possibly this was because of their rural location (just as some stations were painted green and cream in country areas).

86
The attractive station at Bedford St Johns, formerly LNWR, seen in LMSR days. Poster boards and 'Gentlemen' sign in black and white, upper part of canopy, with decorative cast iron support, and fencing, probably in deep cream or portland stone; cast iron columns and doors probably in venetian red or middle brown; although sometimes these rural stations were painted in mid-Brunswick green. *British Rail*

87
A similar colour scheme in either the venetian red, the brown or the green, would have been applied to St Albans Abbey station with the slender cast iron columns in venetian red, brown or green and the upper ironwork and woodwork in deep cream, or portland stone. The Stanier Class 2P 0-4-4T No 1908 stands with the 2.45pm push and pull train for all stations to Watford Junction, and is in plain black livery with yellow and red insignia. '1936-style' smokebox numberplate fitted. Photographed on 14 August 1948. *E. D. Bruton*

86

87

88

88
This view of the frontage of Kilburn station is of particular interest because it shows, above the entrance, one of the large hand-painted posters that the LMSR (and the LNWR beforehand) specialised in. Note the monogram made from the letters LMS, a feature of some publicity material but never adopted for rolling stock or locomotives. The station name sign, repeated twice, is almost certainly in black and golden yellow, whilst over the top of 'Williams Drug Stores' a shabby notice in relief aluminium Gill sans lettering reads 'Station Entrance', probably on a dark brown or maroon background. It seems that 'Kemps the Grocers' have succeeded in providing a more legible and simple sign than that advertising the existence of the railway station!
Ian Allan Library

89
Raised sans serif letters, painted white upon a black board were a common feature on LMSR station frontages — many dating from pre-Grouping days, but with the full title of the new railway added. This example, photographed in November 1949 (nearly two years after the LMSR ceased to exist) was over the road entrance to Hampstead Heath station. The name of the station has been erased, almost certainly during the wartime invasion scare, when it was thought that German paratroopers would be able to establish the whereabouts of their landing by reading station names and road signs! *British Rail*

89

90

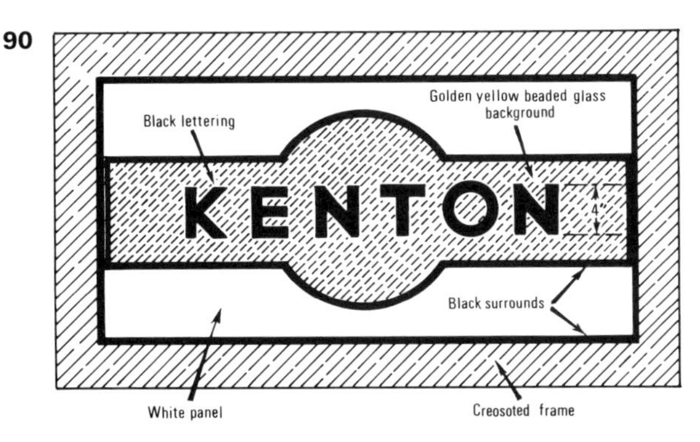

90
The standard 'Hawkseye' station nameboard design, with a 'target' shape rather like that used by London Transport and by the SR; introduced in the 1930s. These nameboards were widespread on the LMSR system. (See also photo 109.) The golden yellow background to the lettering had a beaded glass effect to reflect light and to make the name itself more visually prominent.

91
A variant of the 'Hawkseye' target nameboard was produced for the new stations on the joint LMSR/LPTB electrification to Upminster (District Line). These were either glossy paint finish, or perhaps enamelled, and the background colours were reversed, with the station name in black upon white and the outer surround with the wooden frame in golden yellow. This example was constructed to fit the top of the platform seat below.
Crown Copyright, National Railway Museum, York

91

92

93

92
Watford Junction main line station on 9 September 1946, with the branch to St Albans in the background, and two ex LNWR 0-6-2Ts Nos 6909 and 6725 in evidence. The new station sign in the lower lefthand foreground has white letters and surround on an enamelled maroon panel and white painted supports and frame; a new postwar style, using Gill sans lettering. (Note the abbreviation 'Jn'.)
H. C. Casserley

93
This standard small type signalbox at Aber, on the Chester-Holyhead main line, photographed in 1937, shows the standardised paint scheme of light stone and dark brown.
LGRP courtesy David & Charles

4: Road Vehicles

The LMSR had a very large fleet of road vehicles, ranging from horse-drawn carts to buses and coaches, with of course delivery vans being the most commonplace. The company placed considerable reliance upon the cart horse until the end of its days, and it was BR that quickly got rid of the large stud it inherited; replacing them with 'mechanical horses'. From 1928 onwards omnibuses were an important feature of operations; following the passing of the 1928 LMSR Road Transport Act, which enabled the railway to operate competitively on the roads, as well as the rails. A selection of road vehicles are illustrated, to give a basic idea of the liveries carried at various times.

Buses

Basically in crimson lake livery, with gold (gilt) lining and lettering; black mudguards and trim; white roof. However variations were commonplace, with cream used for bodywork above the waist, and with red lining added to the gilt. LMSR crest sometimes carried.

Horse-drawn vehicles

These featured crimson lake for the main wooden bodywork and wheels, but black was used for fabric hoods and weatherproof protection A mixture of lettering, some in white sans serif or serif, and some in yellow or gilt serif form was used. (The white version usually being on the black portions.) Lining was in gilt on the crimson lake.

Motor vehicles

These followed much the same basic style as the horse drawn vehicles (which they were developed from) with crimson lake as the main body colour and with black hoods, mudguards; etc. As a rule lettering was sans serif or serif white on the black areas and serif gilt, or yellow on the crimson lake. A 1930s development was the use of red shading to the yellow insignia (which became a deeper chrome yellow, resembling 'old gold').

NB In the postwar period all types of road vehicles assumed a plain maroon livery, with white lettering and black trim; it is probable that the maroon paint originated in wartime, just as in the case of the passenger rolling stock; it appeared to be more opaque and slightly bluer.

94
This Leyland Motors 'L' or 'Lion' type bus was introduced in 1925, with pneumatic tyres and a purpose-built chassis (not the usual adaptation of a goods vehicle chassis). The LMSR received this example, resplendent in crimson lake, with gold and red lining-out and black beading. The wheels were in crimson lake with a fine gold line and polished metal hubs. The roof and roofboard were in white, with the letters 'LMS' in black. Crest applied to bodyside. *Ian Allan Library*

95
This superbly elegant Albion six-cylinder 24-seater bonnet-type coach for the LMSR was exhibited at London Olympia in 1929. The livery is crimson lake for the main body and roof, with gold lining and gold sans serif lettering, shaded black. The bonnet, the mudguards, the driver's windscreen surround, and wheels were black. The gold line continued along the bonnet to the chromium plated radiator. *Ian Allan Library*

94

95

96

96
The 'Karrier Ro-Railer' was a road vehicle adapted to run on both road and rail, and was tested on the LMSR Harpenden-Hemel Hempstead branch in the winter of 1930/31. Afterwards it went for a while to Stratford-on-Avon to work a service to the LMSR Welcombe Hotel. The livery was crimson lake with a white roof, gold lining to the beading and gold serif lettering shaded black. The front mudguards and the wheel centres were black. This curious vehicle ended its days in engineer's service on the LNER West Highland line. *British Rail*

97
The LMSR had the largest stud of horses in the country, and until its final days it was an intensive user of horses. This line-up of horse drawn vehicles for city deliveries shows the white sans serif lettering used on the front weatherboard (where fitted) whereas the letters 'LMS' on the sides (wherever a covered body was used) were in serif form in white on the black canvas hood. The lower part of the bodywork (wood) was finished in crimson lake. The vehicle on the extreme right of this picture carries the legend 'Express Parcels Traffic'. Wooden drays (flat wagons) had the full title 'London Midland and Scottish Railway Company' in white upon the crimson lake side raves, and the letters 'LMS' on the end raves; together with the number. *Real Photos*

97

98
A photograph taken in 1923, and therefore showing the earliest LMSR livery for horse-drawn vans. The main body and the shafts and wheels are painted in crimson lake, with pale yellow (to resemble gilt) lining and lettering. Note that the shading effect of 'LMS 23' is *all* in yellow, as is the italic script giving the name and address of the railway company. Inner black band to the lining on the wheel rims. The hood was black with white lettering. *Crown Copyright, National Railway Museum, York*

99
A 1929-built Karrier Motors Ltd lorry, with white sans serif lettering and numerals. Basic livery of crimson lake and black, probably with yellow lining. Note the solid tyres fitted and the canvas roof to the cab, which has no windscreen and a rolled tarpaulin to protect the driver in bad weather. *Ian Allan Library*

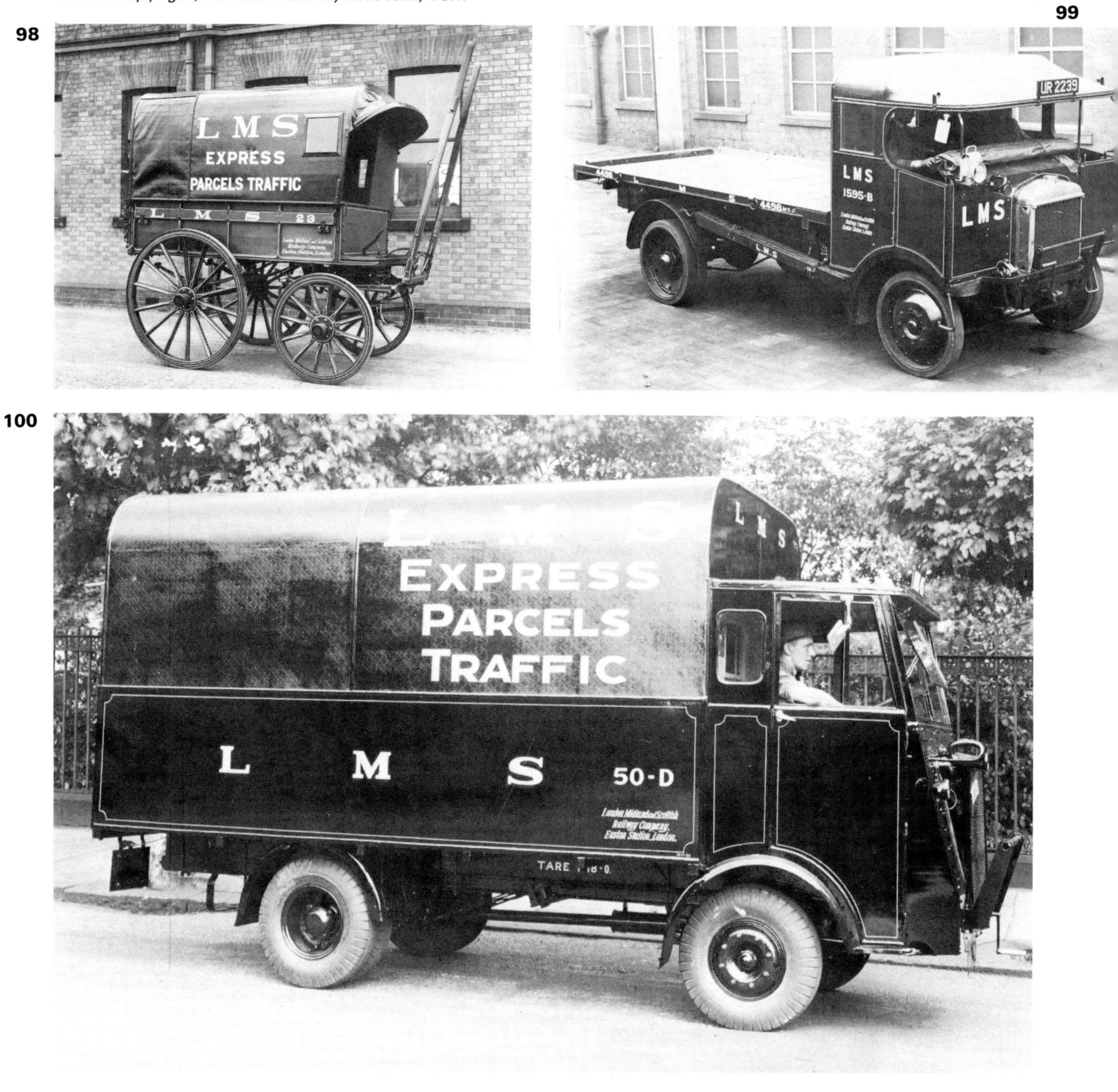

100
A Karrier 'Bantam' van for express parcels traffic, delivered to the LMSR in the summer of 1934. The bodystyle still owes much to its horse-drawn predecessors but the driver now has a fully enclosed cab, and pneumatic tyres are fitted. The livery appears to be the same as for the horse drawn vehicles, with the fabric upperpart in black with white lettering and the main body in crimson lake with pale yellow (gilt shade) lining and lettering. *Ian Allan Library*

101

101
A picture that speaks for itself! The container was in crimson lake, with deep chrome yellow (or possibly gold leaf) lettering; complete with LMSR crest. The side rave on the lorry has white lettering and numerals, and the rear tyre wall has been painted white. All the lettering on the container is shaded to the right and below in black.
Ian Allan Library

102

102
A rear view of one of two Leyland 'Cub' horse boxes, with excellent bodywork by Vincent's of Reading, supplied to the LMSR in 1934. White roof to driving cab and horsebox; plain crimson lake livery with black mudguards and fuel tank. The lettering is in deep chrome yellow with red shading to the left and below for LMS. Crest on rear door. *Ian Allan Library*

103

103
The 'Mechanical Horse' was the designed replacement for the faithful four-legged animal — and only required *three* wheels! This 6ton example was photographed in October 1941, complete with wartime white paint additions to make it more conspicuous in the blackout. Basic livery of crimson lake (perhaps maroon by now — see text) with white sans serif lettering. The female driver (another wartime feature) wears an LMS white metal badge on her cap. *Ian Allan Library*

5: Miscellany

A few associated elements in the overall livery of the LMSR are shown, in order to give added detail. However, the reader in search of 'in-depth' descriptions for which space does not exist in this series, must search through contemporary publications where quite often a description of a new ship, for example, will have some limited livery detail included. For the printed publicity of the prewar and postwar periods, a useful source can be found in the specialist journals of the day produced for the commercial art world. Much information on uniforms can be gleaned from the study of people in the backgrounds to photographs taken at stations, despite the fact that these nearly always concentrate upon the locomotive and train as their main subject. Recently a splendid book entitled *LMS Miscellany* by H. N. Twells (Oxford Publishing Co) has appeared, giving much fascinating background material to the day-to-day operations of this great railway; it is thoroughly recommended as a source of much rare and accurate historical detail.

104
For the period 1925-1947 the standard livery for LMSR ships was a black hull with white/varnished teak upperworks, and a buff coloured funnel with a black top. Between 1923-1925 there was a red band between the buff and the black, and this was retained for the Goole based ships, which also carried the letters AHL (Associated Humber Lines) on the red band from 1935 onwards. The LMSR House Flag for ships had a horizontal white cross on a red (perhaps crimson lake) ground and an LMSR device in the centre of the cross in a circle. Illustrated is the ill-fated steamer *Princess Victoria*, built for the LMSR by Denny Bros Ltd in 1947. Six years later she was sunk by a heavy gale, off the County Down coast, with the loss of 128 lives, when the extremely rough seas burst open the inward-opening rear doors used for loading and unloading road vehicles.
British Rail

104

105
The publicity department sometimes made a monogram of the letters LMS (see also photo 88) but it was never properly adopted, unlike that created for the GWR for example. This mileage board at Wick station shows one early version; photographed in July 1931.
H. C. Casserley

106
Before the arrival of the neon sign upon the streets, large advertising displays were created by lamp bulbs, arranged to flash on and off in sequences, and in differing colours. This LMSR display in Leicester Square, London in the late 1920s, had the lights arranged to make the wheels and valve gear on the locomotive appear to move, also the smoke! (The price of a luncheon or dinner cannot go unnoticed!) *Author's collection*

107
Two typical LMSR posters of the late 1920s, in a style which carried on until 1947, with the use of many famous poster artists, as well as some Royal Acadamecians. The poster for the hotels is by Horace Taylor, and the fishing scene is by Norman Wilkinson RI, who did a magnificient series on this Sport theme, as well as many for the LMSR shipping services.
Author's collection

108

108
Two top-link Camden enginemen look at the Engine Arrangements board at the shed, which shows them which locomotive is rostered to them for the day and which train they will haul. The uniform of the driver was typical of the LMSR period and it is interesting to note that both he and his fireman (left) have white shirts beneath the overalls!
Author's collection

109
Although the tender of the 'Princess Coronation' Pacific is lettered 'British Railways' the locomotive is still in the final LMSR black livery with maroon and straw lining. No M6230 *Duchess of Buccleuch* pounds through Berkhamsted station on 25 March 1948; three months after the LMSR ceased to exist. The picture is included because it shows several distinctive LMSR features: the 'Hawkseye' station nameboard, angled at the platform end; the black and white named train board carried on the leading carriage of the 'The Royal Scot', and the LMSR crest and final livery style on the carriage itself.
H. C. Casserley

109

LONDON &
NORTH
EASTERN
RAILWAY
FORWARD

Previous page (inset)
The London & North Eastern Railway Company coat of arms incorporating the former Great Central Railway's motto 'Forward'.

1 Below:
Ex-GNR Ivatt Class C1 Atlantic No 4419 is seen with a rake of Pullman stock. The LNER grass green livery was particularly suited to these fine machines.
P. Ransome-Wallis

The Grass is Greener

The board of directors of the newly created London & North Eastern Railway were amazingly quick off the mark when it came to selecting a new livery for the company in 1923. In fact some thought was apparently being given to this subject *before* the 'Big Four' were actually in being, because a display of locomotives in various colour schemes which took place at York at the end of January 1923, with eight engines on view for their choice, was the result of some preliminary studies at the end of 1922. Not surprisingly, the locomotive colours were the first thing to be considered, and it seems that the colours of carriages and wagons were accorded less priority, being selected to harmonise with the chosen locomotive colours, perhaps.

The constituent companies of the LNER (as it soon became known in abbreviated form) had varied livery schemes, but green (of varied hues) was predominant, along with black and grey; the latter a wartime austerity colour scheme which both the Great Northern and the Great Eastern Railway had resorted to as a matter of expediency. If green was an obvious candidate in the eyes of the selection committee, it still had to be resolved in terms of a definite shade, or hue. The grass green of the GNR was quite distinct in its appearance from the more subtle Brunswick green of the Great Central, and then there was that deep and mysterious shade, almost a brown in fact, which the North British Railway had used with the title of bronze green. The North Eastern Railway had used Saxony green, but of two different shades (or tones) for passenger or goods engines. To each of these distinctive greens, equally distinctive lining-out and secondary colours were added, giving still more individuality. Even the black locomotives, such as were to be found on the Hull & Barnsley, or the Great North of Scotland for example, had beautiful lining schemes to enrich them. (The Hull & Barnsley actually described *its* black as 'invisible green'!)

It was perhaps unfortunate that the Great Eastern Railway had ceased to use its splendid Royal blue (a deep ultramarine) because of the 1914-18 wartime shortages, and this lovely colour was not presented to the LNER directors for their consideration. Greens were predominant, with lined black as a secondary choice. It could be argued that the LNER board showed much conservatism, and one wonders why some alternatives, in the red or blue spectrum — or even yellow — were not even tried out on an experimental basis. One can only guess that personal preferences played a strong part, perhaps allied to old pre-Grouping loyalties, even in these initial displays. Or then again, perhaps expert opinion (from such men as J. G. Robinson of the GCR or Nigel Gresley of the GNR) was in favour of green because of its excellent wearing qualities in the harsh environment of the steam railway; undoubtedly a truism. Personally, I wonder if any account at all was taken of *public* opinion, or whether the livery selected for the LNER was entirely a matter between professional railwaymen and the board of directors.

The matter was settled, for locomotives at least, very quickly indeed, with a second display held at Marylebone station on 22 February 1923 for the director's benefit. At this display only the former GNR grass green and the former GCR Brunswick green were shown; with lined black again shown but limited only to the former NER style, with red lining. By May 1923 the former GNR grass green was officially adopted for principal passenger locomotives and the former NER lined black for tank and goods engines.

Grass green is the unofficial description of GN Standard Light Green, stemming from GNR days and lasting until the final hours of the LNER, in December 1947, and this book will refer to the colour as such. This confronts the Author with something of an enigma, because since boyhood days, he (and his colleagues) have always known, and referred to, the LNER locomotive green as *apple* green. Exactly how, and when this contradiction arose in our minds I have been unable to establish, although I have found printed references to the colour as apple green in the period 1947/8; so we were not alone in this assumption.

Earlier in this book, I forewarned the reader of the dangers of using names for colours (eg what shade is olive green?) and the LNER presents an excellent example. Doubtless the shade known as grass green can be compared to the colour of fresh grassland — but so may it be equally compared to an apple of the cooking variety! I must settle for the official description, and the shade shown by Ernest F. Carter in his book *Britain's Railway Liveries 1825-1948*, in which he depicts it as No 10* on

**Actually Mr Carter lists no less than three different shades of green : Nos 5, 10 and 15 on his chart. No 10 is the one which he gives for the GNR locomotives, and I think this can be assumed to be the correct shade, although it certainly varied from works to works.*

3
A fine work of art in every sense of the word! Gresley's Class A1 Pacific No 4472 *Flying Scotsman*, specially groomed for exhibition at Wembley, with polished metal details such as spring hangers, brake gear, wheel rims and bosses adding a further sparkle to the already immaculate grass green livery, with black and white lining. A fine single red line is added to the black areas of the framing, but the cylinder covers are plain black, with polished metal detail. No 4472 carried the LNER coat-of-arms on the cabsides, at this time, (from 1924 until 1928). *Real Photographs collection*

the colour chart. Throughout this book I refer the reader to Mr Carter's colour chart, which is unsurpassed as a colour reference. To this I add from time to time my own colour specimens and numerical references. Thus LNER grass green is referred to as C10/LNE1, whilst the original silver/grey colour for the 'A4' Pacifics (not included in Mr Carter's chart) is LNE2 and the Garter blue livery is LNE3; etc. (The prefix 'C' denotes a colour shown on Mr Carter's chart; eg C5.)

In the Southern Railway section I have discussed the problems of colour matching, and some of the effects that time, weather and general wear and tear can have upon paint surfaces — a particularly severe problem with railway rolling stock.

Once the newness had worn-off the paint surface the LNER had a difficult time keeping the silver/grey 'Silver Jubilee' train clean and presentable. In particular, the 'A4' Pacifics were a daunting task for the cleaners, because such a colour is quick to display black marks such as oil or soot. On a dull grey day the 'Silver Jubilee' livery would have been equally dull and grey to behold, unless it was positively shining as a result of the cleaner's efforts. Within six months it was badly stained necessitating the coaches to be resprayed silver. Perhaps all concerned were relieved when Nigel Gresley abandoned this colour scheme in favour of blue for the premier streamlined express trains; because although the garter blue chosen also demanded a high standard of cleaning, it remained more effective in dull light conditions, or after some months in traffic.

The 'standard' livery for LNER passenger trains was curiously old-fashioned when compared to the streamlined trains which they operated alongside of in the 1935-1939 period, in particular because the carriages echoed pre-Grouping practice, being finished in varnished teak to emphasise their mostly wooden-bodied construction.

There were quite a number of steel panelled prewar coaches painted in mock teak, but this was to reach the heights of absurdity in the final years of the company's existence, when brand new flush-sided steel carriages were carefully painted, 'stained and grained', to simulate a teak finish! From late 1938 the finish was spray painted and was increasingly inferior. LNER men said that the postwar finish was very poor by comparison. This was not to say that the LNER teak livery was in anyway unattractive. On the contrary, when in pristine condition it was very beautiful indeed, and possessed a rich glow of colour beneath the varnish layers; whilst the lettering and numerals were veritable works of art on their own account. The problem was that the finish darkened-down considerably in everyday service, so that one rarely saw two carriages with exactly the same shade, unless a set, such as an articulated one, was all shopped at the same time. Badly stained teak panels were bleached with ozalid acid. Some inherited stock was painted brown (see pages 36/37 of *Gresley Coaches* by M. L. Harris). In early BR days it was still possible to find the occasional prewar teak carriage stored-away (usually an inspection saloon or a special of some description) and it was always a pleasant surprise to see the skilled work of the LNER carriage paintshop lasting so well in these conditions; so far removed from the daily toil of the majority of passenger rolling stock.

The LNER suffered from the effects of the depression in Britain's affairs as much as the other three of the 'Big Four' railways, and the need for economies and a more down-to-earth attitude towards liveries were reflected in the change to

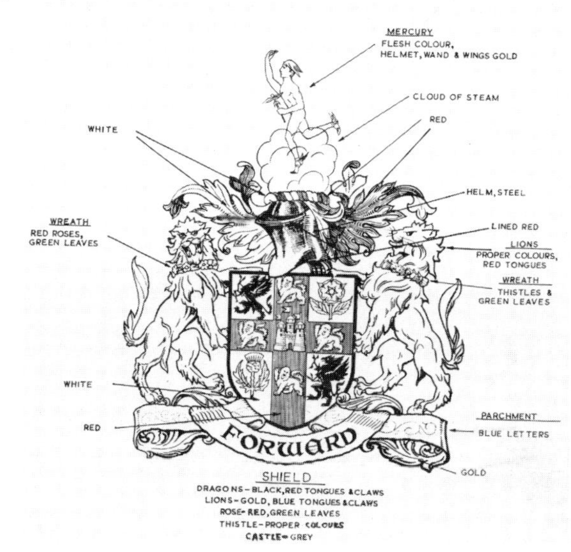

4

The LNER coat-of-arms explained. The College of Arms technical description was: 'Argent on a Cross Gules between in the first and fourth quarters a Griffin segreant Sable in the second a Rose of the second leaved and slipped proper and in the third quarter a Thistle also leaved and slipped proper the Castle of Edinburgh proper between Lions passant guardant Or. And for the crest On a Wreath of the Colours Issuant from Clouds of Steam the figure of Mercury Proper.' *Author's collection*

5

Nigel Gresley chose a silver-grey (metallic aluminium) livery for the first four of his Class A4 Pacifics, which appeared in the 1935 Silver Jubilee year, and which were used on the similarly-liveried 'Silver Jubilee' express. A mid-grey was used for the streamlined valances over the driving wheels and bogie, and a charcoal grey for the wedge-shaped nose. Some metal fittings such as the cab window beadings were brass, and the silver-white lettering and numerals were shaded blue. No 2509 *Silver Link* is illustrated, when new. *LPC*

5

lined black for many passenger locomotives in 1928, leaving the grass green only on the premier classes. Goods engines then became plain black, devoid of all lining. Despite this the LNER managed to keep a generally presentable appearance for its trains in the prewar period, and there was a greater variety of colour schemes than on the other three railways, in part because of the special streamlined trains, and in part because of the varied colour schemes of the steam and diesel railcars, electric trains and tourist trains. Indeed the effect upon the morale of staff and public alike which the appearance of the streamlined trains created was truly splendid, and gave a badly-needed boost to the image of rail travel in the late 1930s, when alternative modes of transport were fast developing. It was a tragedy indeed when the outbreak of World War 2 brought an abrupt halt to all such progress.

Perhaps the greatest contribution the LNER made towards improving the public's image of railway affairs (nowadays referred to as a 'corporate identity') was the revolution that took place in its printed matter, with the adoption of the Gill Sans alphabet. Eric Gill was an artist of extraordinary abilities; a stone-carver and sculptor

6
A drawing by Eric Gill, dated 1927, showing his 'Gill Sans' alphabet, which he intended to be 'absolutely legible-to-the-last-degree'. *Monotype*

in stone and wood as well as being a copper engraver and typographer. Today he is best remembered for his typeface designs, which include Gill Sans, Perpetua and Joanna, but his sculptures can also be readily seen, in the 'Stations of the Cross' in Westminster Abbey for example, or on Broadcasting House ('Prospero and Ariel') together with many war memorials he designed in various parts of Britain. As a child, Gill drew pictures of steam locomotives; beautifully executed studies of LB&SCR types, because the family lived at Brighton, then later at Chichester and Bognor. At this time (late 1890s) the LB&SCR locomotives still carried names, in sans-serif gilt alphabet, with beautiful shading in red, green, white and black. Gill, I feel sure, was appreciative of the beauty of these locomotives in their ornate Stroudley-inspired livery, and the drawings show very careful attention to the lettering and details as well as the overall shape of the locomotive. As an art student, Gill was taught the craft of lettering by Edward Johnston, who became a friend. Johnston designed the sans-serif lettering for exclusive use on the London Underground Railway publicity, signs and station nameboards, in 1916, and Gill had been involved in the early discussions on what form this lettering (still in use today on London Transport) should take. In 1928, at the request of the Monotype Corporation, Gill designed the simple sans-serif alphabet that he gave his name to, and which was undoubtedly influenced by the Edward Johnston design of 12 years earlier.

The LNER had at this time a progressively-minded advertising department led by Mr C. G. G. Dandridge, and they decided to 'adopt' the Gill Sans alphabet to establish a commercial house-style for all painted and printed signs and notices; in fact for printed matter of *all* descriptions. This was an immense programme of letter-standardisation, carried out over a period of years; commencing in November 1932. Eric Gill was himself commissioned to paint a headboard for the 'Flying Scotsman' train; this he duly did and his fee included a trip on the footplate!

The use of Gills Sans by the LNER was not so complete in rolling stock applications as it was in printed matter and station signs, etc. In prewar days, apart from some goods wagons only a select few streamlined locomotives and trains carried it — beautifully applied in stainless steel — and the rest of the locos and passenger stock continued with the previous styles of lettering. The postwar period was equally haphazard in this respect: with the garter blue 'A4' Pacifics receiving the stainless steel letters and numbers once again, but with the new Thompson Pacifics and other types still carrying the original shaded block characters in many instances. A modified version of the Gill Sans, with slightly condensed numerals also appeared during the Thompson period, on a few green and some black locomotives; this can be recognised by the narrower shape of the 3, 6 and 9 numerals. The final period, under A. H. Peppercorn saw true Gill Sans, in unshaded yellow, once again used upon the green-liveried engines. Nameplates featured the Gill Sans letterforms; also some named train headboards.

The use of Gill Sans did not end when the LNER ceased to exist, as it was officially adopted by the new 'British Railways' and examples can still be found in use today in odd corners of the system. What one wishes to acknowledge here is the splendid achievement of the LNER in the adoption of the Gill Sans alphabet. Probably only London Transport could outshine the work of the LNER advertising department in terms of artistic presentation and down-to-earth rules of legibility in the period 1923-1947; particularly in poster design.

I have just mentioned the fact that, where locomotives and carriages were concerned, the Gill Sans alphabet was not adopted in the same dedicated fashion that it was for the publicity and signwriting. Certain special goods wagons and containers did feature the elegant lettering in both prewar and postwar days, however, together with the road vehicles. I suspect that it was regarded as a bit 'too modern' by certain members of the CME's locomotive & carriage staff, who could doubtless

7

Above: MR. **ERIC GILL** PAINTED, AND AFFIXED WITH HIS OWN HANDS, THE NAME-PLATE OF THE MOST RENOWNED TRAIN OF OUR DAY, THE "FLYING SCOTSMAN". HE IS SEEN HERE (AT THE LEFT OF GROUP) AFTER THIS CEREMONY AT KING'S CROSS HAD MARKED THE COMPLETION OF THE GIGANTIC LETTER-STANDARDIZATION DESCRIBED IN THIS NUMBER. AT THE RIGHT OF THE GROUP IS MR. **C. G. G. DANDRIDGE,** ADVERTISING MANAGER OF THE LONDON AND NORTH EASTERN RAILWAY, WHO INITIATED THE REFORM.

On right: REDUCED PHOTOGRAPH OF A TWO-COLOUR PERMANENT SIGN IN THE CABINS OF THE L.N.E.R. STEAMERS SAILING FROM HARWICH.

IMPORTANT.

Passengers travelling to England are reminded that the Customs Examination of Registered Baggage—whether accompanied or sent in advance and irrespective of Destination—takes place at Parkeston Quay (Harwich) and the Passenger must be present; **otherwise the Baggage will be detained there.**

WICHTIGE MITTEILUNG!

Reisende nach England werden hoflichst daran erinnert, dass die zollamtliche Untersuchung des uber Harwich nach London und samtlichen anderen Bestimmungsorten eingeschriebenen Gepacks—gleichviel ob vom Eigentumer begleitet oder nicht—stets in Harwich (Parkeston Quay) stattfindet. Reisende mussen der Zollrevision personlich beiwohnen, **widrigenfalls bleibt das Gepack in Harwich zuruck.**

IMPORTANT.

Il est rappelé aux Voyageurs se rendant en Angleterre que les Bagages Enregistrés, accompagnés ou expédiés d'avance, pour n'importe quelle Destination, sont visités par la douane à Parkeston Quay (Harwich) et que le Voyageur est tenu d'assister à la Visite: **autrement les Bagages seront retenus à Parkeston Quay.**

find many good reasons *not* to use it! Perhaps this also explains the apparent reluctance to use the monogram version of the letters LNER, enclosed in an oval shape, that was produced in the late 1930s (I think to Gill's design) and which only a handful of electrics and locomotives carried. Monograms were much in fashion in the 1930-1940 period, and even the conservative GWR had produced one, which was in no way superior to the LNER version, but which became much wider used. The LNER was for some reason also very reluctant to use its

7
A page from the *Monotype Recorder* (1933) showing the use of the Gill Sans letterforms by the LNER. The photograph at the top of the page depicts Eric Gill himself on the left of the group, and Mr C. G. G. Dandridge, the LNER Advertising Manager, on the right. The occasion was a ceremony at King's Cross to mark the completion of the LNER letter standardisation programme. The named train headboard 'Flying Scotsman' was handpainted by Gill himself. The small inset panel (lower right) shows a standard notice, in two colours, for a ship's cabin on the LNER Harwich steamship service; printed in Gill Sans typeface. *Monotype*

8

coat-of-arms, and only two locomotives displayed it at different times. The first one was the Gresley Class A1 Pacific No 4472 *Flying Scotsman* which was specially groomed for exhibition at Wembley. This had the coat-of-arms on the cabsides (lasting from 1924 until 1928,) whereas the second locomotive, a modified Class D3 4-4-0 No 2000, had the coat-of-arms on the tender between the letter N and E, (later changed to the full LNER.) This locomotive was also specially groomed, in full green livery, for use on special workings such as the haulage of director's saloons, in the postwar period.

During the war years the LNER was forced to adopt the same austerity measures as were imposed upon the other three railways, because their workshops were involved in urgent government work of many kinds, and in November 1941 plain black was specified for all locomotive repainting, with the abbreviated initials NE on tender or tank sides from July 1942 onwards. The totem was also applied to a few locomotives during the war period. The quality of paint was extremely poor and such refinements as varnish layers were reduced to the very minimum — if used at all! As a result, in later years it was not uncommon to see a locomotive with the black paint worn away to reveal the previous lettering or numerals still intact, if somewhat faded, beneath. This state of affairs continued into early BR days, and can be ascribed to the fact that the customary 'rubbing-down' and surface preparation had not been undertaken prior to the repainting. It made life interesting for the train-spotters of the period! The two postwar renumbering schemes added to the confusion; with some locos carrying temporary

8
The elegant simplicity of the Gills Sans letters and numerals enhanced the rich blue livery chosen by Gresley for his 1937 streamlined trains. The locomotives and the lower portion of the carriage sides were finished in garter blue, with Marlborough blue above waist level on the carriages. Stainless steel Gill Sans lettering and numerals added the final touch, together with stainless steel trim. The locomotives had a black finish to the wedge-shaped nose, and a deep Indian red shade for the wheels. No 4491 *Commonwealth of Australia* makes a splendid picture at the head of the 'Coronation' streamlined express. *Real Photographs collection*

9

9
The LNER 'totem', using Gill Sans letters in a cigar-shaped frame; probably designed by Eric Gill himself. This had a mixed reception, and did not eclipse the previous style on locomotives (with a few exceptions) although it was quite widely used in printed matter and on station façades. Colour was usually blue and white, although use of Vermilion and yellow has also been recorded. *Author's collection*

small hand-painted Gill Sans numerals for a while; applied at the sheds; quite often overnight.

Some curious colour schemes appeared on some of the older carriages during the war period and immediately afterwards, in particular on the former Great Eastern lines, where all shades of brown and khaki green were applied to the humbler rolling stock; one can only ascribe this to expediency, because the refinements of the art of staining and graining, or restoring and varnishing a wooden surface were just out of the question; neither time nor skilled labour was available.

An experimental livery of the former GER royal blue, with red lining, was applied by Edward Thompson to his rebuild of the Gresley 'A1' Pacific No 4470 *Great Northern*. This emerged from the Doncaster paintshop in September 1945 and ran in service in the colour for some time. Neither the livery, nor the somewhat austere external appearance of the rebuild (some called it 'ugly') met with much enthusiasm however, and in the following year, September 1946 the LNER announced that the entire engine stock would revert to prewar practice, some 6,400 locomotives, would in due course be painted either green or blue — the blue being the garter blue for the streamlined Pacifics, *not* the royal blue. This bold scheme was never fulfilled because of workshop capacity, and 15 months later it was in any case overtaken by nationalisation, and the grass green and garter blue were not chosen for use by BR. Nevertheless it was a pleasing sight in those austere early postwar days to behold a freshly-painted green or blue locomotive; even if lack of cleaners created a headache for shed foremen who wanted to preserve these attractive liveries in

10
This photograph shows one of the few applications of the LNER 'totem' to locomotives, applied to the bunkersides of the Thompson wartime rebuilds of some of Robinson's GCR Class 8A (LNER Q4) 0-8-0s, into tank engines becoming Class Q1. The 'totem' had white raised letters on a blue background. This photograph shows a false works grey 'photographic' livery, complete with black edging, and white 'condensed' Gill Sans numerals on the tankside. In fact these engines were delivered to traffic in a plain overall black wartime livery with conventional block-shaded numerals — a good example of how misleading 'official' photographs can be when one is researching liveries! *British Rail*

everyday working conditions, if at all possible. A special effort was made with the various small tank engines used as 'station pilots' at important termini and junctions; where they were constantly in the public eye. Green livery and much polish gave them very considerable eye-appeal!

Some general notes on the series must be repeated here for new readers, (who are also recommended to read the Preface).

First of all, a word of warning on the subject of colour research is offered to the reader, regarding the study of old monochrome photographs. These can be very misleading about colours (despite being sepia, or black and white), because if they were taken prior to the invention of the panchromatic emulsion, they do not portray the correct colour *tones*, in relation to one another. Red lining-out or buffer beams, and the background to nameplates appear as dark areas on these old negatives and prints, and in some instances the reds are completely invisible if upon a very dark colour. Blues of the lighter shades are bleached-out to become almost white, or grey. With modern black and white panchromatic film, these colours have their correct tone values.

From time to time locomotives have been released to traffic whilst still carrying a workshop grey livery. This was either due to an urgent need for all available motive power at a peak traffic period, or because the locomotive concerned was the subject of some trials under CME surveillance prior to final acceptance into stock. It would be a mistake to assume that these grey locomotives constituted a livery experiment! In the case of the LNER, however, three types of locomotive *were* delivered to traffic in grey livery. One was the 'Hush-Hush' 4-6-4 experimental locomotive, in dark battleship grey, another was the unique Gresley Beyer-Garratt 2-8-0+0-8-2T Class U1 which was exhibited at the 1925 Railway Centenary whilst still in shop grey; having only just been completed, afterwards it received black livery. The third type was the first of the 'A4' class streamlined 4-6-2s; in a silver/grey shade.

Normally, when a locomotive entered traffic after receiving its livery scheme and final varnishing, a steady process of weathering and wear-and-tear set-in. The longer in traffic, whether cleaned regularly or not, the darker and less contrasting became the individual colours. Painted lining-out and numerals, and gilt transfers of lettering or insignia, also darkened-down with time. In the case of the LNER, apart from the silver-grey already discussed, the most affected livery colour was undoubtedly the garter blue, which darkened-down in the areas adjacent to boiler bands or fittings on the streamlined casing. The grass green livery stood-up to wear and tear extremely well except on very hot surfaces (parts of boilers, fireboxes, etc) where it blackened eventually.

11
In early postwar days the LNER became involved in a very comprehensive renumbering scheme for all its locomotive stock. At one stage it even became necessary to repaint the numbers by hand 'on shed' overnight, and a simple small Gill Sans style was issued to shed painters for guidance. This was a temporary resort, pending the next visit of the locomotive to the works, where the proper transfers could be applied. The temporary small numerals are seen here on the cabside of LNER (ex-GCR) Compound 'Atlantic' Class C5 No 2897 *Lady Faringdon*; photographed at New Holland Pier on 17 April 1947. *H. C. Casserley*

12
Poor quality black paint applied during World War 2 (note the abbreviated letters NE) and a subsequent coat of equally poor quality black in early BR days have resulted in this dual-image on the tankside of Class N15/1 No 69179, photographed at Glasgow on 17 April 1953, with its wartime insignia clearly showing through beneath the BR number. *P. W. B. Semmens*

11

For the LNER there is a most valuable source of written reference for locomotive liveries, which gives very specific details, class by class. I refer of course to the excellent series of partworks entitled *Locomotives of the LNER*, published by the Railway Correspondence and Travel Society (RCTS). Two other valuable reference sources, for the modelmaker in particular are *A Pictorial Record of LNER Wagons* by Peter Tatlow; published by Oxford Publishing Company and *Historic Carriage Drawings in 4mm Scale, Vol 1 LMS & LNER* by David Jenkinson and Nick Campling; published by Ian Allan Ltd.

Some aspects of the LNER do not appear to have been as well chronicled as one might wish, and the present Author must confess to finding the colour schemes of stations, in particular, elusive. Study of contemporary photographs, and in particular colour pictures shows considerable use of cream, or perhaps pale buff, paint on stations, particularly wooden structures; whilst grey seems to have been favoured for ironwork such as station footbridges and roof framework (at least at large stations.) The standard Gill Sans signs were in deep blue and white, or sometimes in black and white. I have not been able to determine whether the emerald green colour that was in use on the lower portions of cream-painted walls and similar surfaces in the early 1950s was in fact an LNER choice, or one introduced at the time of nationalisation by the ER architects.

12

13

An experimental Royal blue livery (matching the dark shade used by the former GER) was applied to Thompson's rebuilt Class A1 Pacific No 4470 *Great Northern* in 1945. This had red lining-out and standard shaded gold numerals and lettering. It is pictured here at King's Cross on 25 June 1946, at the head of the 10.00am 'Flying Scotsman' express. *C. C. B. Herbert*

13

14
The Royal blue livery on No 4470 was evidently disliked, because in the following year (September 1946) the LNER announced its decision to paint *all* locomotives green, (except the Class A4 Pacifics and the solitary Class W1 4-6-4, which were to be garter blue once again). A start was made on this, but nationalisation soon brought it to a halt. One pleasant feature was the choice of some station pilots as early recipients of the green livery, as seen here on Edinburgh Waverley station pilot No 8478, of Class J83. The lettering and numerals were in plain yellow Gill Sans style. *LPC*

1: The Gresley Years 1923–1941

By the spring of 1923 the LNER board had made its decision regarding locomotive liveries for the new company, following an exhibition at Marylebone station on 22 February, when the grass green (C10/LNE1) of the former GNR predominated; together with two black engines both in the lined red style of the former NER. The GNR green had black and white lining, but the frames and footplates were black, instead of the GNR chocolate brown, with single fine red lines. For the first few months locomotives continued to appear in the pre-Grouping colours in many instances, but carrying their new LNER numbers and insignia; presumably to use-up existing stocks of paint. The legend L.&N.E.R. (note the full stops) was at first used, in 7½in shaded letters, but as the use of the grass green became general, the full stops were omitted and later the letters LNER were normally applied (without the ampersand) in 7½in (later increased to 12in) high shaded block lettering. This style remained in use on many locomotives for the rest of the company's years, despite later attempts to change it to Gill Sans, or to use a 'totem'. There were two distinct versions of the block-shaded letters and numerals: gold for passenger engines and yellow for goods. Shading was in red and black on the green engines and red and brown on the black engines; both versions having fine edges of white 'struck' between the gold or yellow and the shading, to give highlights. The decision was taken not to put the LNER coat-of-arms on locomotives (except for very special circumstances) whilst, during the early period 1923/4, a regional suffix was painted to the running numbers: N — Great Northern; C — Great Central; E — Great Eastern D — North Eastern; B — North British and S — Great North of Scotland. The Stratford works of the former GER for some reason continued to paint some goods engines in GER grey livery for several years after Grouping, with yellow numerals (in GER style) and no LNER insignia. (Even today, Stratford has a reputation for diverging from official paint schemes, on its modern diesel fleet!)

During Gresley's regime the contrasts between old and new were sometimes heightened by the use of special colour schemes for the streamlined trains, for tourist trains and for railcars and electrics. Thus, although the grass green remained in use throughout, its applications became steadily more limited, partly because of the need to economise (see later) and partly because of these various exceptional liveries. By the happiest of chance, Sir Nigel Gresley's last locomotive designs were completed in full green livery, despite wartime conditions. Due to his sudden death in 1941 he did not live to see his fine machines smothered in austere overall black and grime.

The broad specification throughout was as follows:

Locomotives:

Express Passenger livery

Basic body colour of grass green (C10/LNE1) including cab fronts, wheels and splashers, tender sides and rear. Black smokebox, Valances, underframes and outside cylinders, (except for locomotives painted by Darlington, which had green outside cylinder covers). Black and white lining and black edging on green areas, fine single red lining on black areas. Buffer beams signal red with black edging separated by a fine white line. (A complete official specification can be found for both green and black locomotives on pages 46/47 of Part 1 of the RCTS *Locomotives of the LNER*.) Variations included green-painted side-frames and splashers continued, above the wheels on some former GER 4-4-0s and 4-6-0s, and black sideframes and splashers on some former GCR 4-4-0s. The size of cabside numerals had to be reduced for the short sidesheets of the Ivatt Atlantics and certain other types; whilst where splasher beading cut across a cabside (particularly on former NER and GER types) the numbers were placed either high above, or low inside the beading. These detail changes did not take place until 1928 onwards when it was decided to move the locomotive running number from the tender side to the cab side at which time the letters LNER on the tender were increased to 12in high to match the numerals. Here again variations occurred, with some smaller types of tender retaining the smaller lettering, lowered, and without the running number below.

The use of the grass green livery was officially restricted to express passenger, and some intermediate passenger engines, when introduced in 1923. These were considered to be types with a driving wheel diameter greater than 6ft 0in; but again there were certain exceptions made, particularly in Scotland. The full list was as follows:

A1 (later A10), A2, A3, B1 (later B18), B2 (later B19), B3, B4, B12, B14, B17, C1, C2, C4, C5, C6,

C7, C8, C10, C11, D1, D2, D3, D4, D5, D6, D7, D8, D9, D10, D11, D12, D13, D14, D15, D16, D17, D18, D19, D20, D21, D22, D23, D24, D25, D26, D28, D29, D30, D31, D32, D33, D34, D36, D38, D40, D41, D42, D43, D44, D49, E1, E5, '901', X1, X2, X3, X4.

By June 1928 the worsening economic situation in Britain was affecting the LNER to the extent that it sought to make economies in its locomotive livery specification, and the number of classes authorised to carry the full green livery was reduced to the following:

A1 (later A10), A2, A3, B1 (later B18), B2 (later B19), B3, B4, B12, B17, C1, C6, C7, C8, C11, D49, X1, X2 and X3. To these were later added, (up to 1941): A4, C9, K4, P2, V2 and V4. (The last two mentioned being Sir Nigel Gresley's final designs.) In addition three 'Claud Hamilton' 4-4-0s remained in green, for Royal Trains.

Other tender and tank engines

Basic overall body colour of glossy black, with a fine red line, and red *inside* frames and bufferbeams. The red line picked out the forms of tanksides and tenders or bunkers, boiler bands, cabsides and cab fronts, outside cylinder covers and footplate edges and footsteps. The front bufferbeam on tank engines was lined in black and white, but not the rear one which was plain signal red. The bufferbeam numerals were in gold with brown and black shading, whereas the main numerals and insignia on tank or tendersides were in yellow; shaded red and brown and picked out in white. This scheme applied to *all* classes not selected for the green livery in 1923, including goods engines. However, in June 1928, when the use of grass green was restricted, as just described, the use of red lining was discontinued on goods engines and small tank engines, which therefore became plain overall black, whilst many former green engines, including the handsome ex-GCR Robinson Atlantics, henceforth carried the lined black livery, until the war brought about a complete halt to this lining-out of black engines.

Variations

Sir Nigel Gresley introduced some variations to the official express passenger locomotive livery, to suit new locomotive designs, as follows:

A Class W1 4-6-4 high pressure compound experimental express passenger locomotive No 10000; introduced in 1929: Overall livery of dark battleship grey, with polished steel boiler bands and handrails. Lettering and numerals in white, shaded black; front bufferbeam unlined signal red with white numerals shaded black.

B Class A4 4-6-2s Nos 2509-12, streamlined express passenger locomotives; introduced in 1935: Main streamlined superstructure, cabs and tender in (LNE2) pale silver-grey (aluminium), side valances in mid grey; nose, or smokebox front, in charcoal grey; lettering in silver/white with dark blue shading; wheels in pale silver grey; external frames and cab roof in mid grey. Bufferbeam on rear of tender, signal red.

C Class A4 4-6-2s: Further new locomotives at first appeared in apple green livery, except one No 4489 *Woodcock* which ran for some two weeks or so in shop-grey with black and white lining and lettering, then it was decided to paint the class in a new shade of blue, entitled garter blue (LNE3) commencing with seven new engines for the 1937 'Coronation' and 'West Riding Limited' services. The main livery of garter blue (LNE3) was applied to the streamlined casing including the side valances, and to the tender. The nose ends were black and so were the outside frames and cab roof, but the wheels on both locomotive and tender were in rich Indian red, with polished rims. The black smokebox/nose area was separated from the blue by a fine red and a fine white line. No other lining was applied, but extensive use was made of polished metal trim, including raised stainless steel Gill Sans lettering and numerals on the 1937 batch. Later engines, and those repainted from grey or green, had standard shaded gold transfer lettering and numerals during the Gresley period.

D Finally, mention should be made of the unique Beyer-Garratt Class U1 2-8-0+0-8-2T, introduced in 1925. Numbered 2395 it was exhibited at the 1925 Railway Centenary still in workshop grey livery, with black shaded white numerals and lettering. Soon afterwards it received full glossy black with red lining out; finally carrying plain black goods engine livery.

Author's note

Unfortunately the character of the black and white film available to photographers during the 1920/30 period was such that, quite often, the camera failed to capture the red lining-out on black engines. Even the closest study of the original print sometimes only reveals traces of the lining, (and the same applies of course to the red lining on the black portions of locomotives in the full grass green livery.) Some LNER official photographs do convey the lining detail, but the best guide now existing is to be found in the collection of copies of original colour slides marketed by *Colour-Rail*; some of which are reproduced in this booklet.

Electric Locomotives

The LNER possessed a mere handful of electric locomotives, all but one of former NER origin, but if the outbreak of World War 2 had not halted the Manchester-Sheffield scheme, a sizeable fleet of

Gresley-designed locomotives was in prospect. A solitary prototype was completed, tested and then placed in storage for the duration of the war. The livery for electric passenger locomotives was the standard green (see illustrations.) Further information upon the livery carried by the 10 Bo-Bo electric freight locomotives on the former NER Shildon-Newport line during the period 1923-1935 (after which the line reverted to steam traction) would be welcomed. It is to be assumed that the locomotives were at some stage repainted by the LNER black with red lining, but positive photographic evidence has eluded the Author. The 10 Newport-Shildon Bo-Bos went into storage and only one saw further use (see page 197). In NER days they carried green livery, as did the two Bo-Bo electric shunters on the Newcastle Quayside branch. These latter two definitely carried black livery in LNER days.

Rolling Stock:

Passenger stock

Once having chosen a slightly modified version of the former GNR livery for passenger engines it was perhaps hardly surprising that the varnished teak finish of the GNR passenger stock was also perpetuated. Varnished teak was also common for ECJS and NE stock so the majority of rolling stock on the East Coast main line was in any case already in such livery, and with the continued use of wood for carriage body construction the LNER directors chose wisely. Natural varnished teak varies considerably in colour, and darkens with age, so to give a definite description is well-nigh impossible. It can be nearly orange in shade, or dull umber brown, and in *all* shades in between! If the modelmaker of the present day wishes to capture it on a scale model, perhaps the most important point to remember is that it was *transparent* in effect, ie shining through layers of varnish. (I would suggest painting a fairly transparent orange-brown all over, and then dragging a dry brush loaded with alternate shades of brown lightly over the surface; finally giving an overall glossy varnish when the paint is dry. An article on the modelling of teak coaches appeared in the July and August 1981 issues of *Model Railway Constructor*.

When a carriage went for repair and a badly damaged wooden panel was replaced, it was almost impossible for the carriage works to match the same shade of teak; therefore it was quite common to see a sort of patchwork effect, with some panels much lighter than others. Only if a complete overhaul took place, with all the wood stripped bare and then revarnished, was it possible to restore a harmony to the finish. For many old carriages inherited by the LNER from the various pre-Grouping companies, the job of stripping layer upon layer of paint of various colours was not considered worthwhile, and a paint finish to imitate teak was applied instead. This was normally somewhere near to a burnt sienna in shade, although dark umber brown and even dark yellow ochre have been recorded by the Author on old carriages which survived World War 2 without repainting.

Without question, it was the lettering and lining-out which gave the teak carriages their final touch. The lettering and numerals were applied in a style so beautiful that it almost defies description, and one which can certainly be described as a true work of art.

Throughout Gresley's time, even when alternative forms of carriage building, using steel or plywood panels, began to make their mark, the worksmanship that went into producing the varnished teak livery continued in excellence. But by the 1940/1 period with wartime conditions prevailing it was obvious that changes had to be made; these are described on page 193.

The basic specification for teak rolling stock was as follows:

Body sides and ends: Natural varnished teak, except for suburban (non-corridor stock) which had black painted ends.

Roof: White lead.

Solebars, headstocks, buffer shanks and wheel centres: Imitation 'teak' paint; actually a burnt sienna shade (with a small admixture of white to give it opacity) *not* red oxide as is sometimes stated.

Frames below solebar level, bogies and steel portions of corridor connections: Black.

Wheel rims and axles: White.
(Obviously the white roof, and the wheel rims and axles quickly darkened in service conditions.)

The finishing touches were as follows:

Lettering and numerals: Gold, with a graduated red, to pink, to white, shading to the left and below. The characters being in an expanded serifed letterform. Additional back shading was in black and brown to the right and below, giving an almost three-dimensional effect. The letters LNER were used; no coat-of-arms.

Lining: A primrose yellow line with a fine red line each side of it was applied to all raised mouldings and casings, (see drawing) except for suburban stock which was not lined after 1923.

Variations:

Apart from the pre-Grouping carriages painted in imitation 'teak' colour, already mentioned, there were some specific variations during the Gresley regime, and these also tended to depart from the traditional style of coachbuilding, using flush panelled sides, of plywood or steel.

Tourist stock:
In 1933 special coaches began to appear for use on 'Tourist trains', the LNER's answer to increasing competition from road coaches for excursion traffic. At the time the cost of teak was very high, and for these carriages Gresley used plywood panelling for the exterior; later replaced by sheet steel because it deteriorated too quickly, though some lasted to 1962/3 with plywood panels. These carriages were painted grass green below the waist and cream above, with black bogies and underframes, white roof, black carriage ends and brown wheel centres with white rims. Some carriages were articulated twins.

The 'Silver Jubilee' (1935): Steel panelling was used, covered with silver-grey rexine; with fittings in stainless steel. Lettering and numerals were in relief Gill Sans with stainless steel finish; the bodyside fairings below solebar level were in charcoal grey, also the bogie frames. Pale grey sheet rubber covered the gap between carriage ends. Wheel centres were grey; white rims.

The 1937 streamlined stock: For the 'Coronation' and West Riding Limited' trains, further steel-panelled streamlined carriages were built. These were finished in two-tone blue livery: garter blue below waist level and Marlborough blue above. Extensive use was made of stainless steel trim, including the window frames. Lettering and numerals were in relief stainless steel Gill Sans. Body side fairings below solebar level, and bogie frames were black; the wheels had dark red centres and white tyres. The roof was in the standard white lead finish.

In addition to the above, some steel-panelled stock was built for normal duties, the first appearing as early as 1927/8. These were elaborately painted and lined out, complete with imitation teak staining and graining; to match the wooden stock.

Other Stock:
Passenger luggage vans, and vans used in passenger train formations were in teak finish or 'teak' paint; without lining except for selected examples used in important trains, which were fully lined to match the carriages. Horse boxes were chocolate brown, with white roof and large white initials NE on the side, and many pre-Grouping examples of luggage vans and similar vehicles had a similar brown-painted finish, or one to simulate teak, without lining; using carriage style letters and numerals.

Railcars
In Gresley's time the LNER had a large stock of steam railcars, and a pleasing feature was that they carried names as well as a distinctive livery. The names were those previously carried by horse-drawn stage or mail coaches in Britain. Between 1924-1930 some 90 steam railcars were introduced. The first livery was imitation teak, fully lined, on the steel panels. Later this was changed to red below waist level and cream above, and finally the same green and cream livery as used for the 'Tourist trains' was applied to the whole fleet. Roofs varied from silver/aluminium to black, and bogies and underframes were black. Wheel centres were dark red, with white rims.

Four diesel-electric railcars were employed; three being very similar to the steam railcars externally, the fourth being a lightweight streamlined vehicle. The livery for these was deep cobalt blue below the waist and cream above, with some gilt lining-out on the three larger ones.

Electric Trains
Even in NER days the Tyneside electric trains had been distinguished by their red and white livery, and when Gresley introduced new steel-panelled stock for Tyneside he used a bright scarlet vermilion red with cream upper panels. This was changed to a mid blue and 'Quaker grey' in 1941, reportedly because the red trains were too easy a target for enemy aircraft! In the blue and grey livery the electric stock was also distinguished by the use of the cigar-shaped LNER 'totem' on the carriage sides

Freight Stock:

Goods wagons: Throughout Gresley's regime the livery for freight stock remained virtually unchanged; only the size and style of insignia was varied. The basic details were as follows:

Brake-fitted stock: Brown red oxide bodywork (changed in name but hardly in shade to bauxite in 1940) for all bodywork above solebar level. This was also applied to brake vans even if they were not fitted with the continuous train brake.

Non-fitted stock: Mid-grey for wagons and vans, including non-revenue earning loco coal wagons, and sleeper wagons. If the solebars and headstocks were of wood these were also grey.

Refrigerated vans: White bodywork with black metal details and black lettering, etc.

Service, or departmental vehicles: Oxford blue. (Soon fading to a very pale shade.)
Yard vehicles/limited trip vehicles: Green.
Breakdown cranes and some service wagons: Black. (The cranes had red lining-out.)

On all vehicles with steel underframes these were painted black; as were the wheels, axles, brake gear, buffers and draw gear, on *all* vehicles. The roofs of vans were lead white, until the introduction of the bauxite paint, when they were painted to match the bodywork.

Lettering and insignia: Block white sans-serif

style, usually 18in×12in with the initials NE. After 1937 this was changed in favour of small (4in) letters in the bottom lefthand corner of the bodyside. Numerals and capacity then appeared below the number. Originally the number had appeared under the large letter E, in 5in characters. Some special high capacity well-wagons, with bogies and a long side frame had the full title of the railway company in white Gill Sans capital letters during the 1930s.

Containers: Early types, known as 'A' (smallest) and 'B' were in brown red oxide to match the brake-fitted flat wagons they travelled on by rail. The lettering and the roof was white. Slogans such as 'Door to Door Transport For Merchandise — Avoids Packing — Ensures Safety' were painted in white block capitals, together with the full name of the railway. With the 'Gills Sans revolution', from about 1934 onwards a much neater style was evolved, using the initials LNER and all other lettering and numerals in the standard alphabet. In his book *A Pictorial Record of LNER Wagons* the author, Peter Tatlow states that the bodywork was thought to be the Royal blue colour (as used on road vehicles) but another authority, Mr A. A. Harrison (in a letter to the Author) states that the containers were a dark grey. Further details, or confirmation, would therefore be welcomed. The lettering was in white. The special type BK containers for furniture removal *were* in the Royal blue. The flat wagons carrying them remained in brown red oxide; later, bauxite. Special insulated containers were white with black lettering, and there were some metal-built containers which were given an aluminium/silver finish with black lettering.

15

15
Former GER Class D16/1 4-4-0 No 1818E, photographed in the new grass green livery, with black and white lining; in 1923 at Stratford. Note the initials L&NER on the tender (in this case, without full stops, however) and the small suffix E after the number. The GER brass trim to the splashers, boiler barrel wrapper and polished chimney cap have been retained; also the white cab roof. The new small LNER oval numberplate is on the cab sidesheet, within the splasher beading. Footsteps and running plate in lined green. *LPC*

16
The new LNER grass green livery was closely based upon that of the former GNR, except that black was used instead of chocolate brown for footplate valances and footsteps, as well as frames. The black had a fine red line to the edges, (except on the cylinder covers, which were plain black). Class A1 4-6-2 No 2555 *Centenary* displays the first standard style for express passenger locomotives, with the locomotive number painted on the tender, and with the legend LNER above, and with just a small oval numberplate on the cabside. Brass builder's plate on the smokebox side and brass nameplate on central splasher. Polished metal fittings on the smokebox door. *Author's collection*

16

17
Raven's Class A2 Pacific No 2402 *City of York* in the first standard livery, with number on the tender. Note that the cylinder covers are painted green, edged black and white; a persistent practice at Darlington, whereas Doncaster painted them black. There was also some slight variation in the shade of green used at Darlington, which was generally considered to be somewhat yellower.
Ian Allan Library

17

18

18
No 6383 of Robinson's GCR 'Director' Class 4-4-0, built after the Grouping by Gresley for service in the Scottish area; LNER Class D11. The deep sides to the footplating and lower driving wheel splashers are painted black with a fine red line, unlike the GER 4-4-0s and 4-6-0s which had this feature in fully lined green. When names were applied to this class they were in gold handpainted shaded block letters, along the upper splasher sides.
LPC

19
The small cast oval numberplate, with the full name of the railway company, and the place and date of construction or rebuilding, which was standard for all locomotives from 1923 onwards. On tank engines it was on the bunkerside; on tender engines on the cab side, to begin with. This particular example is of added interest because instead of displaying a number, it merely carries the letter 'C'; belonging to a departmental Class J92, ex-GER, shunting engine at Stratford Works.
H. C. Casserley

19

20

20
When the decision was taken to place the number on the cabside instead of the tender, the initials LNER were made larger on the tender, to match. Class C49 4-4-0 No 256 *Hertfordshire* shows the revised layout, with the small oval numberplate relocated on the driving wheel splasher below the nameplate. Darlington-style green painted outside cylinder covers. Special excursion train billboard carried on the smokebox top. *LPC*

21
Detail of standard cabside numerals, which were in gold with red and black shading and white heightening, on green engines. On black engines the same style was used, only in yellow with brown and red shading.

21

22

22
Tender detail on Gresley Class B17 4-6-0 No 2812 *Houghton Hall*, showing the black and white lining and black panelling on the rear as well as the sides. On such a small tender the letters LNER appeared very large indeed! *E. R. Wethersett*

23
Detail of the 12in-high gold, shaded cabside numerals and letterforms used on green painted tender engines. For black engines the letters were yellow and the shading in brown and red. *LPC*

23

24
Gresley's Class B17/4 4-6-0s in the 'Football' series had the club colours painted on the wheel splasher below the nameplate, and carried a brass football in demi-relief. The small works/numberplate was therefore moved forward to the leading driving wheel splasher. No 2859 *Norwich City* displays to utter perfection the LNER prewar standard green livery; in this instance with green outside cylinder covers. This particular locomotive was one of two subsequently given streamlined casings, in 1937. (see photo 36) when it was renamed *East Anglian*. *Real Photographs collection*

24

25

25
Close-up of a nameplate on Class B17/4 4-6-0 No 2852 *Darlington*, showing the club colours painted on the splasher, each side of the brass football. The style of sans-serif lettering had been introduced by Gresley on the GNR, for his pioneer Class A1 Pacifics in 1922. *Alec Swain*

26
In this cab and tender detail of a Class B12, ex-GER Holden 4-6-0, we see three variations from the standard green livery. Two are due to the prominent brass wheel splasher beading on the cabside: namely the number placed very high above it, and the small numberplate still in position below the beading. Third variation is the use of small lettering for the initials LNER on the tender side; although centrally placed. *LPC*

26

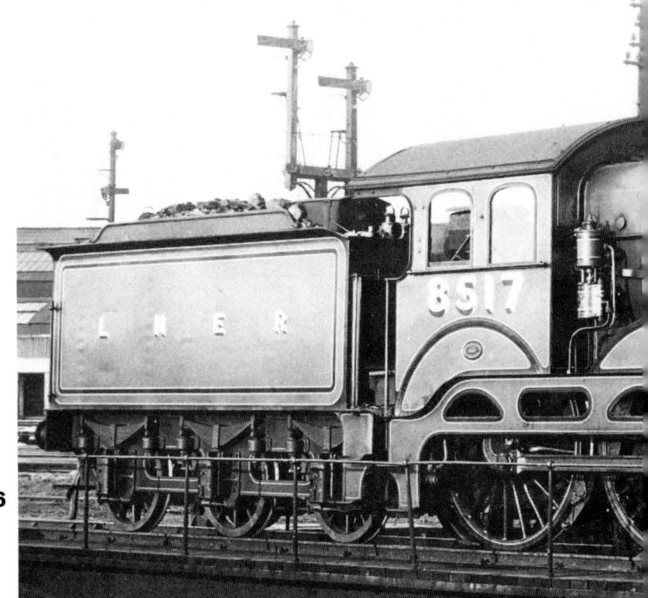

27

27

A complete exception to the rules was made for the Gresley/Yarrow 'Hush-Hush' high pressure compound 4-6-4 No 10000. This experimental locomotive was given a unique livery of dark battleship grey with polished metal boiler bands and handrails, and black and white lettering and numerals. No 10000 displays its unique form to the camera entering King's Cross station. When rebuilt in 1937 as a more conventional streamliner, in Class A4 style, it was given the new garter blue livery.
E. R. Wethersett

28

The standard green livery was applied to Nigel Gresley's superb 2-8-2 Class P2 heavy passenger engine No 2001 *Cock O' the North*, with the green extended right to the front of the semi-streamlined shroud surrounding the smokebox and chimney. A point to note is the use in 1934 of Gill Sans letterforms for the cast brass nameplate, and also the location of the brass worksplate on the cabside below the numbers. The cab roof, and the upper fairing to the tender, were black.
Real Photographs collection

28

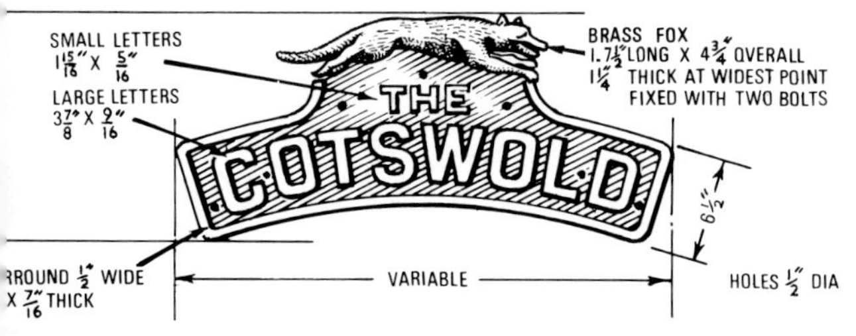

29

Two typical nameplates showing (a) the style adopted for the Gresley D49 'Hunt' class 4-4-0s and (b) the much simpler style with Gill Sans lettering that was used on later express passenger engines, commencing with No 2001 *Cock O' the North*. A nice touch for the 'Hunt' Class D49s was the addition of a brass casting of a fox above the name; the fox facing forwards on both sides of the engine.

29

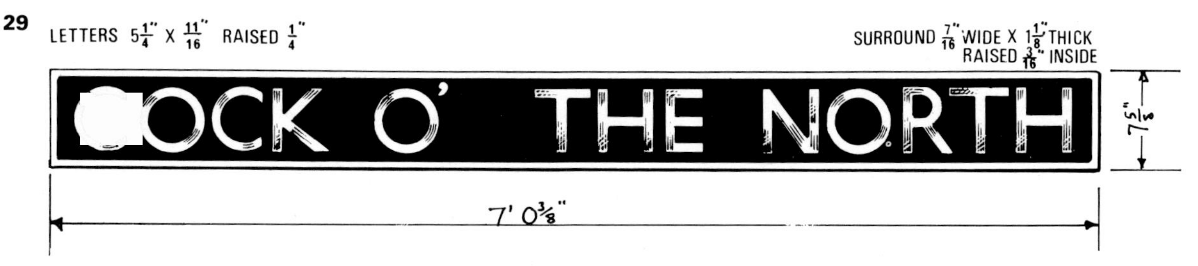

30

Class A4 4-6-2 No 2509 *Silver Link* in the silver-grey (metallic aluminium) livery first adopted in Silver Jubilee year for the new steamlined high speed express train. Four locomotives received this treatment. Compared with photo 5 this picture shows a later version with the charcoal grey of the nose (smokebox) extended around the sides to meet the mid grey valance. The name was handpainted on the boiler sides, in silver-white with blue shading. (When first exhibited at Doncaster this locomotive carried nameplates in the style later adopted for the whole class; for some reason they were not carried in traffic, whilst the engines were in the silver-grey livery.) *Real Photographs collection*

30

31

31

When further Class A4s were delivered, Gresley at first chose the standard green livery, complete with boiler bands lined-out. The nose end and valances were black, but the cab roof and tender top were at first painted green (later black.) On Nos 4483-4487 a variation was that the black was extended around the sides as far as the first boiler band, to create an entirely black smokebox area. No 4482 *Golden Eagle* displays the more elegant version. All the green engines were later repainted garter blue. *Modern Transport*

32

The garter blue livery was introduced in Coronation year, 1937, when further Class A4s were built for new high speed trains. A particularly high standard of finish was bestowed upon them, and stainless steel relief Gill Sans lettering was fixed to the sides of the cab and tender, as well as used for the nameplates. The lower edge of the valance was given a stainless steel trim over the driving wheels and this was carried along the bottom of the tender to match. The only lining was a single red and single white from the rear of the chimney to the top of the valance, separating the black front from the blue boiler sides. All the wheels were deep Indian red with polished rims. Illustrated is No 4496 *Golden Shuttle*; built for the 'West Riding Limited'. *British Rail ER*

32

33

34

33
Although the garter blue was eventually applied to all the Class A4s, and to the solitary Class W1, they did not all receive the stainless steel letters and numbers during Gresley's time. Illustrated is the most famous of them, No 4468 *Mallard* when new; fitted with a Kylchap double chimney. The letters and numbers are in standard gold shaded characters. Photographed at King's Cross.
P. Ransome-Wallis

34
When Gresley rebuilt his Class P2 2-8-2s, giving them 'A4'-style front ends, he gave them the standard green livery. Seen here is the front end detail of No 2003 *Lord President*, showing the shaded letters and numerals in gold on the black front.
Modern Transport

35

36

37

35
Standard shaded numerals for engine bufferbeams. On the Class A4 Pacifics with stainless steel lettering these were not applied, a painted version of Gill Sans being used instead.

36
In 1937 two Class B17 4-6-0s were given 'A4'-style streamlining to work the new 'East Anglian' express. Green livery was chosen for them, with black. The valance had a fine red line following its contours. No 2859 is illustrated renamed *East Anglian* (compare with photo No 24). The other engine was No 2870 *City of London*; formerly *Tottenham Hotspur*; (at first it was named *Manchester City*.) *British Rail ER*

37
Sir Nigel Gresley's two final designs, the superb Class V2 2-6-2, and the smaller Class V4 version, both carried the standard green livery, although in fact they were mixed traffic engines in concept. (The name *Green Arrow* was also applied to a new fast goods train service.) No 4771 shows the elegant lines of the V2 design, with Gills Sans used for the nameplates. *Modern Transport*

38

39

40

41

38 (Previous page)
The 'Claud Hamilton' 4-4-0s used for Royal Train working were kept in immaculate green livery although the rest of the class were relegated to lined black after 1928. Pictured here at Cambridge on 19 April 1938 is Class D16/2 No 8783 in typical Royal engine finery. The cab roof was white and all copper and brass was polished, including the chimney cap and the smokebox-top snifting valves. The brass beading for the rear splasher had been removed from the cabside, allowing room for the standard numerals. *E. R. Wethersett*

39 (Previous page)
When the use of grass green was restricted to certain classes only (as described in the text,) the remaining passenger engines were given black livery with red lining. Robinson's graceful 'Atlantics' were amongst those so treated, and Class C4 No 6083 is seen here; nonetheless beautiful! *Real Photos collection*

40
The lined black livery (always difficult to photograph in monochrome) was well suited to Gresley's tank engines, as seen here on Class V3 2-6-2T No 390 photographed when new, in 1939. On black engines the lettering and numerals were yellow, with brown and red shading.
Crown Copyright: National Railway Museum

41
After an initial public appearance in shop grey livery the magnificent Gresley-Garratt No 2395 was given fully-lined black livery. Note the letters LNER along the side of the frames.
Crown Copyright: National Railway Museum

42

Between 1923 and 1928 even goods engines had red lining-out on the black, and the style suited the huge Class P1 2-8-2s very well indeed. No 2393 shows this livery, with the numerals on the tender and small numberplate on the cabside. Later all the goods engines ran in plain black. *British Rail ER*

42

43

43

Plain black became the lot for the smaller tank engines, of varied origins, although *some* received full red lining (station pilots, or for special events) even in the 1930s. The numerals were normally on the tankside below the letters LNER, and the small oval numberplate was on the bunkerside. Illustrated is Class J88 No 8328. To make the yellow insignia stand out from the black, red and brown shading was used, with a fine white line picking out the shadow areas in order to give them an illusion of depth.
P. Ransome-Wallis

44

For its remarkable tram engines on the GE Section the LNER gave a 'teak brown' paint finish to the wooden portions and black, with a single red line for the metal surfaces. The roof was painted white. No numbers were painted on the sides, and the small oval number/worksplate was fixed centrally on the wooden body. LNER Class J70 No 7126 is illustrated, fresh from the paintshop. *Ian Allan Library*

44

45

45
Sir Vincent Raven's huge express electric locomotive, No 13, built for the NER but never used for anything after some initial trials, due to the collapse of the Newcastle-York electrification project. Kept in store by the LNER, it had a brief outing, steam-hauled at the Railway Centenary exhibition in 1925. For this event it was repainted in standard green and black livery, and lettered LNER. Afterwards it went back into storage!
F. R. Hebron

46
For the Manchester-Sheffield electrification, Sir Nigel Gresley produced a prototype Bo-Bo electric locomotive, No 6701 (later No 6000) and this emerged in 1941 in green livery with black and white lining. The LNER totem was in gilt on the cab doors and the brass worksplate was placed centrally on the cab front. The bufferbeams were in red, lined black and white, with the standard style numerals. The locomotive number and lettering LNER were in shaded block characters on the centre of the bodysides; the number being smaller than normal.
LPC

46

47

47
Side-corridor third class carriage No 4173, built at York in 1931, in the standard lined teak finish, with white roof. Large shaded numerals on each door to denote third class. *LPC*

48
When seen fresh from the workshops, the varnished teak livery was very beautiful to behold. enhanced by the lining-out on all the beading, and the elegant shaded lettering. This particular example is No 6119, a first class Kitchen/Restaurant car built at Doncaster in 1929 for the 'East Anglian' service. *Modern Transport*

48

49

49
Grass green and cream livery was chosen for the special stock built for the 'Tourist trains', with a white roof, black carriage ends, underframes and bogies. Wheels had dark red centres with white rims. The lettering and numerals gave an added touch of colour to these already colourful carriages. Pictured here is an articulated-twin Nos 21263/4, built by Metro-Cammell in 1934.
Ian Allan Library

50

51

50
Gresley continued to build some stock in his traditional teak finish even in the late 1930s, when such wooden construction was very expensive indeed. This third class open No 60525 was built at York in 1936, this was one of the special 52ft 6in Gresleys built for use on the GE Section. Photographed on SR metals at Bromley on 21 June 1936, the carriage was in a through working, and judging by the white roof, had only recently entered traffic. *H. C. Casserley*

51
The magnificent stock produced for the 1937 'Coronation' included 'beaver-tail' observation cars with a Bugatti-inspired streamlined end. The livery was garter blue below the waist and marlborough blue above, with stainless steel trim, and raised Gill Sans letters and numerals. A stainless steel band separated the garter blue from the black used below solebar level.
Ian Allan Library

52
For many older, pre-Grouping carriages, the cost of removing layers of various coloured paints was not considered worthwhile, and a brown paint scheme was applied, to resemble the colour of teak. This varied quite a lot in shade, and fairly typical was a mid-brown tending towards chocolate. Former GER six-wheeled third non-corridor carriage No 61119 is seen in this brown livery at Stratford on 12 March 1938. *H. C. Casserley*

53
Corridor brake third No 52236, built Doncaster 1934, was photographed in May 1939, as the leading vehicle of the 12.15pm Marylebone-Manchester express; leaving Princes Risborough. It is of interest in showing the lined-out varnished teak livery and lettering, also the white roof destination boards, with black Gill Sans letters. The locomotive is Class B17 4-6-0 No 2862 *Manchester United*. *H. K. Harman*

54
Typical layout, and detail of the teak prewar carriage livery, showing also the shaded numerals applied.

52

53

54

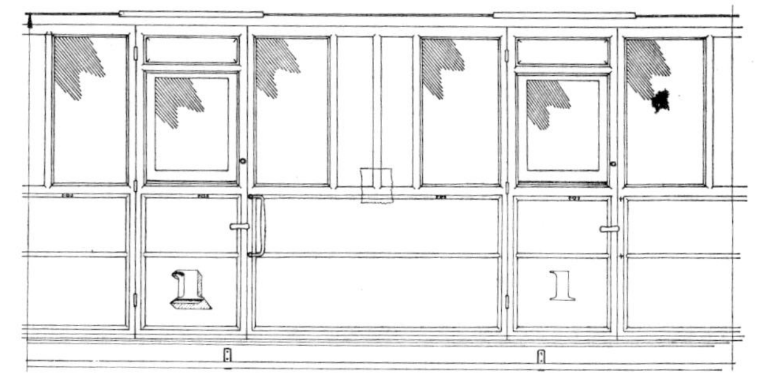

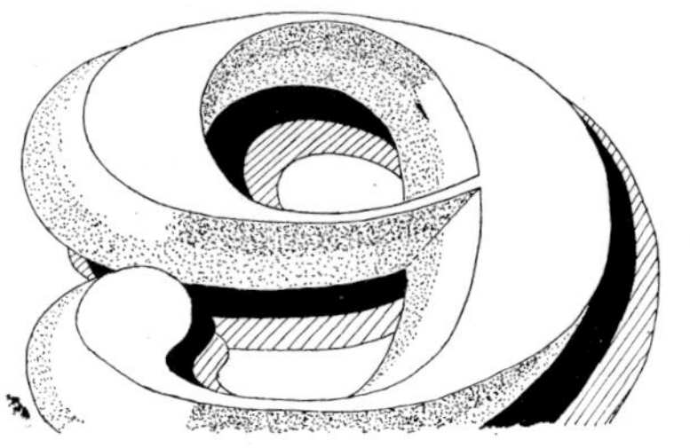

55

55
Sentinel 100hp steam railcar No 22 in the original livery of imitation varnished teak, with full lining and standard carriage style lettering. No name carried as yet; later it became *Brilliant*. Note the articulation between the engine portion, and the carriage portion behind. *LPC*

56
The Clayton steam railcars had a bizarre layout, with an external bunker ahead of the cab at the engine end. This example, No 296 *Wonder*, was delivered to traffic in the second livery of bright scarlet/vermilion red and cream, with grey/aluminium roof; black underframes and bogies and white wheel rims. Very fine black and gilt lining was applied to the cream, to simulate a panelled effect, and the bunker had black edging and gilt lining on the red. *Real Photographs collection*

56

57

57
Gresley finally settled-upon a grass green and cream livery for the steam railcars. No 220 *Defence*, a 200hp twin-engined Sentinel car is seen here in steam at Scarborough. *Ian Allan Library*

58

58
For the new steel-bodied articulated-twin electric multiple units in the Newcastle area, Gresley used the bright scarlet/vermilion red and cream livery, with aluminium/grey roof and black guttering. A fine black line separated the red and cream at waist level. A new train is seen here at Monkseaton in July 1937. Standard shaded numerals and letters were used, with the class designation alongside the sliding doors. Note the Gill Sans lettering on the station building (left).
Modern Transport

59
The bright scarlet/vermilion red and cream livery was considered to be too conspicuous for enemy aircraft raiding Tyneside, and the colour scheme was altered to blue and 'Quaker grey' in 1941. (Perhaps black would have been a wiser choice!) The roofs were grey, with black guttering and a band of black separated the blue from the grey at waist level. Numerals were in black Gill Sans, just above the solebar at one end of the carriage side. The LNER 'totem' was applied to the centre of the bodyside, on the blue; in black and white. Parcels van No 2424 is seen at Tynemouth, hauling a six-wheeled trailer. *W. Hubert Foster*

59

60

60
The first style of LNER-designed covered goods van, with 9ft wheelbase. This is an unfitted version and was therefore finished in mid-grey livery, including the solebars and headstocks, with a white roof and black wheels and undergear, etc. The white wheel tyres were specially applied for the official photograph, and were not a commonplace sight on freight stock in traffic conditions. The large letters NE are in white, 18in × 12in, and the running number in white 5in numerals, (with the chalk lines to guide the painter still visible). The inscription 12ton is in 4in letters. Fitted vans were in brown red oxide with the same lettering layout details. *British Rail ER*

61
A 10-ton 'Loco Coal' wagon, seen standing on a retarder. Mid-grey bodywork, with black headstocks and solebars and undergear. White lettering. *Modern Transport*

61

62
A 1928 Doncaster-built 8ton refrigerator van, in overall white livery for the bodywork and black lettering. The entire underframe area was black, also in some cases (not this photo) some of the ironwork on the white body, such as ladders, latches and angle-irons, were also painted black. *LPC*

62

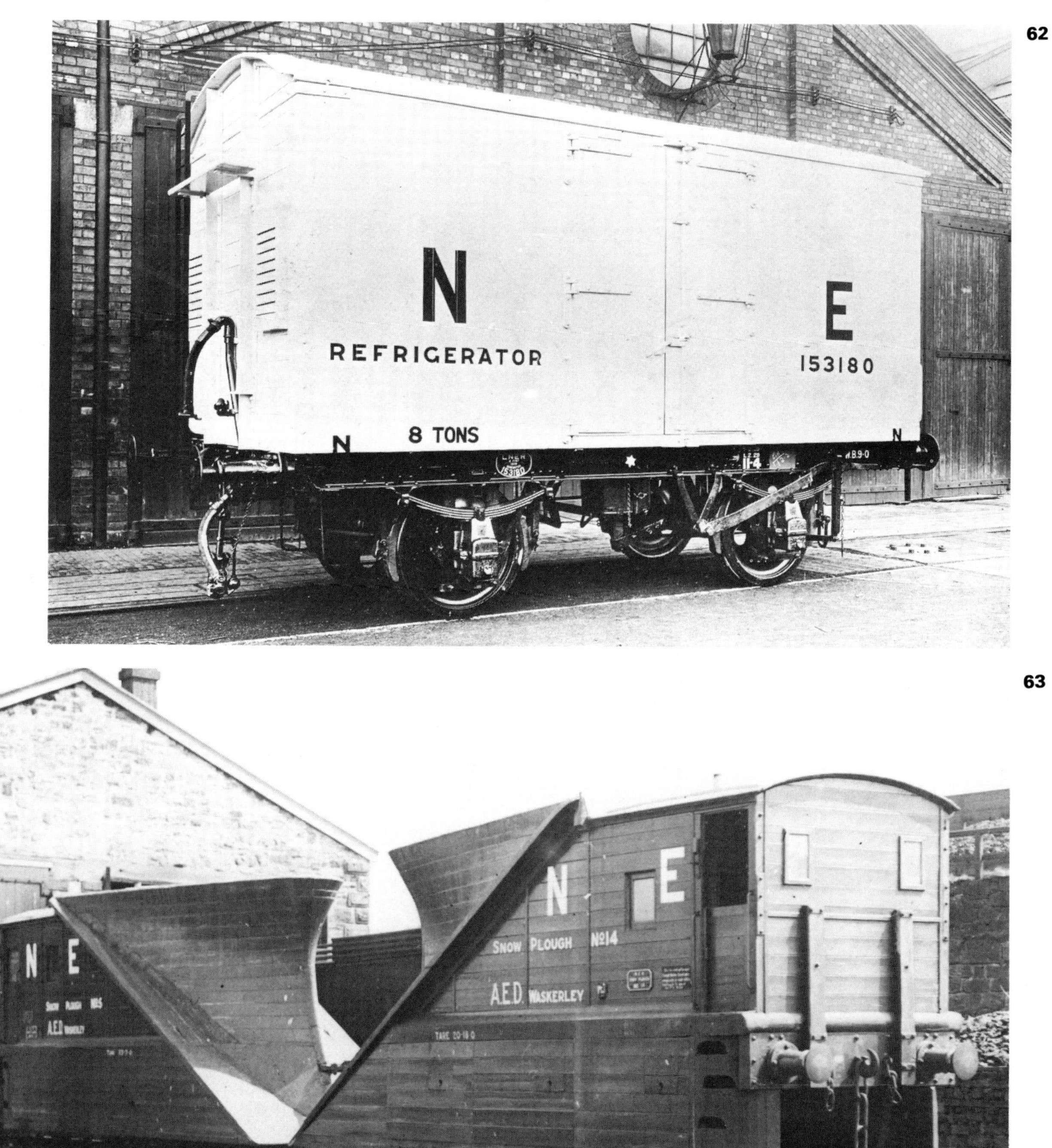

63

63
Snowploughs Nos 14 (nearest) and 5, at Waskerley on 31 May 1935. They are apparently in a dark grey livery, with white lettering. These snowploughs had a six-wheeled layout, and were of NER design.
H. C. Casserley

64

65

66

64
Commencing in 1937 the large initials NE were reduced in size to a mere 4in and relocated on the bottom left hand corner of freight stock, together with the running number (4in) and capacity (3in). Illustrated is a 1938-built Sleeper wagon, with the modified insignia, finished in a rather light version of the grey livery, including solebars and headstocks. *British Rail ER*

65
The LNER experimented with pressed steel road-rail containers in 1929. The original livery was aluminium/silver paint with black lettering, later they received the Gill Sans style on either a dark grey or an Oxford blue background; (see next photo). *Modern Transport*

66
The LNER letter standardisation scheme, using the Gill Sans alphabet was very suitable for containers, being legible from a considerable distance. For these type BK furniture containers the background colour was Oxford blue, with white lettering. (The 'Conflat S' wagon being in bauxite and black.) Note the full stops centrally placed between the initials L·N·E·R. Photographed in 1940. *British Rail ER*

2: War and Postwar 1941-1947

World War 2

Sir Nigel Gresley was still in office when World War 2 broke out, and continued as CME of the LNER until his death in April 1941, (he was actually due to retire just two months later). Edward Thompson succeeded Gresley as CME, and he could hardly have taken-on the job at a worst time! After the initial 'phoney war' period, by 1941, events were taking a very serious turn indeed and Britain was being severely pressed to utilise all her manpower and resources to repel the Nazi threat. Workshop routines were completely disrupted and maintenance and cleanliness were difficult to sustain beyond a make-do-and-mend basis. New construction was concentrated upon freight and mixed traffic types, with the LNER Gresley Class V2 2-6-2 showing its true worth at this time. The streamlined trains — pride of the prewar LNER — were withdrawn, and the carriages put into storage. The Class A4 Pacifics were however needed too much to be 'mothballed', but it wasn't long before some pieces of the streamlined casing were removed to make shed maintenance easier. However, unlike the LMSR, which completely de-streamlined its Stanier Pacifics, the Gresley engines did survive the war in streamlined form.

Locomotives: The garter blue and grass green locomotive liveries were abandoned in November 1941 in favour of overall plain black, and in the following July the initials NE replaced the full legend LNER on tenders and tanksides; also on carriages. The only deviation was the use of the cast metal cigar-shaped 'totem' on the 'Q1' 0-8-0T rebuilds (see photos 9, 10). The quality of the black paint was extremely poor in many instances, and of course some engines actually survived the war period without complete repainting, but it was difficult to judge what livery was carried under the accumulated layers of grime and grease.

Passenger Stock: Passenger carriages were put back to traffic after workshop visits in unlined teak, or in the case of older stock, plain brown paint. (A tour the Author made of the carriage sidings in the vicinity of Stratford, East London, in the early 1950 period, revealed quite a lot of old stock still in wartime colours; it ranged from chocolate brown, to yellow ochre and even khaki green.) Roofs were no longer painted white and such refinements as dark red wheel centres and white rims were a thing of the past! Some steam railcars were repainted in plain brown.

Freight stock

For freight stock constructed during the war, the paintbrush hardly existed; plain wood sufficed, with black for ironwork and just a patch of bauxite or grey, where the numerals and data were applied. Raw material shortages resulted in the use of plywood to construct the bodywork on some 12ton vans; these *did* receive overall bauxite paint, for protection.

Note

Fear of enemy invasion in 1940 led to the removal of station name signs, road signposts and similar notices giving the specific locality; a situation that made travel in the hours of darkness, when the 'blackout' was in force a very hazardous business! They were replaced in due course.

The Postwar Period 1945-1947

The prevailing mood of austerity, once peace had been declared, did not deter Thompson from making one 1945 livery experiment, although the dark blue colour was not popular; perhaps being too prone to go black in service conditions. The same year, 1945, saw one of Gresley's Class A4 Pacifics restored to prewar garter blue, complete with stainless steel lettering and numerals. This was No 4496 *Golden Shuttle*, which was renamed *Dwight D. Eisenhower*. Thompson also introduced the first of his Class L1 2-6-4Ts resplendent in lined grass green livery, but retaining the wartime style of NE, instead of LNER, on the tanksides to begin with.

Locomotives

In September 1946 the LNER board announced that the whole of the engine stock would be painted either grass green, or garter blue (the blue for streamlined Class A4 Pacifics, and Class W1 only) and all would have the prewar style of lining-out. Amidst a flurry of publicity a representative batch of engines was beautifully repainted and exhibited, but afterwards the workshops seemed unable to cope, and by nationalisation the scheme was still in its infancy; although those engines so treated certainly brightened-up the scene. A special effort was made in the case of the 'A4' Pacifics, in blue complete with new Gill Sans stainless steel letters and numbers, and dark Indian red wheels. A unique engine was the Class D3 4-4-0 No 2000 which was used to haul the special director's saloon. This received full green livery *plus* the LNER coat-of-arms on the tender sides. At first the letters NE flanked it; later changed to the full LNER in gilt Gill Sans.

Note:

Mention of Gill Sans leads me to one confusing feature of the postwar scene. It seems clear that *officially* the Gill Sans alphabet and numerals had been adopted for rolling stock but the majority of locomotives, and virtually *all* the carriages, that were repainted between 1945-47 received the old-style transfers. It must be assumed that there were quite considerable stocks of these still to be used-up; or then again perhaps someone in authority held diverging views on the suitability of the Gill Sans, (such attitudes are not unknown to this very day!). Use of the Gills Sans was further confused in Thompson's time by the modified 'condensed' (ie slightly narrower) numerals that he attempted to introduce (see photo 9). The true Gill Sans was applied by Thompson's successor, A. H. Peppercorn to new locomotives of the 'A1', 'A2' and 'B1' classes, and some existing smaller types received the correct version, in plain yellow on black, or gilt on green. When the newly-created 'British Railways' swallowed-up the LNER in January 1948 one of the things they took for future standard use was the Gill Sans alphabet, not only on locomotives but also on rolling stock, station signs and printed publicity.

Passenger Stock

Passenger carriages presented an odd sight in the immediate postwar period, some bedraggled specimens still boasted full lining-out, or at least vestiges of it, whilst much was in plain wartime brown or plain teak with the gold initials NE. The use of the designation '3' for third class had been abolished in 1940, but the 'I' was retained for first class identification. It was commonplace to see elderly teak carriages running in the same train formation as modern flush-sided steel stock, and it was probably this that prompted Edward Thompson to give an 'imitation teak' paint finish to his new steel-bodied carriages. In some cases this livery was elaborately 'stained and grained', but without any lining-out. Carriage roofs reverted to white for new stock, and the solebars, if revealed, were in burnt sienna, as were the wheel centres; the bogies being black. The streamlined stock, taken out of storage, began to appear in ordinary, often quite mundane trains and the special high-speed services were never resumed. The surviving Sentinel steam railcars were soon withdrawn, being life expired; the last one being scrapped in 1948. The diesel railcars had been withdrawn in 1939, but were stored and were not broken up until the war ended. On Tyneside the blue and grey livery was still applied to electric trains, complete with the LNER 'totem', and we may assume that this livery was in prospect for the new Liverpool Street-Shenfield electrics, then on order; if nationalisation had not intervened.

Freight Stock

Freight stock saw little or no livery change, and presented for the most part a very down-at-heel appearance, having suffered the brunt of wartime loading and intensive use. It was still possible to find the odd example showing pre-Grouping initials, and many still carrying the large letters NE, used in prewar days. A considerable amount of freight stock had been built for war use, and after the war the LNER commenced building a fleet of steel-bodied mineral wagons finished in grey livery.

Note

The LNER was just getting itself back into real shape when it was nationalised. The 'Flying Scotsman' train had been restored; new main line carriages were coming off the production line; two major electrification schemes were underway and a general smartening-up of stations was in progress. It is a matter for debate whether the standard BR livery, locomotives and rolling stock, etc, that soon replaced the LNER standards, were in any respect an improvement upon what was in prospect in 1947.

67

67
Wartime plain black livery on Gresley's Class A4 Pacific No 4901 *Charles H. Newton* (formerly named *Capercaillie*) showing the abbreviated initials NE on the tender. The need to ease the time taken for maintenance and repairs led Thompson to remove the streamlined valances ahead of the cylinders and over the coupled wheels, to expose the wheels and motion. The standard block-shaded style transfers were retained, and the brass worksplate on the cabside was still highly polished. The chime whistle was replaced by a smaller standard one. *British Rail ER*

68

69

70

68
All classes of locomotive large and small, received the same livery treatment in the 1941-1945 period; plain black, with just the numerals and the initials NE, after July 1942. (See photo 9 for the exception to this rule.) This former GER 0-6-0T LNER Class J69 was photographed at Parkeston Quay on 20 July 1947, still carrying the wartime lettering, but since renumbered to No 8596. The larger image of the old number — 7305 — is still visible beneath the new patch of black paint applied to the tankside, when the new numerals were put on. *C. C. B. Herbert*

69
One Class A4 Pacific was restored to garter blue livery as early as September 1945. This was because of the decision to rename No 4496 as *Dwight D. Eisenhower*, in honour of the wartime associations the LNER had with him during the planning of the Normandy invasion. (Eisenhower had used a special armour-plated LNER Gresley sleeping car as his wartime mobile office whilst in Britain.) A further nine months elapsed before any more 'A4s' received the blue livery. They were all given new stainless steel numerals and lettering (being renumbered Nos 1-34) and deep Indian red wheels. The streamlined valances were not, however, restored to the locomotives. *Modern Transport*

70
Class A4 Pacific No 29 *Woodcock* displays the postwar style of front end numerals, in painted Gill Sans, also the class description: A4 and the shed allocation: King's + painted below. Despite being repainted in the garter blue with stainless steel letters, etc, the locomotive is very shabby, and this picture serves as a vivid reminder to the reader just how difficult it was to find cleaners in the early postwar period. *E. R. Wethersett*

71

For the first of his Class L1 2-6-4Ts, Thompson re-introduced the full prewar grass green livery, except that only the initials NE were used; (later this was changed to the full LNER on this engine.) No 9000 appeared from Doncaster works in 1945 — the first completely new locomotive design to be introduced after the war by any of the 'Big Four' railway companies.
Ian Allan Library

71

72

72

Class B12 4-6-0 No 1511 is seen here at Kittybrewster shed on 10 December 1947, in fully lined grass green livery. Having announced their intention to paint *all* the locomotive stock (except the select few garter blue locomotives) in this style, some of the workshops found it impossible to cope with the work involved. (The Scottish area seemed able to produce more green engines then the Southern area of the system could manage.)
Ian Allan Library

73

It was perhaps a shortage of green paint that delayed the LNER scheme (shortages of *all* kinds were rife in Britain at that time) and one has only to compare this picture with the preceding one to see that whereas in Scotland the Class B12s were receiving the 'new' colours, their brethren on the GE Section were still emerging in overall black; albeit with the full initials LNER restored to the tender sides, and with quite a respectable varnished finish to the black paint! No 1512 is seen at Colchester on 19 July 1947 at the head of the 2.30pm Colchester-Clacton working. *Ian Allan Library*

73

74

74
This official photograph of the pioneer Class B1 4-6-0 No 1000 *Springbok* repainted in the postwar green livery shows the intended standard Gill Sans lettering. At the time this was taken, newly-built locomotives of the same class were still being painted black, and these still had the old-style shaded letters. *British Rail ER*

75

75
In this instance the correct postwar Gill Sans lettering and numerals have been applied (in yellow paint) but the locomotive still retains its overall black livery. Class D15 No 2502 is seen quite soon after out-shopping from Stratford Works. *E. R. Wethersett*

76
The finalised postwar livery for green engines is seen here on Class A2 Pacific No 525 *A. H. Peppercorn*. (Peppercorn was the last CME of the LNER.) Correct in every detail, it shows the intended appearance for all the non-streamlined 'Pacifics' and other types. Unfortunately BR had other ideas and the grass green livery was not adopted for general use. Once existing supplies ran out, the long time famous livery soon disappeared from the British railway scene, that is until the advent of the preservation societies! No 525 was photographed at King's Cross. In this livery the bufferbeam numerals were in yellow Gill Sans. *E. R. Wethersett*

76

77
Cab detail of Class A2 Pacific No 525 *A. H. Peppercorn*, showing standardised Gill Sans primrose yellow numerals, with brass worksplate below, and route availability RA9 in small characters on bottom right hand corner of the cab sidesheet. Photograph taken at Doncaster works on 31 December 1947; the very last day of the LNER's existence. Not easily spotted in the photograph is the very fine red lining applied to the axlebox covers and the outer edge of the frames, on both locomotive and tender.
Crown Copyright: National Railway Museum

78
Class J45 (later reclassified DES1) 0-6-0 diesel-electric shunter No 8003, introduced by Thompson in May 1945, in full wartime black livery including abbreviated initials NE. *H. C. Casserley*

79
Until the outbreak of World War 2 intervened, it had been Gresley's intention to rehabilitate and employ the 10 stored Newport-Shildon, ex-NER, Bo-Bo electric locomotives for use on the new Manchester-Sheffield route. Only one example was actually dealt with, No 6498 (formerly No 11) at Doncaster, in 1941 and this was turned-out in plain black goods engine livery. Seen here in the company of the prototype Gresley Bo-Bo (on the left), this locomotive subsequently became a depot shunter at Ilford, Essex and lasted into BR ownership. The rest of the class were never put to traffic again, because it was subsequently decided not to use them; new Gresley Bo-Bos being built instead in BR days. *E. V. Fry*

77

78

79

80
The prototype Thompson-designed 'Newton coach' (produced at the instigation of Sir Charles Newton, Chief General Manager of the LNER in 1945.) A gangwayed side-corridor main line coach, with doors mid-way down the sides, No 1531 was a first class version and is seen in the original imitation teak brown paint, with pale grey roof and black bogies and undergear. No 'staining and graining' to the teak colour, and no lining, but with gold letters and numerals, (with NE abbreviation.) Rectangular opaque toilet windows at each end on this example.
British Rail ER

81
A second example of a steel-bodied Thompson main line carriage, this time with the characteristic elliptical lavatory windows, using opaque white Triplex glass. The imitation teak brown paint finish (devoid of lining, or graining) was carried around the body ends to the gangway connection. The roof was mid grey on this example, bogies (Thompson's single bolster design) and solebars and undergear were all in black. No class designation shown on this third class corridor compartment coach; completed in May 1945.
British Rail ER

82
This picture shows the first dining car service restored after the war, on the 'Flying Scotsman', in 1945. The coaches comprise one of the 1938-built Restaurant Car triplet sets. Plain teak livery, with full lettering, and white roofboards, with black Gill Sans. *Ian Allan Library*

83
Third class sleeping car No 1348, completed in December 1947, with the painted steel panels 'grained' to imitate a wood finish. White roof; burnt sienna solebars, and black bogies and underframes; black carriage ends on this particular example.
Ian Allan Library

83

84
Nationalisation overtook the LNER's plans for the 1948 'Flying Scotsman' train, which was given new rolling stock of improved design and comfort. Although finished in LNER imitation teak livery, with white roof and brown fairing over the solebars, the small prefix E was painted ahead of the numerals 1706; denoting BR Eastern Region ownership, and it was to be the final essay in LNER carriage livery before being replaced by the first BR scheme of carmine red and cream. This Buffet Car was delivered to traffic in May 1948 — five months after the LNER had ceased to exist — and it shows the final LNER design for rolling stock. It is questionable how much longer the LNER would have continued to paint these modern steel-bodied carriages in such bizarre imitation wood finishes! *Ian Allan Library*

84

85

85
Plywood-bodied van No 283525, a 12-ton covered goods van design which was produced during (and after) World War 2, when there was a shortage of raw materials for freight stock construction. This brake-fitted example, with screw couplings, is in the standard bauxite brown livery, with small white lettering and numerals on the lower left-hand corner of the bodyside. The white roof is an illusion, created by a fresh layer of snow! In fact the roof was also finished in Bauxite; black underframe, wheels, etc. Photographed in Berkhamsted goods yard on 23 February 1947. *H. C. Casserley*

86

86
From 1945 onwards the LNER (and the LMSR) produced a very large quantity of all-steel 16ton mineral wagons. These were unfitted, and finished in mid-grey livery with black underframe, headstocks, etc. This example, No 274579 was built in August 1945, and this official works photograph shows the pressed-steel side and end doors in the open position. *Redpath Dorman Long Ltd*

87

87
Finally, this picture is included to show the sorry condition of much of the wagon fleet in the immediate postwar period. This hired 10ton coal wagon still carries the pre-1937 large white NE insignia as well as the later small initials (incorrect in having full stops: N.E.), and no paint has been applied for at least the past 10 years. (Note the bare wood of the uppermost plank, which has been replaced at some stage.) No H6544 was photographed in Berkhamsted coal yard on 20 July 1947. *H. C. Casserley*

3: Road Vehicles

Goods vehicles

Between 1923 and 1932 there was not a standard livery for railway goods vehicles on the LNER system, and the three main Areas tended to continue using pre-Grouping schemes. In the North Eastern area, for example, the horse-drawn pulleys were still painted in a light red shade, whilst in the Southern area they were painted grey.

The introduction of the Gill Sans lettering in 1932 was accompanied by a standard colour scheme of Royal (ultramarine) blue, using white lettering. This was sometimes brightened-up by a red panel carrying the full name of the company, and by red wheels; although study of contemporary photographs shows the use of either black or grey as alternatives for the wheels. Exceptions to the rule were the dozen or so horse boxes in the North Eastern area which were mixed in colour (with royal blue predominating,) whilst the District Motor Representatives in the same area used vans painted in NER green with gold lettering.

By the outbreak of World War 2 the LNER road vehicle fleet had a very concise 'house style' and it proved possible to retain this for the postwar period; one latterday addition being the use of the LNER 'totem' in white on the blue.

Buses

Available photographic evidence shows the livery to have been very similar to that carried by the Sentinel steam railcars, except that an imitation teak finish was sometimes given to the waistline. The lettering was in shaded serif form, exactly the same style as used on the railway carriages.

Tramcars

The teak colour was used, and standard gold shaded carriage style lettering was applied until about 1946/7, when plain yellow Gill Sans lettering began to replace it on the Grimsby & Immingham cars.

88

88
Between 1923 and 1932 there was no standard LNER livery for road vehicles; the three Sectional areas tended to continue using various pre-Grouping colour schemes. In 1932 a deep shade of blue was adopted as standard, and these two Morris-Commercial four-tonners, delivered in 1932 for service in London, must have been amongst the first to receive the new colour. The side rave with the railway company's name in full was probably vermilion red with white lettering in block sans-serif, but not yet Gill Sans, (note the slightly larger letters for L, N, E, and R in the words London & North Eastern Railway.
Modern Transport

89
The introduction of the standard Gill Sans alphabet gave a very smart and modern look to the LNER road vehicle fleet, as can be seen on this 1933 Thornycroft Platform Lorry, in the blue livery with red side raves and red wheel centres, underbody and chassis area in black.
Ian Allan Library

93

94

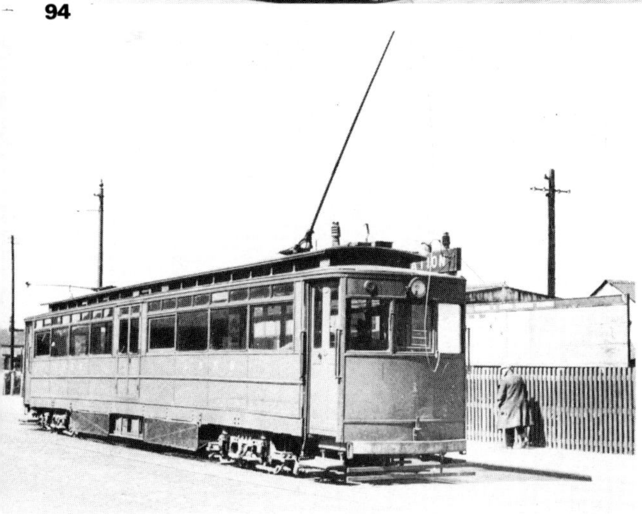

93
Perhaps the most fascinating feature of this 1929 AEC single-decker for the Newcastle area is the painted 'ersatz teak' finish at waist level! The livery is presumed to be grass green lower panels and white above (including the roof) but it is not absolutely confirmed. The lettering and numerals are in standard LNER railway carriage style. The driver's cab front is in black below the windows and there is a black ladder at the rear of the bus, to reach the roof rack. *Modern Transport*

94
The Grimsby and Immingham tramcars, operated by the LNER were in teak brown livery. (They actually finished their days in BR ownership painted malachite green). Car No 1 is seen here at Corporation Bridge station Grimsby on 16 April 1947. There are some interesting notices in the background, including a long poster hoarding with the full name of the railway in white Gill Sans on blue. *A. F. Cook*

95
In 1899 the Great Northern of Scotland Railway opened a tramway service to its Cruden Bay Hotel, using small single-deck tramcars. They lasted until 1940, but latterly only carrying laundry baskets. The final livery was teak brown with standard carriage-style shaded serif lettering. Note that the car is standing on a small turntable, with the line going-off at right angles behind it. Photographed in August 1935. *W. H. Whitworth*

95

4: Miscellany

The LNER's decision to adopt Gill Sans lettering for all its printed and painted signs, notices, posters and timetables has already been described in some detail in the introduction on pages 160-162. Without doubt this was a most important contribution to the advancement of good railway design standards, and it can be considered as one of the earliest transport 'house styles' or 'corporate images', exceeded in quality and thoroughness only by the generally similar work done at the same time for London Transport. By the late 1930s the use of Gill Sans had become synonymous with the LNER, who did *not* however own the copyright of the lettering, and so there were many other applications of Gills Sans then to be seen in Britain.

The road vehicle fleet, just mentioned, was striking in its blue livery, and a similar consistency of style was beginning to emerge for stations, with the façades carrying large Gill Sans letters. In some cases (such as on the Shenfield line) the new LNER 'totem' was used, in blue and white glass with back illumination. Poster boards, information boards and similar station furniture all conformed to the house style, and station name signs were progressively changed to the Gill Sans standard. War interrupted the programme, but a good start had already been made on further station improvements when the LNER was nationalised.

A consistently high standard of artwork was a source of pride to the LNER publicity, or advertising department, and exhibitions of their poster designs were held from time to time. These posters ranged from highly finished 'classical' landscape and seascape paintings, to quite abstract designs, but all gave colour and interest to railway station hoardings, and all carried clear messages to the public. The use of Gill Sans was extended to the pictorial posters, although not rigidly adhered to by some artists. The Gill Sans 'totem', or monogram, was widely used in its printed form, and there had actually been an earlier version of this (see picture 102) which seems to have been restricted to use on posters, and which was more ornate in concept. One curiosity, used both prior to, and with, the Gill Sans style was the placing of full stops *centrally* between the initials LNER; particularly on posters and printed leaflets.

96

96
What greater tribute could be paid to Eric Gill's Gill Sans lettering than that it was as easy to read on a timetable sheet, as it was on a large station façade! Here the lettering is spaced across the entire frontage of Fenchurch Street station, London; in white on dark blue. The picture was taken at 7.25pm on 8 July 1950. The wooden canopies below are painted cream. *H. C. Casserley*

97

97
In this instance (and many others) the Gill Sans lettering is applied in relief lettering direct on to the brickwork, with the letters LNER flanked each side by the station name. Yarmouth South Town was photographed on 1 September 1951 The entrance awning is in cream, with standard blue poster boards on each wall area of the frontage.
H. C. Casserley

98

98
What a lonesome scene Alexandra Palace station made when this picture was taken, in early BR days, with a very down-at-heel Class N2 0-6-2T No 69519 wearily running-round its two coach train! The foreground shows a typical painted station nameboard with Gill Sans letters in white on (faded) blue. The Palace building looms large and forlorn in the background. *Ian Allan Library*

99
I have included this delightful study of a Kelvedon & Tollesbury Light Railway train, in Tollesbury station, because it shows some fascinating contrasts. The wooden station building on the left, painted in a two-tone colour scheme (perhaps green and cream) displays a smart standard poster board, with white Gill Sans letter on blue. (The letters LNER have the full stops placed centrally: L·N·E·R.) Adjacent are two vintage four-wheelers, originating from the Wisbech & Upwell Tramway) both in peeling brown paint, and neither they, nor the Class J69 0-6-0T ahead of them seem to have been cleaned for months! It is impossible to read the number on the tankside of the locomotive, which is still in wartime black livery. *Cyril W. Footer*

99

100
The commemorative plaque which was attached to the boiler sides of the Class A4 Pacific *Mallard*, in 1948. This was perhaps the final example of the use of the LNER 'totem' on a locomotive. *British Rail ER*

101
The carpets in the prototype 'Newton coach' (see photo 80) featured the initials LNER, woven in Gill Sans style. However, the lettering on the inside of the carriage door is in the time-honoured gilt serifed, shaded form. Note the leather strap to open or close the door window, a relic of Victorian days. *British Rail ER*

100

101

102

102
A typical LNER poster of the late 1920s; in this instance by Fred Taylor. The quality of the artwork purchased by the railway for publicity purposes was extremely high. Note the ornamental surround to the letters LNER in the bottom right-hand corner. This was frequently used in the 1920s, and it appears to be the forerunner of the later 'totem' (see photo 9). *Author's collection*

103

103
A truly splendid poster by Tom Purvis, using very bold shapes and colours to portray a simple message; easy to understand when seen from a carriage window, for example. The LNER motif is used again; very small in the left hand lower corner. Note also the full stops placed centrally between the initials L·N·E·R.
Author's collection

104

105

LONDON by L·N·E·R
IT'S QUICKER BY RAIL
FULL INFORMATION FROM L·N·E·R OFFICES AND AGENCIES

106

107

104
Gone are the days when so much fish travelled by rail! (The Author well recalls the constant aroma of fish that was to be found on some LNER station platforms, including King's Cross; particularly on hot days.) This decorative poster by 'Shep' uses a very simple, free, style of lettering to suit the design; circa 1927.
Author's collection

105
Once the Gill Sans lettering was officially adopted a more uniform appearance was given to printed publicity of all kinds. Here the lettering certainly reads extremely clearly, and it is placed in a simple frame, surrounding the painting of London's Rotten Row, by Anna Zinkeisen. It makes an interesting comparison with photo 102.
Crown Copyright: National Railway Museum

106
The ships of the LNER fleet were characterised by a black hull, with white upperparts (or varnished wood) and the funnels were in buff yellow with black tops. The LNER house flag consisted of the St Andrew's saltire with the initials LNER (latterly in Gill Sans inside the cigar-shaped totem) in red at the centre of the cross. Variations probably existed in different areas; for example the GE Section (Harwich) is believed to have included the GER coat-of-arms in the forward section of the flag. Illustrated is the steamship *Vienna*. *Ian Allan Library*

107
The time-honoured pose of the steam locomotive driver; typifying many a boy's childhood dream! The style of clothing did not change during the LNER's days. Of interest is the foreground detail of the locomotive, showing the black and white banding and lining-out on the grass green livery, including the wheel centres. The locomotive is the Class P2 2-8-2 No 2001 *Cock O' the North*; photographed in May 1934.

89

90

90
One of the first of the ubiquitous Scammell 3-ton 'Mechanical Horses', delivered in 1933. Full standard blue livery, but with black wheels, front bumper and mudguards and black panel carrying the full name of the railway company on the trailer-wagon side. White cab roof and white lettering. These attractive little machines steadily displaced the faithful railway horse in crowded city streets. *British Rail ER*

91

92

91
A service department Ford 5cwt van for the Manchester area; in blue, with black mudguards and wheel centres; white lettering. The carriage behind shows the full prewar lined teak livery, and the white roofboards complete with Gill Sans lettering. Photographed in November 1934 at Marylebone station, London.
Ian Allan Library

92
The LNER kept their standard blue road vehicle livery until nationalisation; also the Gill Sans white lettering and numerals. Of added interest on this 1947 'Brush-Bred' electric Parcels Delivery Van is the use of the LNER 'totem' on sides and front. Note the single central headlamp carried! Wheel centres either mid-grey or red; mudguards black. *Ian Allan Library*